ST MARTIN'S
TRUE CRIME
CLASSICS

SUDDENLY GONE

THE KANSAS MURDERS OF SERIAL KILLER RICHARD GRISSOM

DAN MITRIONE

St. Martin's Paperbacks

Published by arrangement with Addicus Books, Inc.

SUDDENLY GONE: THE KANSAS MURDERS OF SERIAL KILLER RICHARD GRISSOM

Copyright © 1995 by Dan Mitrione.

Library of Congress Catalog Card Number: 95-31805

ISBN: 0-312-96052-2

Printed in the United States of America

Addicus Books trade paperback edition published in 1995
St. Martin's Paperbacks edition/September 1996

St. Martin's Paperbacks are published by St. Martin's Press, 175 Fifth Avenue, New York, NY 10010.

10 9 8 7 6

*To Henrietta and Janet
for their unwavering
support and patience.*

Acknowledgments

Writing this book involved interviewing many people, and I wish to thank all who contributed. I'd like to emphasize my appreciation to those who felt the impulse to retreat from painful memories of this story, but who overcame their fears and trusted me to tell their stories.

I owe a debt of gratitude to the police investigators, forensic specialists and prosecutors who assembled an incredible circumstantial case and shared their insights and memories with me. In particular I must thank the mainstays of the investigation. Detectives Ken Landwehr, Bill Batt and Pat Hinkle, who unselfishly committed hours of personal time to insure that I had the facts necessary to tell this story thoroughly and accurately. These officers are some of the most dedicated and professional individuals I have ever worked with, and I thank them for their invaluable contributions. A thanks to Walt Coffey for sharing some investigative material and his insights with me.

I must thank Rod Colvin and Tom McFarland at Addicus Books for not only recognizing the importance of this story and taking on the project, but also for their unwavering support and guidance along the way. Their experience proved to be the guidepost needed to see me through the various stages of this project.

I wish to thank the victims' parents and family members for working through the pain and sharing their unique insights and emotions with me. It was precisely through their openness and their loving memories of Terri, Christine, Theresa and Joan that I learned about these very special women. It is a gift I will always cherish.

Author's Notes

This is a true story. The account I present has
been carefully reconstructed after going over
more than 1,700 pages of investigative reports
and court transcripts as well as physical evidence. I've
also interviewed everyone whom I believed could contribute information about this case. If key individuals
were missed, it was not due to oversight, but to either
scheduling changes or individuals' reluctance to talk
about the case.

None of my efforts to make contact with Richard
Grissom has produced results. I have written him numerous times, asking for interviews, and I've made
attempts to reach him through his court-appointed attorneys. He has, however, remained unwilling to provide comment or meet with me.

For reasons of privacy, five individuals in this account have been assigned pseudonyms. The names
Sherry Cash, Karen Marshall, Jessie Barnes, Joe Collins
and Ruth Silvers are not real.

Dialogues in the text were reconstructed from interviews as well as from police reports and court transcripts. As in most homicide cases, some individuals
have differing memories of the same events. When

such conflicts occurred, I based my narrative on considered judgement of the differing claims.

On several occasions while writing this book, I was asked why I chose to write about this case. My answer has always been straight-forward and simple. From the time in 1989, when I first saw a "missing person" poster of Joan Butler, I felt drawn to this story. I stared at that poster for several minutes, memorizing details, unable to say exactly why I was so moved by Joan's picture.

I followed the news accounts about Joan and those pertaining to Theresa and Christine as they became the lead stories on the evening news for several weeks. As years passed and the stories became "old news," personal interest in their story never waned. If anything, I felt a certain need to tell their story as truthfully and accurately as possible.

It is impossible to write an account such as this without becoming emotionally involved. I have trouble reconciling that the young lives of several, loving women were cut short by a ruthless killer whose senseless motives might never be understood. It is difficult to not be affected by the sorrow and grief that have invaded the lives of the families and friends left behind. In truth, hundreds of lives were instantly affected by the kind of unthinkable acts committed by a serial killer.

I continue to take an occasional journey into the rural areas of Johnson and Douglas counties, where some authorities believe Grissom may have buried the bodies of his victims. I drive along dirt and gravel roads, looking and listening. Sometimes, I stop and stare off into distant fields and try to convince myself that just maybe a message or a sign of some sort will bring news of the missing women.

However, at the end of each journey, I deal with the unsettling reality that I may never know the whereabouts of Joan, Christine and Theresa.

I took on this project, knowing that the young women in the case were dead. Many of the details will always rest with them.

D.M.

But O for the touch of a vanished hand,
And the sound of a voice that is still!

Alfred Lord Tennyson

1

For most of the evening of June 6, 1989, Terri Maness, clipboard in hand, made her way door to door, canvassing the residents of her town house complex on East Lanston in Wichita, Kansas. The air was cool, a welcome reprieve from the scorching daytime temperatures already invading south-central Kansas two weeks before the beginning of summer. Terri wore a light, summer dress, a bright, flower print reflective of her warm, spirited character. An energetic young woman, in her mid-twenties, she stood around five-feet-five inches, and had thick, curly brown hair, wide, brown eyes and a well-proportioned figure.

Terri covered the complex systematically, as if on a mission. She had purchased her own town home in the complex just three months before and already had been appointed secretary of the town house association. The trash-collection rates had reached an unacceptable high, and Terri was circulating a petition to get them lowered.

Terri had little trouble collecting her fair share of signatures for the evening. She returned home to finish a few other association projects. It was after 10:30 P.M. when she finally put aside her paperwork and got ready for bed. Having slipped into a favorite nightshirt, Terri headed from her second-floor bedroom back down to the main floor to turn out the living room lights. When she heard a car door slamming, she moved the curtain back a few inches and caught sight of her next-door neighbor, Wichita Police Officer J. C. Stevenson, as he stepped out of his pickup truck. Terri had twice tried to reach J.C. at home much earlier that evening before ending her signature drive. Both attempts had failed to catch the hard-to-track police officer. Right then was as good a time as any to get his signature, she reasoned. Terri gathered up her clipboard full of signatures and ran out the front door before J.C. could get inside.

J.C. Stevenson, a twenty-year veteran of the Wichita Police Department, was a good, responsible cop who made time for other people when they needed him. He stood an inch shy of six feet and his 180-pound frame showed that he kept himself in pretty good shape. The veteran cop had not known Terri long, but in the few short months since her arrival at the complex, he'd enjoyed having her as a neighbor. And Terri, like others at the complex, certainly felt more secure having a police officer living close by.

It was just after 11:15 P.M. when Terri said good night to J.C. He had willingly signed her petition, watched as Terri returned safely to her home and closed her door. The officer would see Terri just one more time. The circumstances would be immeasurably different, and the encounter would significantly alter his life.

By 9:30 the next morning the law offices of former District Judge Paul Thomas in downtown Wichita were a buzz of routine activity. In addition to Paul Thomas, the office was staffed with two other attorneys and seven secretaries, including Terri Maness. Everyone in the law firm appreciated Terri's dependability, as well as her upbeat personality. Of the secretarial staff, Terri was the one who nicknamed her typewriter and computer and adorned them with happy-face stickers.

In spite of the hustle and rush of the day's early preparations, a couple of Terri's co-workers noticed she had not arrived for work. Terri was always one of the first to arrive and one of the last to leave. Her co-workers automatically assumed that she had called someone else in the office to explain her tardiness. It would have been inconceivable that Terri had not called. A doctor's appointment, car trouble, a personal errand that couldn't wait, Terri always called to let someone know.

Later that morning, another of the office secretaries, having finally asked her co-workers which one of them had heard from Terri, became alarmed to find no one had. The young woman immediately dialed Terri's home phone number. After several rings, no one answered and, to her surprise, Terri's answering machine did not intercept the call. She tried again but heard only the repetitious rings from the other end of the line. She next dialed Terri's parents, Bonnie and Gene Maness, who lived in Augusta, a small, Kansas community located about twenty minutes north of Wichita.

No, announced Bonnie Maness, they had not heard from Terri and thought it surprising that Terri had not gone to work or called someone there to explain why. Bonnie Maness knew that if her daughter was sick or something was wrong, she would call home to tell them. It was an agreement they had. Terri always called. Bonnie Maness was worried now. Still, she thanked Terri's friend for the call and asked that he please have Terri call home as soon as anyone heard from her.

Hanging up the phone, Bonnie Maness paced the floor, uncertain about what she should do next or how much time was considered a "reasonable" period to wait before taking steps to locate Terri. She and her husband both knew just how uncharacteristic it was for Terri not to show for work without calling someone. Their daughter had been steadily employed since moving out on her own several years before, and Terri had never failed to show for work. The Manesses were also realists. They knew the police and most other people would not consider a single morning long enough to declare someone missing or, for that matter, be concerned.

At the risk of overreacting, Bonnie Maness called the Wichita Police Department. She was not calling to file a missing persons complaint, but to talk to her daughter's neighbor, Officer J.C. Stevenson. Learning that Stevenson had taken the day off, she dialed his home and was grateful for the sound of his voice when he answered. Bonnie knew he could help. Trying to remain as calm as possible, she expressed her concerns to J.C. and asked if he would go next door to see if Terri was home and if so, if she was OK. J.C. agreed and promised he'd call back as soon as he'd checked.

Fifteen minutes passed before Bonnie Maness picked up the phone and once again heard J.C. Stevenson's voice. No, he told Terri's mom, Terri was not at home. No one had answered her door and, more important, her car was not parked in its usual spot in front of her unit. He told Bonnie that he left a note on Terri's front door, asking that she call her parents as soon as she arrived home.

J.C. had seen this situation before, played out between a host of parents and their suddenly unpredictable children. But he also knew Terri, and he could sense the anxiety in her mother's voice. J.C. made a concerted effort to reassure Bonnie that everything would be OK. He told her about having seen Terri late the night before when she came after him for his signature. He tried to assure her that Terri was probably out taking care of an errand or an appointment. "After all," J.C. said, "her car is not out front. She must have driven it somewhere this morning."

"I'm sure you're right," Bonnie replied. "It's probably nothing more than a miscommunication. We'll just sit and wait for her to call us." She thanked the officer for his help but could not shake the feeling that something was wrong.

Terri's parents knew their daughter like no one else. They doubted she had gone off to some mysterious appointment. If Terri had to be someplace besides work, she would have made certain someone knew where she was. Bonnie and Gene struggled to believe that everything was all right, but parental intuition was getting the best of them. They sat together by the phone with foreboding anticipation.

By 2:00 that afternoon, Bonnie Maness could not wait a moment longer. Hours had passed with no word from Terri. She again called J.C. Stevenson at home. Far too concerned to be apologetic, Bonnie asked J.C. to once again check Terri's town house for any sign of her return. The officer told Bonnie that he would take another look next door, but added that Terri's car was still not in the parking lot. Still, J.C. asked Bonnie to wait on the line while he ran to see if the note he had left was still on the door. It was, and within minutes he returned to tell Bonnie that nothing had changed.

"J. C., this is Terri's father and we really need you to help us out here," said Gene Maness breaking into the conversation from an extension phone. "We want you to go into Terri's house and have a look around. You have our permission to go in, whatever it takes, and see if she's there. Something is wrong, J.C.," continued Gene Maness, his voice cracking in distress. "We just know it. This is not like Terri, and I think you know that. Please do this for us," Gene Maness asked.

J.C. told the Manesses he would help; if they authorized his entry, he would be willing to go inside and have a look around. He could feel their anxiety building by the minute, and he knew he had to help them. Before hanging up he agreed to call them as soon as he had finished. That call would be delayed. Nothing in his training, nothing in his twenty years of police experience would prepare him for what he would confront inside the town house next door.

Approaching the front of Terri's house, J.C. glanced once again at the note taped to the front door. Instinctively, he tried the lock a third time. He rang the doorbell repeatedly before going around to the rear of the unit. He approached the sliding glass door that separated Terri's kitchen from her concrete patio. It too was locked, but J.C. knew how to maneuver the door off its track. Sliding it back just far enough to gain entry, he slipped inside the kitchen and began calling out Terri's name even though he was convinced she was not at home. He continued calling her name as he walked through the dining room and into the living room at the front of the house.

J.C. had been inside Terri's house a few times before and from what he recalled of the living area, nothing seemed out of place. He worked his way upstairs to the bedrooms where he was careful to check inside closets and under beds. He felt a bit uneasy about looking in every nook and cranny of his neighbor's house but reasoned that he needed to tell Terri's parents that he checked everywhere.

Returning to the main floor, J.C. nearly left without checking the downstairs laundry and recreation rooms. He was already uncomfortable and felt certain that Terri would come home while he was looking around. Again, he remembered the promise of a complete search made to Terri's parents and proceeded to the lower level.

Stepping from the stairs into the recreation room, the veteran officer was shocked to an abrupt halt. His eyes widened, his breathing stopped. He remained motionless, frozen by what he saw. When he moved, it was backward, falling against the landing. As he hit his head, he gasped for breath and locked his palms against the wall to keep from falling. NO, NO, NOT THIS! his mind screamed. He closed his eyes, trying to convince himself that the scene before him was not real. Terri had been brutally murdered.

He clutched his stomach, knowing he was very close to becoming sick. He thought about leaving, about going back outside, if only long enough to catch his breath and regain his senses. He wondered for a moment whether he could muster the courage to come back if he left. He fought the urge and remained in the room making every effort to control his breathing and remain calm.

J.C. took several deep breaths and stood as erect as his legs would permit. He began talking to himself, convincing himself that right then, more than ever, he needed to be a cop, a good, strong, thinking cop. J.C. wanted nothing to do with the horrific crime scene before him, but knew that its preservation depended on his professional, common-sense approach.

Bracing himself, and with slow, rigid steps, he made his way to the center of the room. He stopped when he found himself standing directly over the lifeless body of young Terri Maness. He could feel his heart try to beat its way out of his chest as he searched for a "clean" area within which he could squat close to the body.

Terri's body was colorless. It was apparent she had been dead for several hours, but J.C. nevertheless felt for a pulse. Part of him remained unable to accept the finality of the horrid scene. Squatting next to the body, J.C. turned his focus to a note, a piece of paper with several lines of scribbled writing apparently left behind by Terri's killer. The note rested on top of her nude, bloodstained body. He noticed that the first few lines of the note were a rash of obscenities. He suddenly stopped reading. For the moment he could not read on. The officer remained totally overwhelmed by the complexity of the picture in front of him. Multiple stab wounds covered Terri's body, and her blood, which just hours before coursed through her body, now saturated the carpet in a dark red pool beneath her.

J.C. stood to allow the circulation to return to his legs. He tried hard to make sense of it all as he stared blankly into the contrasting whiteness of a far wall. Something very abstract and vague was now calling for his mind to focus, to make the leap, to adjust to what was *really* in that room. The veteran cop had felt for years there was little on the streets that could shock him. His lengthy career had taught him that anything was possible. But not this, he thought to himself. Not Terri! He again tried to focus. Why this? Why Terri?

J.C. backed away from Terri's lifeless body and looked around the room. He could sense the anger and the hatred that had invaded this young woman's life just hours before. Somehow those emotions still saturated the room like a sickening odor. Whoever did this, he thought, was an angry, hateful person. Why? Why Terri? How could so much anger be suddenly thrust upon this happy, young woman? Terri simply could not have had this kind of enemy in her life.

The police officer gathered himself. He understood that the job of finding out what happened was just beginning. He needed to get out of the room and make the necessary calls. Thinking ahead about the crime scene, which potentially included the entire town house, J.C. returned to his own house to make his calls.

First, he called 911, identified himself and reported the crime for an immediate response by an on-duty police unit. Next, he contacted his superiors. J.C. knew his department would be pulling out the big guns for this murder. In less than ten minutes, a battery of cops and crime scene experts, including the county medical examiner, would begin invading the house next door. They would pick it apart methodically from top to bottom. The house where Terri had lived, the rooms that once held her warmth, and the walls that reflected her spirited, peaceful presence soon would be wiped clean of her distinct personality.

His calls made, J.C. prepared himself to return next door and wait. Just then, he remembered Bonnie and Gene Maness. My God, he thought. Terri's parents are waiting for my call. They begged me to see if everything was OK. Jesus! J.C. thought, things are as far as they can get from OK. The officer searched his mind for a way around the inevitable, what he knew was his responsibility. He toyed with the idea of waiting until the crime scene was secure and getting someone else to officially notify the Manesses. He knew deep inside, however, that he couldn't do that. They had been waiting for him, counting on him. He had to make the call himself. J.C. knew the Manesses lived twenty miles away. It would take them awhile to get here. It would be ample time for the police to secure the area and control the crime scene. He did not want Terri's parents to see their daughter the way he found her. He would not have them forced into remembering that horrid scene for the rest of their lives. They would have their share of demons to confront without seeing Terri's body.

When Gene Maness answered the phone, J.C. could not bring himself to reveal the true details about what he found. He would not tell them over the phone what happened. It would be better if they were around other people when they found out, he reasoned. He simply asked Gene if he and Bonnie could meet him at Terri's house as soon as possible. Silence followed. Gene asked no questions. J.C. knew it had been well over forty minutes since they had asked him to check Terri's house. It was time enough for the Manesses to conclude that something was terribly wrong. J.C., fighting back tears, said good-bye to Gene and returned next door to wait.

Having heard the obvious distress in J.C. Stevenson's voice, Gene Maness set the receiver in its cradle and remained motionless. He didn't need things spelled out in bold letters. He could hear the alarm in the officer's voice. Something had happened to Terri. Gene's voice and face betrayed him as he turned to his wife. "J.C. Stevenson wants us to meet him at Terri's place," he said quietly before looking away. "We'll have to go there right away."

"OK," she replied. She did not ask questions. She did not want to be told anything when there remained the slightest glimmer of hope that the unthinkable had not happened to their daughter.

Before leaving, Gene Maness placed a phone call to Attorney Paul Thomas, Terri's employer, and asked if he would meet them at Terri's house. Gene Maness could not tell him why. He could say only that a police officer had called and asked them to meet him there. Terri had been missing all day, and it was his guess that something had happened to her. Gene Maness then took his wife by the arm and helped her into the family car. For Terri's parents, the ride from Augusta to Wichita seemed like the longest ride of their lives.

Paul Thomas arrived at the scene well before the Manesses. He was accompanied by Gina Adams. She was one of Terri's co-workers, and Thomas had asked her to show him where Terri lived. Thomas, was a middle-aged man of medium build, had a full head of reddish-gray hair and beard to match. He studied the scene taking place directly in front of Terri's town house. Police cars filled the parking lot. Red and blue lights flashed from every direction. The place was swarming with officers.

Thomas approached a policeman who was marking off the area with yellow, crime-scene tape. "I'm Attorney Paul Thomas," he said, introducing himself to the officer. Pointing up toward the front of the town house, he added, "The girl who lives in this house works for me. Can you tell me if anything has happened to her?"

The uniformed officer paused and glanced back toward the town house as if stalling for time. He turned back around, looking first at Gina Adams and then at Paul Thomas before responding. "I don't know the identity of the individual inside this unit," the officer said. "But all of the initial indications are that the woman who lived here has been murdered."

Gina gasped and backed away wrapping both arms around her stomach. Thomas put his arm around her and led her away from the building. Gina was a close friend of Terri's. She trembled and began to cry. Her legs grew weaker with each step until finally Thomas was supporting her as they moved toward his car. Once at the car, it began to sink in that he had seen Terri Maness, one of the sweetest and most promising young women he had ever met, alive for the last time the day before. Sweat poured from his forehead as he tried to calm Gina and reconcile in his mind that Terri had been murdered. How could that be? he asked himself over and over as he held fast to Gina.

Thomas thought about Terri's parents, by that time only minutes away. He surmised from the brief phone call from Gene Maness that Terri's parents did not yet know what had happened. He knew that he and Gina might be the only ones there for them when they arrived. "Listen Gina," Thomas began. "Terri's parents are going to arrive any minute now. We have to be strong for them. We might be the only ones here that they can talk to or hold on to." Thomas handed Gina a handkerchief. "Let's gather ourselves and be strong for Terri's mom and dad, OK?"

Gina took the handkerchief and patted her eyes. "OK," she replied, trying to regain her composure. "I'll do my best." She and Thomas stood side by side and watched as Bonnie and Gene Maness drove into the parking lot.

When the Manesses entered the parking lot, they realized that their worst nightmare had become a reality. What little hope they had that Terri was somehow all right was dashed by the sight of flashing police lights and yellow, crime-scene tape blocking the entrance to their daughter's home. The Manesses, paralyzed with fear, sat in their car, staring in disbelief toward their daughter's town house. Gene would be the first to get out but not right away. He would wait awhile. He needed courage.

The Terri Maness murder was assigned to Wichita Police Detective Ken Landwehr who worked robbery-homicide on the Investigations Division. Landwehr was a consummate professional whose career in police work had spanned a course from behavioral science to investigations of serial killings. The detective stood around six feet, with a trim, athletic build and soft-spoken demeanor. He was always well-dressed, sporting nicely cut suits and coordinated shirts and ties.

At the time of the Terri Maness murder, he was marking his third year as a detective with the Wichita Department, having come from the department's behavioral science unit where, following eleven years of service, he had long been considered an expert. In the behavioral science field he had worked many difficult investigations, including the multiple murders committed in Kansas by a serial killer known as the "BTK (bind, torture, kill) murderer." When the prudent detective first saw the Maness crime scene, he wondered whether the gruesome murder might be another in the BTK series, or possibly the work of another serial killer.

Solving the Terri Maness murder would depend largely on Landwehr's methodical, textbook approach: gather all potential evidence at the crime scene and submit it to forensic labs for analysis; pick apart the crime scene and surrounding areas for any other pieces of evidence or clues; interview the victim's neighbors and residents within an expanded perimeter; find her car and conduct interviews and a crime-scene investigation; retrace the victim's patterns just prior to the murder; compile a list of names of anyone involved in any aspect of Terri Maness's young life; interview everyone and when that's done, interview them again. In brutal, enigmatic murders such as this one, Landwehr knew that no piece of evidence could be overlooked.

Of immediate concern to Landwehr was the note left behind on the victim's body. In addition to a few hand-written lines of hideous obscenities, the note also expressed a deadly threat which, in part, read: "...the judge is next!" In the Maness case, the immediate focus of the threat was believed to be Terri's employer, former District Judge Paul Thomas.

The possibility of Paul Thomas being the murderer's next target was taken very seriously by Landwehr. The former judge was interviewed extensively, and a team of investigators combed through his law offices with special concentration on Terri Maness's work space and desk. The team examined files, personal and business, stored in cabinets and on computer disks. Thomas and his legal staff were litigators of primarily civil cases, not criminal. No solid leads came from the office and file searches.

The investigation at the town house continued. No fingerprints other than those safely eliminated as belonging at the scene had been recovered. Physical evidence obtained was minimal and weak at best. There had been no apparent forced entry into Terri's unit, leading investigators to the early assumption that Terri knew her killer and may have let him in.

A neighbor two or three houses from Terri's reported that she saw Terri's car back out of the parking lot around 5:30 A.M. on June 7. The witness could not identify the driver. She said she just assumed it was Terri.

They found Terri's car later in the day. It had been abandoned just two blocks away at another complex. Inside the car the police recovered Terri's telephone answering machine and a few other personal items they believed had been removed from her house. Verifiable prints could not be obtained from either the car or the answering machine. Also, a woman whose car was parked a few spaces from where Terri's was found, reported that her license tag had been stolen from her car sometime during the previous night. It was, at least, another lead.

The medical examiner's report established the time of Terri's death as just before midnight, on June 6, or just after, on June 7. The examiner was able to determine that Terri died from strangulation and not from multiple stab wounds.

Within the early stages of the investigation, Landwehr and his team successfully eliminated Paul Thomas as the "judge" who might have been the killer's "next" target. They determined the note was simply a ploy designed to lure them onto another course.

While the investigators awaited results of other findings in the case, they began compiling a list of people to be interviewed and checked out. The list grew long as they added Terri's friends, neighbors, associates, coworkers, boyfriends and members of her church group. Several names were recorded from Terri's address book and still others were found in her purse. When finished, the team had compiled three type-written pages of names, each and every one to be tracked and interviewed. Landwehr's premonition that Terri's murder might just be the first in a string of sexual murders would be right on the mark.

2

June 12, 1989, Michelle Katf sat with her fiancee, Jim Temossi, watching TV on the sofa in her apartment. The couple had decided to spend a quiet evening together and had tuned in a sports program. Michelle moved about on the couch, unable to sit still. For reasons she could not explain, she felt on edge, easily distracted, unable to relax.

When the program was over, Jim knew that something was bothering Michelle, so he stood and announced that he should go home and get some sleep. He sensed it would be better for him to leave. Somehow, they both knew it was just an off night. They stood in the apartment doorway and kissed good night.

Walking away from the apartment Jim turned back to Michelle. "Are you going to be OK?" he asked.

Michelle smiled. "Yes, I'll be fine. I just need some sleep. I'll talk to you tomorrow."

"All right then, get some rest," Jim added as he headed down the stairs to the parking lot below. He moved across the parking lot toward his car, completely unaware that he was being watched.

Michelle's apartment was located at the end of a string of apartments in the Apple Creek complex at 9933 Locust, in Kansas City, Missouri. The building arrangements varied throughout the large complex. The end units were the only ones with parking lots in the back. At night the lot was normally lit by a series of floodlamps extending from the rear of the building, but many of the bulbs were either very dim or burned out, making the area darker than the residents liked. In fact, not enough light was available to illuminate a small, brown Toyota parked on the far side of the lot. The Toyota was not empty.

A lone occupant sat slumped and well-hidden in the driver's seat. He had watched Jim Temossi leave the building and drive out of the lot. The stalker had carefully chosen his surveillance spot. The car sat seventy feet across the lot from the building's entryway. The car was further obscured by an old Sycamore tree whose branches extended well into the lot. The stalker knew exactly where and when to wait. He had watched the comings and goings around the end units for some time, and now was focused on the activity in unit number 4207, the apartment of Michelle Katf.

It was just after 11:00 P.M. when Michelle closed the door behind Jim. She secured the deadbolt, the only lock on the door. After tugging on the door a few times to satisfy herself that it was indeed locked, Michelle continued her nightly ritual of checking all doors and windows in the apartment. She checked the sliding-glass door and double-checked the piece of wood Jim had placed between the door and wall to insure that the door could not be slid open. Her apartment was not a fortress by any stretch, but with everything locked up tight, she felt secure. Her ritual completed, Michelle turned off the living room lights and made her way to the bedroom.

Having watched Jim Temossi drive out of the area, the man in the brown Toyota re-focused his attention on Michelle's apartment as he watched the lights go out. He adjusted his position in the front seat and sat back to wait. He had been to the building many times, but never for the reason that brought him here tonight.

It was midnight by the time Michelle finished a quick shower, then threw back the bed covers and jumped naked into bed. After a few minutes of tossing, she reasoned that whatever was bothering her probably would disappear with a good night's sleep. She molded her body into a favorite position and drifted off to sleep.

It was just past 2:00 A.M. when Michelle was startled awake. She fought to bring her mind into focus. The overhead light was on. What was it? Had she heard something? Why was the light on? Had Jim returned for something? She rubbed her eyes, as she turned toward the bedroom doorway. Her heart began pounding rapidly and a rush of adrenaline shocked her wide awake. A man! A big man! A man she didn't know was standing at her bedroom door! For a brief second she wondered if she might be dreaming. She tried to scream but nothing came out. Frozen in place, she thought to herself, this must be a dream. Before she could move, the man sprang with the speed of a large cat, landing on Michelle, pinning her beneath the covers. In the same motion, one of his hands covered her mouth and pressed her head against the mattress.

Though only half awake and deathly afraid, Michelle would not be a passive victim. She resisted, at first trying to bite her attacker's hand. She kicked and squirmed but found herself trapped by the assailant's strength and the confinement of her own blankets. Finally Michelle freed one arm and began hitting him and trying to push him off.

Defending himself against her blows while still try-ing to hold her down, the attacker loosened his grip around Michelle's mouth. She managed a deep breath and a muffled scream before he could return his hand to her mouth. The attacker left Michelle's arm free to pummel him while, with his other hand, he tried to gather her up in the web of sheets and blankets formed by the struggle.

She continued to kick and squirm, trying to slide under him to free herself. Michelle knew she could not stop fighting. She could not give in. She had to keep moving, trying to escape. She slid from side to side as far as possible and then tried to roll over first to one side, then back to the other. Suddenly, Michelle felt the bed give way from under her. With her attacker still on top of her, she fell to the floor at the foot of the bed. Caught inside the bundle of sheets and blankets and struggling to breathe, Michelle lay still with her eyes closed, hoping the man would relax his vice-like grip over her mouth. Michelle let her body go completely limp.

The tactic worked. Suddenly the man relaxed his grip slightly. For Michelle, however, it was just enough for her to take several deep breaths of air. Pinned to the floor and wondering what was to come, she made a conscious effort to focus her eyes away from her assailant. She knew it might be better for her if she did not look at him directly. As she focused on the wall, she pulled from some deep memory the notion that she stood a much better chance of surviving this ordeal if her attacker believed she could not recognize him. Michelle's strength had momentarily abandoned her, but not her resolve. Just let me catch my breath and I'll get away from him, she convinced herself.

"I have a gun!" he said, speaking in a loud whisper as if he knew he could be heard through the thin walls separating the units. "Don't keep fighting me," he ordered. "I have a gun and I'll use it." Just then the man released his grip on the bundle of bed clothes holding his victim and began tugging at something in the side pocket of his jacket.

Michelle did not look to see what he was pulling out but suddenly felt something being pressed just under her chin. The attacker now kept his other hand over her mouth.

"Go ahead, feel it," the man insisted, still talking in a loud whisper. "Put your hands on it. See for yourself that I have a gun."

Michelle prepared for the worst, but was surprised by her attacker's attempt to convince her that he had a gun. Could he be bluffing? she wondered. She made an effort to obey his command and focus on the object pressed against her throat. Looking down, Michelle noticed the thin leather-looking gloves worn by her attacker and his deeply tanned forearms exposed between his gloves and jacket sleeves. She closed her eyes and reached up slowly with her free hand to feel the gun. Placing her fingers on the underside of the gun and along the barrel, she was once again struck by the notion that something wasn't right. The object didn't feel like a real gun. She had expected to reach up and feel cold, hard steel, but the instrument she touched felt phony—like a cheap, plastic imitation. Michelle lowered her hand, and kept her eyes focused away from the man's face.

Apparently satisfied that his gun would guarantee his victim's cooperation, the man relaxed his grip around her mouth. "Don't scream!" he ordered. "Now you know I've got a gun and if you scream, I'm gonna have to blow your brains out."

Michelle remained still under her attacker, but she was not giving up. She was just waiting for the right opportunity to present itself.

"Get up slowly," he ordered, making a halfhearted attempt to help her out of the blankets. The attacker stood and kept the gun pointed directly at Michelle's head. "Leave the blankets on the floor." Any opportunity for Michelle to cover her naked body faded with this latest command. When his victim was on her feet, the assailant grabbed her arm and then quickly pushed her away from him. "Get dressed. Get something on," he ordered.

His words produced momentary relief for Michelle. She could not comprehend the man's motives, but his latest command was a good indication that he had not broken in to rape her. She moved immediately, demonstrating her willingness to cooperate before he could change his mind. She turned toward the bedroom closet.

"Wait! Don't go in there," he said walking up behind her.

Michelle froze, dreading that he might have suddenly changed his mind about raping her. He didn't touch her, but rather pointed toward a chair in the corner, away from the closet. "There," he said, pointing to a suit coat draped over the back of the chair. "Put that on!"

Michelle did as instructed. She felt less vulnerable now that she had been allowed to cover herself.

"OK, we're getting out of here," said the man, motioning for Michelle to leave the bedroom.

Michelle hesitated at first, then with stiff, awkward steps began moving slowly toward the living room. Just inside the front room she felt the assailant's hand wrap around her arm. His grip was tight, pinching her arm just above the elbow.

He pulled Michelle closer to him before speaking once more. "We're going to walk out of here now," he said. "If you try anything stupid, I'll shoot you."

Michelle nodded that she understood.

As the man opened the front door of the apartment, Michelle realized he had not unlocked it first. She had double-checked the door before going to bed. He must have come in through the door, she thought.

Tugging at her arm, the assailant forced Michelle along the outside corridor toward the central staircase. At the top of the stairs Michelle stared four floors below to a dark, desolate parking lot. I can't go down there with him. I can't let myself be taken, she thought. As she was being forced down the stairs, she could only guess at this madman's intentions, but she sensed the worst. At that moment Michelle knew only one thing for certain. If she allowed herself to be dragged off in the middle of the night, she was not coming back.

As they approached the last set of stairs, Michelle knew that time was running out. Her next moves might be the most compelling of her life. Thoughts of the gun sprang to her mind. She had to believe it wasn't real. She had to believe that confronting him right then would not result in her lying at the bottom of the stairs in a pool of her own blood. She had to take the chance. What choices did she have? She had to fight him.

Michelle tried to jerk her arm away from her attacker's grasp but he managed to hold on to the sleeve of her coat. She pulled again, first up, then back, trying to free herself from his grip.

"What the hell are you doing?" he yelled, no longer concerned about who might hear him.

A feisty Michelle continued to fight. "I don't believe that gun is real!" she yelled as loud as she could.

"You're not taking me anywhere! You let me go, you bastard!"

"This gun is real!" the attacker yelled back, still trying to hold fast to his victim's arm. "Are you crazy? I'll shoot you if you fight me! I'll blow your head off!"

"I'm not going anywhere!" Michelle screamed again. "It's not real. I know it's not real!"

The attacker let go of Michelle's arm and brought the gun around pointing it directly at her chest.

"Help! Someone help me!" she cried out.

The man paused, then fired twice at point-blank range. Michelle expected her body to react to the shots, but was at once surprised and relieved. There had been no loud bangs, no sharp, burning pain. The gun had sounded snap, snap, like a child's toy cap gun. She was right. The gun was not real!

Michelle continued to struggle and screamed out for help as loudly as she could. "Help me! Please help me! Rape, Rape, Fire, Fire! Please help me!" She had convinced herself she was not going to lose this battle.

Her attacker was, likewise, not ready to concede defeat. As Michelle screamed and fought, the man raised the gun above her head and brought it crashing down against her skull. The blow forced Michelle to her knees. The man swung twice more but landed only glancing blows as Michelle fell away from him. A large piece of the gun broke away and landed on the steps next to her.

Michelle was dazed but managed to raise an arm above her head to ward off any more blows from her crazed attacker. Everything began spinning around her. As she regained a sense of awareness, she realized that the man had walked away from her and out into the parking lot. She told herself to get up and run back up the stairs, but she couldn't move. She remained stunned, the ground still spinning beneath her. Suddenly she heard footsteps. She looked up again to see her attacker coming back toward her. Oh God! she said to herself. Please God, let it be over, please! She didn't look up as he approached. She covered her head and braced herself for more blows. With her other arm she clung to the stair railing to prevent him from pulling her away.

The man came up next to Michelle, but simply bent down and retrieved the broken piece of his weapon. Picking it up, he turned away from his bloodied victim and walked slowly back across the lot as if nothing had occurred.

Realizing she may not be given another chance to get away, Michelle summoned the strength she had left, pulled herself to her feet and climbed back up the stairs as fast as she could. Before reaching the top landing, Michelle heard the sound of a car engine. She turned toward the darkened parking lot below and watched as a small, dark car drove off without its lights on. Struggling to get down the corridor to her apartment, Michelle placed a hand on her throbbing head. Her hair was matted and sticky. She felt a trickle of moisture running down her temple and on to her cheek. She pulled her hand away. Her fingers were covered with blood.

Back inside her apartment, Michelle first hurried to her bedroom closet for clothes—jeans and a top. She was too frightened to clean herself up. She stared at the chaotic picture of her bedroom. It wasn't a dream, she thought. This really did happen to me tonight. I came within a push and a scream of losing my life. She touched her fingers to the sticky knot on her head; she was still unable to truly comprehend it all. Her head throbbed. She hurried to the front room to call the police but discovered her phone was dead. She wondered if that too was the work of her assailant. Unable to stay by herself a moment longer, Michelle left her apartment and headed to a neighbor's. She would awaken someone, anyone. She desperately needed to feel safe.

Michelle eventually learned that other residents in the building heard her screams that night, but were unable to determine where, or if, anything was really happening. It wasn't until hearing Michelle's second set of screams, that one neighbor got out of bed to look out the window. Another resident saw what he believed to be a light-skinned black man walking across the parking lot to a car parked under the tree on the far side. The witness watched as the man, apparently carrying something in a white cloth, got into a dark Toyota and drove, lights off, out of the lot. From his vantage, the witness could not see Michelle on the stairs just above the lot.

Michelle and other witnesses eventually gave their statements to police officers from the Kansas City, Missouri, Police Department. A worn and haggard Michelle gave her initial statement to an officer who walked her back through the sequence of events. Michelle emphasized that she could not figure out how her assailant got into her apartment. Windows had not been broken. The front door had not been forced. The sliding-glass door remained secure with its protective cross-bar still in place.

During the initial search of the apartment, which in Michelle's opinion was not at all thorough, a flashlight was discovered at the foot of the bed. Michelle pointed out to the officers that the light was not hers, that the assailant must have brought it. The police left the flashlight in place. Michelle initially surmised that this action was not an oversight but a purposeful investigative procedure in which everything is left in its place until the last moment, when it is all taken in as evidence.

As the cursory search continued, Michelle's concerns and frustration grew with the apparent indifference of the investigating officers. She did not care that no one was there to comfort her, but she did care that the police, in her opinion, "...just didn't seem concerned that it happened, period." To her, the officers acted as if they were forced to be there, that the investigation was keeping them from something else they wanted to do. The officers not only had failed to search the bed clothes scattered at the scene of the initial attack, they left without taking pieces of evidence. As the officers left her apartment, Michelle, head still throbbing, ran after them with the flashlight left at the scene. "Here," she cried out in frustration. "It's not mine! Don't you understand? It's not mine! You forgot it!"

Finally, and with a seemingly tired if not condescending "OK," one of the officers took the evidence from Michelle.

Later that morning, Michelle spoke with Gina Kelly, the manager at Apple Creek. Neither woman could come up with an explanation for how the assailant got into Michelle's apartment. Michelle already had made the decision not to spend another night in the apartment, and there would be no discussion about breaking her lease. Offers from Gina Kelly to change locks were falling on deaf ears. It would be a long, long time before Michelle could forget just how close she came to losing her life.

Michelle's boyfriend, Jim Temossi returned that morning to be with her and help her get a few necessary things out of the apartment. He would return later for the balance of her possessions. As they attempted to gather up the scattered bed clothes, they shook out a blanket and heard something fall to the floor. Jim looked down and noticed a large pocket knife. "What's this?" he asked, looking toward Michelle.

Her eyes widened as she stared at the knife. "It must have fallen, or he dropped it during our struggle on the bed." She shook her head. Her frustration had reached a saturation point. "Damn police!" she said. "They should have found that. They just don't care!"

From the manager's office, Jim Temossi telephoned the Kansas City, Missouri, Police Department to tell the investigating officer about finding the knife. He was told to drop it off at the police station when he got the chance. Then, two weeks later, when returning for the remainder of Michelle's things, Jim discovered two pellets on the stairs just above the parking lot. He surmised that they were the pellets fired at Michelle. Jim phoned the police to tell of his discovery. Again, he was told to drop them off at the station when he could.

3

Joan Butler held down two jobs after relocating to Kansas City from Wichita. Her primary job was in advertising. Joan worked in the media design department at the Montague-Sherry Ad Agency in downtown Kansas City. Her second job was working part-time at a gourmet specialty shop called "The Better Cheddar," located in the fashionable area of Kansas City known as the Country Club Plaza. She worked the part-time job a few nights a week and on weekends. On Sunday, June 11, 1989, Joan was scheduled to work at the Plaza store. It was just before noon when she left her apartment in Overland Park, Kansas, a suburb of Kansas City, located in Johnson County, just south of the Plaza.

Today was to be the start of a very bad week for Joan. A light spring rain had been falling, causing slicker roadways. Joan had traveled about a third of the way to the Plaza when she stopped for a red light. At the intersection, Joan's small Honda was rammed from behind by a tailgater. The reckless driver might have pushed Joan's car out into the intersection had it not been for the presence of another car just in front of her. The crash caused extensive damage to her car and Joan suffered facial cuts and bruises. Following emergency treatment at the Shawnee Mission Medical Center in Overland Park, Joan returned to her apartment and phoned her parents in Wichita to tell them the bad news.

Ralph and Jada Butler had once lived in Kansas City, but had moved to Wichita when "Joanie," the oldest of their four children, was just four. They were loving, caring parents completely sympathetic to Joan's plight. They consoled her and invited her home to Wichita to recuperate. The truth be known, Joan's parents would have rather had her living closer to home anyway and took advantage of every opportunity to persuade her to that end. They silently hoped the accident would serve as a catalyst for Joan to move back to Wichita. They also knew that events many times more harrowing than a minor traffic accident were more likely to occur in the "big city."

Prior to graduating from high school in Wichita, Joan told her father she wanted to follow in his footsteps and pursue a career in advertising. Joan was the apple of her father's eye, and nothing could have pleased him more. Ralph Butler had maintained a long and successful career in advertising with KSNW, Channel Three, one of the top-rated TV stations in southern Kansas. His talent, perseverance and likeability helped him survive the turbulent world of ratings and the pressures of advertising quotas. His ability to provide a comfortable living for his wife, their two sons and two daughters was not lost on young Joan. As a teenager, she believed that she had what it took to step into her daddy's shoes.

Following high school, Joan enrolled at the University of Kansas, the sprawling university campus was located in Lawrence, a small, quaint town of tree-lined streets with well-preserved, turn-of-the-century homes. While at KU, Joan attended the William Allen White School of Journalism, graduating with ease in the class of 1987. At graduation, Joan was more than ready to take the next step toward her advertising career.

From college, Joan returned initially to Wichita to seek employment. She had convinced herself that in Wichita she might enjoy an easier, less competitive start to her career. She knew a lot of people there, and most of her friends and family were in the area. She found immediate employment with a cable TV company but, in time, grew dissatisfied with the company's lack of opportunity for growth and advancement. A job change landed Joan with the Stephan Ad Agency in Wichita and, for a while, afforded her the opportunity to do the kind of work she really wanted.

One hot summer weekend a little more than a year after graduation, Joan accepted an invitation to visit a few friends from college who had been living and working in Kansas City. She was excited about the opportunity. To Joan, it was more than just a chance for her to visit close friends. She had been growing increasingly restless in Wichita and wondered whether her current job or the town itself held the opportunities for career growth and social interaction she had been striving for.

Joan Butler was, if anything, enthusiastic and ambitious. She had told her parents that by the age of thirty, she would be directing her own department in a large ad agency. Few days went by in which Joan was not considering the possibilities and opportunities in Kansas City, just two hours to the north. She loved her family and believed her initial choices to remain close to home and gain early work experience had indeed been the right ones. It would be hard to leave, but something was pulling her away. She would make the trip north to play for a weekend with her college friends. She also would talk to them about a move and look around the city.

During one of the social activities that July weekend in Kansas City, Joan was introduced to Brett Wittman, a tall, athletic, pleasant-looking young man who was drawn to Joan almost immediately. The entire weekend was a happy and inspiring time for her. The fires of change were being fueled and she could feel the heat. For weeks after their meeting, Brett and Joan maintained contact and saw each other occasionally. Their relationship grew and contributed to the push toward her inevitable migration north.

Almost immediately after moving to Kansas City, Joan was hired by the Montague-Sherry Ad Agency, located in downtown Kansas City, Missouri. Though not one of the largest ad agencies in the metro area, it had a good reputation as an upstart company with promise and great growth potential.

At the agency, Joan specialized in purchasing time on TV and radio for clients. The department was headed by Gary Coleman, a young, energetic vice president who supervised a small, close-knit group of young, advertising and design people with whom Joan blended nicely. Joan was excited about her new position. She jumped in with both feet.

After living for a while in the home of Brett's mother, Joan eventually found a place of her own. She took a small one-bedroom apartment in the Comanche Place Apartment Complex located in Overland Park. To her satisfaction, the complex had around-the-clock security-guard service that included a manned guard shack at the main entrance. The complex also had installed tire-puncturing spikes designed to prevent cars from entering any unguarded exits. Her apartment was small but, to Joan, it was home for now. She had her own parking space at the front of her building.

Months passed and Joan had settled into her new job and apartment. However, she found herself with too much extra time on her hands. Her relationship with Brett had broken off, and she was not ready to establish another one right away. Though she dated, Joan did not spend a lot of time and effort looking for Mr. Right. She reasoned that when the time was right, he would find his way into her life. Joan opted for part-time work to fill some hours. That's when she was hired by The Better Cheddar on the Plaza.

The morning after the car accident, Joan decided to rent a car while waiting for the insurance company to make a decision about her Honda. A neighbor of Joan's at Comanche Place drove Joan to Enterprise Leasing in Overland Park, Kansas, where she contracted for a new, maroon-colored Chevrolet Corsica.

Back to work at Montague-Sherry following her accident, Joan could not seem to get into the swing of things. Her timing was off. Whether speaking with clients or designing programs, she just felt out of step. She decided she was just riding a slow wave of depression as a result of the accident and her facial injuries. News she received during the balance of that week would not help.

Just prior to her accident, Joan had made a deposit to hold another apartment closer to both of her jobs. But a few days after the accident, she learned she could not break her lease at Comanche Place. She would have to continue paying rent until another tenant was found for her apartment. Then, days later, Joan was notified by her insurance company that her Honda was a "total," which only added darker clouds to her already dispiriting week.

Looking for a way out of her emotional slump, Joan decided to resume her aerobic workouts. She returned to "The Body Works," a favored athletic club located in the city's popular Westport district. Joan had been a member of the club since moving from Wichita. Putting herself through a light workout, she wondered why she had waited so long to return to the one activity outside of work that always invigorated her.

Days later, Joan ran into a friend, Celeste Becker, during her workout at "The Body Works." Afterwards the two sat together at the club's juice bar. Joan caught Celeste up on the week's dismal events. Celeste listened, shaking her head.

"I think you need a night out. You need to come out dancing with us this Saturday," Celeste insisted. Celeste filled Joan in on the plans she and her boyfriend had made for the coming weekend and invited Joan to come along.

Joan really wanted to go out dancing but felt awkward about tagging along without a date. "I don't know," Joan replied halfheartedly. "I don't have a date, and I have to work at the Cheddar until nine that night."

"Oh, come on," said Celeste, unwilling to take no for an answer. "You know you don't need a date. There will be plenty of guys there to dance with, and you know we never start before ten anyway. You need a break, Joanie. Bring an extra set of clothes to work on Saturday, change at my place and then we'll go out. It will be lots of fun, you'll see."

Joan conceded without too much persuasion. Celeste's suggestion was really what she needed. She already was laying out Saturday's schedule in her mind as she drove from Westport to her apartment in Over-

land Park. I really owe this to myself, Joan said to
herself convincingly. Saturday morning she would begin looking for a new car. Saturday night, after work,
she would be out dancing. Finally, something sounded
good. Joan Butler believed she may have just turned
the corner on her gloom and anxiety. A string of unfortunate events might just be behind her, she thought.
She sang along with a song playing on the car radio.
She had no idea.

4

Saturday, June 17, 1989, was another sticky, pre-summer night in Kansas. A small, brown Toyota Hatchback pulled into the parking lot of a popular night spot near the University of Kansas campus in Lawrence. The lot offered parking for Pizazz, a dance club and bar frequented more by local residents than university students, though a handful of students drifted in and out on any given night during the school year. The driver of the Toyota made no effort to park his car near the club's main entrance. He preferred parking spaces on the outer edges. He purposely sought distance, some obscurity for the business he would transact prior to entering the club.

The brown Toyota had not been parked long when a man approached. The man opened the passenger-side door and slid in next to the driver.

"You got anything for me?" the driver asked. The question was vague but each knew why the other was there.

"I got a good lead for you, man!" said the passenger excitedly, apparently pleased with himself for having come through. "But I gotta get something off this one man. I'm strapped, and I really need a piece of this one."

"Depends," replied the driver, known to his passenger only as Rick or Ricky. The driver was calm and matter of fact about the set-up. "You already know what's there?" he asked casually. "Have you seen the place? What can I expect? Besides, you still owe me," he added before the passenger could respond.

"I know, I know," said the passenger in an apologetic tone. "But I have to put in some time on these scores. This information doesn't come in the mail. I gotta do my homework man, and that takes time and money! I'm not asking for a lot from this one man. I just need to make some ends meet, cover some things, you know? You gotta at least see what you can do for me if the score is hot."

"What's the score?" asked Ricky coldly, all but ignoring his partner's pleas.

The passenger reached inside the pocket of his dress shirt and pulled out a small, folded piece of paper. He unfolded it, read it over once in the dim light of the parking lot, paused for a moment and handed it to Ricky. "It's a broad's place up in Overland Park," the man said as Ricky took the piece of paper and stared down at the writing. "Her name is Carla, and she lives alone man!" the passenger said, a renewed enthusiasm returning to his voice.

The driver's eyes grew wide with interest as he listened to his source's lead for the burglary. Ricky began bombarding his source with a flurry of questions having more to do with Carla than the score. "Is this Carla home alone a lot?" asked Ricky, excitedly. "How old is she? What does she look like?"

"That doesn't fucking matter!" shot back his partner. "She won't be there. That's the deal here man. You have to hit the place later tonight or not at all. The broad has taken off for the weekend, due back sometime tomorrow but I don't know what time. I'll tell you about the place man. It should be an easy hit."

Ricky sat back, staring out the window at two young girls walking toward the club. He knew better than to ask any more personal questions about Carla. He would not draw that kind of attention to himself. For a brief moment he had become aroused by the prospect of catching Carla home alone, but he'd leave that for another time. Right then he needed his partner to believe they were on the same playing field—that they were going after the same score. Ricky took a deep breath and relaxed, allowing his source to finish detailing the night's target.

"The number of the broad's apartment is on that piece of paper," he said. "The place is called Comanche or the Comanche Apartments or something like that. They have a guard shack at the main entrance, but there's never anyone in there after midnight. If you don't want to go in the front, there's an exit right on Eighty-first Street. The exit has those spikes in the road that are supposed to take out your tires if you try to go in that way, but most of them are broken and, with this little car, you can get around them anyway, no sweat. You have to hit the place from the back. There's a small patio at the back of the apartment and it's got a six or eight foot wall behind it so people can't see in. Once you make the patio man, you're home free. No one can see you then. You should be in and out in a flash," he added, while Ricky listened, wondering whether he would end up doing things his own way in the end.

"This Carla broad is supposed to have a lot of jewelry stashed in a jewelry box in her bedroom. This one should be a piece of cake, in and out man! So if you do it and score, man, give me a little cut. I'm really hurting, man."

"Yeah well, let's see how it goes," said Ricky, once again stone-faced and feigning disinterest. "I'll have to see what's there and what I can get for it, and that's if I decide to do the score at all man." Ricky started rolling up his window, announcing that the meeting was, at least for him, all but over.

"It's an easy score Ricky! One of the easiest yet and she's supposed to have a lot of valuable shit man!" the passenger said, in a last-ditch effort to convince his cohort to follow through and do the job.

Ricky shrugged. He would not be pressured into anything. He already was disappointed that the opportunity included only a simple burglary. He had been distracted by the prospect that this Carla had a lot more to offer him than jewelry. "I'm going dancing," he said, opening his car door. "I'll call you if I do the job."

Both men entered Pizazz, but did so separately, with Ricky passing the ID checker five minutes before his partner. Both had arranged to meet women at the club that night and, once inside, no one would have guessed the two men even knew each other.

Ricky, now assuming a friendlier mask, met with a sometime girlfriend named Cathy Arenal. Cathy had come to Pizazz with a girlfriend but would spend most of the evening dancing and talking to Ricky. She was a KU student but also lived and worked in Lawrence. She was not a regular at the club but did enjoy an occasional night of dancing there. She had known Ricky for only a short time and had dated him only a couple of times. The man was a bit older than Cathy and not a student, but she found him easy to be around and certainly attractive.

Ricky stood just under six feet with the upper body build of a well-conditioned athlete. He possessed a formidable, natural strength, well-hidden at times, by his choice of loose, baggy and colorful dress shirts. By wearing colorful shirts, Ricky liked to pass himself off as a Polynesian, or someone from a South Pacific island even though he had no foreign accent. He was, in fact, dark skinned but not black in appearance. His hair was curly but grouped in longer, looser curls which he kept well-oiled, allowing them to curl up on the back of his neck. His facial features were attractive—high cheek bones, coal-black eyes and a beguiling smile.

Women considered him sexy. Ricky was soft-spoken and had a smooth, seemingly effortless way about him, lending the appearance of someone not easily ruffled. He was, on first impression, composed, willing to stand back and let others dominate conversations. He let his image do his talking for him. What he had worked for him, and he knew it. He had little trouble getting close to women; their protective edges were easily softened by his magnetism and charm.

Cathy Arenal danced and talked with Ricky until the club closed at 2:00 A.M. He walked Cathy and her girlfriend out to the parking lot, stopping short of Cathy's car. Her girlfriend, acknowledging the attraction between Cathy and "the islander," walked ahead to wait in the car while Cathy spent a few extra moments talking to Ricky. He did not make a move to convince Cathy to leave with him that night. Nor did he solicit an invitation to her apartment. To Ricky, the night was still young and he already had decided what he would do in the remaining hours before dawn.

Cathy may have assumed that the evening of dancing and talking had brought her a little closer to Ricky. Yet, she sensed there was something mysterious about him, something veiled and indistinct that she could not bring into focus. To Cathy, it was not threatening but more a part of the allure, part of her attraction to him.

Ricky's tactics were good, but Cathy did not know how good. In less than two weeks, she would discover the gravity of her error in judgment. The young coed would learn a shocking lesson about her own vulnerability.

Ricky drove his Toyota out of the parking lot at Pizazz and out of the city of Lawrence. The night would not end before he took his shot at Carla's apartment. Earlier, when talking to his source, Ricky did not let on that he already was very familiar with the Comanche Place complex. He had driven through it several times to case it. His own apartment in Lenexa, Kansas, was just ten minutes away. To men like Ricky, multi-unit apartment complexes housed not people, but victims. Every unit, every resident was, to him, a potential target; he considered any women he found inside the units simply bonus babies, prizes to be enjoyed at his discretion. To him, their bodies and their lives had no greater value than the necklaces around their necks, the baubles in their jewelry boxes or the credit cards in their purses.

Ricky stopped at his own apartment to change clothes before moving on to Comanche Place. It was now 3:30 in the morning. Arriving at the target complex, he steered his car into the exit road and around the road spikes. Had anyone been watching at that late hour, the maneuver would appear to have been performed by a resident, experienced at avoiding the spikes and using the exit as a quicker way into the complex. Driving into the complex, he registered the location of the target unit, number 177, as he passed it. He then turned the Toyota left, away from the apartment and down a slight hill to another part of the complex. His path took him into a section that dead-ended into a horseshoe loop lined with resident parking spaces. He spotted an open space and backed into it. He felt his adrenaline pumping more with each passing minute. He cut his engine, exited the car and began a casual seventy-five-yard walk back up the incline toward unit number 177.

Once there, Ricky made his approach from the side of the building and ducked behind the patio wall. Once behind the barrier, the experienced thief waited a few minutes before executing his next moves. He knew if he had been spotted, lights might come on in nearby units or windows and doors might open to allow the curious to determine if the man they had seen belonged there. He would not make any noise. While waiting, he studied the buildings across the way, watching for the reflection of headlights bouncing off them. Headlights would indicate someone, maybe police or security, had turned into the complex and were heading his way. He knew the difference between a charge of trespassing and one of breaking and entering. It would pay to wait, and he knew it.

A few minutes later, Ricky broke a small section of a rear window, unlocked it and slid inside. Then, he unlocked the sliding-glass door off the patio and opened it slightly. If forced to make a quick exit, he did not want to be slowed by locks and closed doors. With a small flashlight in hand, the thief moved toward Carla's master bedroom. To him, it was the only room that contained both the items he intended to steal, and those he wanted to inspect. First, he took a few pieces from Carla's jewelry box—those which appeared most valuable to him. Then, he spent the rest of his time performing his own unique, ritualistic inspection of Carla's most personal items before slipping out the back door and down the hill to his car. The routine left him excited and, although in possession of a score, unsatisfied.

The successful thief did not immediately leave the area. He calmly remained seated behind the wheel, meticulously inspecting the pieces of jewelry from his score. He was holding a necklace up to the light of a distant street lamp when another flash of light bounced off a building across the lot.

A car was coming into the complex. As the car turned toward the loop, its lights again bounced off buildings across from him. It was coming his way. For the first time that evening, the thief felt a pang of nervousness. He glanced down at his watch. It was just before 4:30 on Sunday morning. He reasoned that if it wasn't the newspaper delivery, it had to be the cops. Ricky squeezed the gold necklace in the palm of his hand and slid down in his seat just far enough to not be noticed, but still able to see who was pulling into the dead-end lot. Seconds later, Ricky breathed a sigh of relief. It wasn't the police or security patrolling the lot. It was a resident returning home. A resident driving a maroon Corsica.

5

June 19, 1989, 7:30 A.M. Judy Sherry, co-founder and ad executive of the Montague-Sherry Ad Agency, pulled into the agency's parking lot near downtown Kansas City. The sun was up, the air cool, and the week ushering in the summer was about to begin. Judy had a smile on her face. Business was good, and each new week had brought with it the promise of steady, satisfying growth for the agency. She was proud that the business had grown to a size deserving of attention from competitors in Kansas City. Her employees numbered twenty-two, a statistic of which she was most proud.

As Judy stretched her legs, she scanned the parking lot for Joan Butler's Honda. Joan usually pulled into the lot about the same time as she did. Joan was not there yet. Unusual, she thought. Then Judy remembered Joan's accident and recalled that Joan had been driving the red, rental car for the past week. But she saw no red Corsica in the lot either. Judy recalled Joan's black eye, her facial cuts and generally somber mood of the previous week, and wondered if maybe she decided to extend her weekend a day or two. Whatever the reason, it was probably a good one for Joan not to be at work early.

Gary Coleman, Joan's boss at Montague-Sherry, arrived about half an hour after Judy. He headed straight for the media design division to prepare for an early meeting. His group in the division worked as a service team, and Joan was the media agent. The design team occupied the upper floor of the agency and maintained a degree of independence from the other departments at Montague-Sherry. The upper-floor team also had its own coffee bar, which Gary noticed was empty. His immediate thoughts were of Joan. Gary thought it odd. Joan was always there when he got in. Her work habits were so consistent and reliable that her absence, even for one day, created a conspicuous void.

Gary made coffee and prepared for his meeting. Following the meeting, he overheard members of his staff talking about Joan's absence. They all had noticed that Joan had not arrived at work and had not called. Gary waited until 9:30 A.M. and again asked his staff if anyone had heard from Joan.

One of Joan's co-workers replied that she had tried calling Joan at home, but her answering machine had picked up the call. Gary asked if anyone remembered Joan saying she might go home to Wichita for Father's Day. Gary knew how close Joan was to her family and wondered whether she had decided to pop in on her dad for the weekend. But no one had heard Joan mention the possibility. In fact, another member of the team said she was certain that Joan was scheduled to work at her other job the previous Saturday and had talked about going out dancing Saturday night.

Sensing something was wrong, several members of the team dropped what they were doing and began a full-scale effort to contact Joan. Although concerned, they were convinced there was a reasonable explanation for why Joan was not there and why she had not called anyone.

By 10:30 A.M., Gary Coleman had asked for and received directions to Joan's apartment in Overland Park. A half hour later, he arrived at Comanche Place and went directly to the apartment manager's office. Gary did not mention his concerns about Joan to the on-duty manager; he simply asked for Joan's apartment number and directions to get there.

Before parking near Joan's place, he circled the lot but could not find the rental car Joan had leased the previous week. He parked and hustled up the stairs to Joan's apartment, number 230. He noticed that delivery people and door-to-door solicitors already had made their rounds that morning. A phone book had been placed on the concrete pad just in front of the door, and a packet of promotional ads, stuffed inside a clear plastic bag, dangled from the doorknob. Gary knocked on Joan's door several times. When there was no response, he tried the door and found it locked. He knocked several more times while calling out Joan's name but again, no reply.

Puzzled, Gary returned to the manager's office where he expressed his concerns about Joan Butler. He asked if someone might "officially" enter Joan's apartment and have a look around. "I just need to know if she's in there and if she's all right," he pleaded. "It's just not like her to not show up for work and not call anyone to tell them why," he explained. "Couldn't someone just go in there and have a quick look? That's all I'm asking! I don't have to go in myself, I just want someone to look inside."

"I'm sorry sir," explained the manager. "Our regulations are quite specific about when and how the management can enter a tenant's apartment. Without specific authorization or formal notice, we can't go in and look around. I appreciate your concerns, but I can't help you with your request," the manager replied with bureaucratic indifference.

Realizing he and the manager would never reach common ground, Gary gave up at Comanche Place and called his office to see if anyone had heard from Joan. Learning that nothing had changed, Gary asked one of his staff to call Joan's parents in Wichita. Just maybe, Gary thought, Joan had indeed made a last-minute decision to go home for Father's Day and was simply running a bit behind schedule while trying to return to Kansas City. Still, Gary's fears mounted. He knew it was a stretch that Joan had gone home. She would have called if she was going to be late or was not coming in at all.

Returning to the agency, Gary was not surprised by the news that Joan had not gone to Wichita. He was, however, somewhat shocked by the news that Joan had not even called her father, as promised, the previous day. Ralph Butler told one of Joan's co-workers that Joan had assured her mother the previous Friday that she would be calling on Father's Day. Hearing this, Gary suspended his schedule for the day and announced to his staff that he would be concentrating his efforts on finding Joan Butler.

Gary first called Enterprise Leasing to determine if anything had been reported on Joan's rental car. He was told that the lease status of the car had not changed and that the renter had not contacted the company. Gary explained his concerns about Joan and asked for all of the identifying data available on the car. Next, he retrieved Joan's file from her desk and began compiling an extensive list of individuals to be called. Gary copied the names and numbers of Joan's friends, relatives, clients, hairdresser, and anyone whom he believed might be able to shed some light on her whereabouts. For Gary Coleman and the staff at Montague-Sherry, this would be just the beginning of a long, determined effort to locate their friend and associate. Joan had been missing for half the workday. They knew something had to be wrong. They were like an extended family, and they knew when something had happened to one of their own.

In Wichita, Ralph and Jenelda "Jada" Butler, troubled over their daughter's sudden and mysterious disappearance, began calling everyone they hoped might help them locate "Joanie." One of their first calls was to Ralph's cousin John Mura and his daughter Beth who lived in Kansas City. Ralph knew that Joan and Beth were very close. Joan may have contacted her. He also knew that John may have been the last family member to see Joan when he helped her look for a new car the previous Saturday.

John told Ralph that he had helped Joan on Saturday but that he had said good-bye to her as she hurried off to her part-time job early in the afternoon. He also mentioned that Joan told him she might go dancing with a girlfriend that evening. To the Butler's disappointment, however, neither John nor Beth had seen or talked to Joan since Saturday.

By Monday afternoon, with still no word from their daughter, the Butlers placed three additional phone calls. The first was to the management office at Comanche Place. Unfortunately, Ralph Butler's requests for a cursory search of Joan's apartment were met with the same indifference encountered earlier by Gary, Ralph persisted, however, registering his unwillingness to take no for an answer. Unlike Gary Coleman, Ralph was able to argue from the vantage of a desperate father looking for his missing daughter. If the management would not check Joan's apartment, he would ensure that the police did. His determination forced a break in the administrative gridlock, and the manager finally acquiesced, indicating she would go and have a look around apartment number 230.

The subsequent report that Joan was not inside her apartment and that nothing in her apartment seemed out of the ordinary provided Joan's parents a measure of relief. The news did verify that Joan was not found hurt or somehow trapped. They would not allow themselves to think about any scenarios with endings worse than that. To the Butlers, there was still hope. Something minor might be amiss, they reasoned, and it would all be explained in time.

The second of their three phone calls was made to the Overland Park Police Department. The Comanche Place complex fell within their jurisdiction. Joan's parents had decided that enough time had passed without word from their daughter to warrant filing a missing person's report. Unfortunately, filing the report would be another obstacle for them.

Most metropolitan police agencies were not motivated or prompted into action by a report of a young person missing for less than twenty-four hours. Response and reporting policy were dictated accordingly. A parent's insistence that their child was not the kind to run off did not carry much weight in most cases.

In addition to the twenty-four-hour stipulation, the Butlers faced another obstacle when advised that a missing-person complaint could not be registered over the phone. They had to be filed in person. To the Butler's credit, their persistence once again won them a mild concession. The Overland Park Police agreed to take preliminary background information on Joan to have on record until the Butlers could appear in person the next day to file a formal report. If clues surfaced overnight, the police at least would have some data on Joan.

By early Monday evening, the Butlers placed a third call, this time to Joan's friend and next-door neighbor, Deborah Stryker. They had heard Joan speak about Deborah on numerous occasions. Joan and Deborah had grown close since becoming neighbors at Comanche Place. The Butlers knew that it was Deborah Stryker who drove Joan to Enterprise Leasing to pick up the rental car.

In addition to questioning Deborah about whether she knew of other places where Joan might have gone, they asked if she had a key to Joan's apartment or, if not, could she find a way to get in and look around. Deborah did not know where Joan might have gone, but when asked whether or not she could, or would, go into Joan's apartment for their sake, her answer was a unreserved "yes."

Deborah immediately contacted Sarah Blanz who leased the ground-floor apartment just below Joan's. Sarah agreed they should somehow get into Joan's apartment. Sarah dialed a friend named Jerry who lived nearby. Around 10:30 that night, with Deborah and Sarah looking on, Jerry hoisted himself up onto an exterior patio wall and squeezed through an open window leading into Joan's kitchen.

Once inside, Jerry opened the front door for Sarah and Deborah and their search began. Nothing struck them as unusual. They did notice that only one of Joan's contact lenses could be found in its case atop the bathroom vanity. They noted that a piece of half-eaten toast sat on a plate on the kitchen counter. A table knife stained with jelly rested beside it. A cigarette, only slightly smoked, lay in an ashtray near the plate. Following a good look through the apartment,

Deborah Stryker played back Joan's messages from her answering machine. She copied the ones not from Joan's parents with the intent of giving the list to them.

Using Joan's phone, Deborah called the Butlers in Wichita to let them know what had transpired. Before leaving, Deborah removed a picture of Joan from the bulletin board by the phone. She would hang the picture, along with a hand-printed notice, in the mail-box area of the apartment complex. She wanted everyone to be aware that her friend was missing and that help was needed in finding her.

In Wichita, the Butlers spent the first of many sleepless nights worrying about their oldest child, Joanie. During the late-evening hours, final preparations were made for their trip to Kansas City. They had someone to look after their younger children. They telephoned their son, who was working and studying on the East Coast, and told him about the day's events. They promised to keep him apprised of developments concerning his sister.

Executives at KSNW-TV where Ralph Butler worked were notified and told that Ralph would be taking some time off in Kansas City. He and his wife would be leaving the next morning and would be gone for however long it took to find their daughter. If they could have seen into the future, they would have told everyone they would be gone from home for a very long time.

6

To the Overland Park Police, the sudden, unexplained disappearance of Joan Butler did not send up a warning flag or elicit a major case investigation. For much of the week after Father's Day, the Joan Butler case was in limbo. It was not that the police were cold or indifferent to the needs of family members or friends. Rather, in order for them to be of help, they had to have a lead to go on, something they could piece together to recreate a logical sequence of events. The Overland Park Police did open an investigation into the Joan Butler disappearance, but the clues left behind provided no hint of what might have happened.

The police conducted a walk-through search of Joan's apartment and interviewed several individuals who had knowledge of her habits and activities leading up to the time of her disappearance. The police did express concern about possible contamination of a potential crime scene, since no less than seven people had gone through the apartment prior to their arrival. The walk-through, however, did not reveal any signs of foul play within the apartment. The apartment, in fact, appeared normal. In addition, Joan's car was missing, prompting the assumption that whatever happened to her, happened outside the apartment.

The early investigation also revealed that Joan had made it home after leaving Celeste Becker's place the previous Sunday morning. An interview with Celeste confirmed that the black dress with gold sash-belt found hanging on the back of Joan's bedroom closet door, was indeed the dress she had been wearing Saturday night. The black pumps she had worn also were found on the closet floor. Note also was made of the partially eaten toast and the half-smoked cigarette found atop Joan's kitchen counter. Adding to the belief that once home, Joan again left her apartment, was the fact that neither her purse nor her car could be found.

The only evidence remotely suggestive of foul play was not obtained from inside the apartment, but came from an interview with Joan's downstairs neighbor, Sarah Blanz. Sarah told police that sometime around 4:30 in the morning she was awakened by a loud crash or thud, which sounded as if someone or something had hit the floor above her with a good deal of force. Sarah was forced to admit however, that waking at that hour of the morning from a deep sleep, she could not be certain what she had heard. She also reported that after getting out of bed to look into the parking lot, she noticed nothing out of the ordinary. Sarah told police she also vaguely remembered that Joan's car was parked in front of the building that morning when she looked out.

Information obtained early on by police produced a variety of assumptions but no new leads. The Joan Butler case was in danger of being assigned the "missing person" label and placed in a "pending" file until new leads could be developed. It might have indeed gone that route and remained there, were it not for the efforts of Joan's family, friends and co-workers.

Joan Butler's disappearance was starting to alter the lives of many people close to her. Ralph and Jada Butler, continuing their exhaustive efforts to find their daughter, stayed on in Kansas City. They moved in with John Mura and his family who, likewise, were doing all they could to help in the search for Joan. Except for a few brief and necessary trips home to Wichita for the sake of their other children, the Butlers committed themselves, for however long, to an aggressive, continuous search. As time passed, they presumed the worst, but would not give up hope.

Gary Coleman, Judy Sherry and Joan's co-workers at the ad agency also proved to be dedicated and unselfish in their commitment to finding out what happened to their friend. In the first three weeks after Joan's disappearance, small groups handled the day-to-day business at the agency while the majority of the staff's time was dedicated to finding her.

It was inevitable that the paths of Joan's parents and the staff at Montague-Sherry would cross. By Tuesday afternoon, June 20, Ralph Butler and Gary Coleman sat facing each other across a conference table at the ad agency. The two compared notes and picked each other's brains for ideas and possible leads. They acknowledged that the police had opened an investigation into Joan's disappearance and were aware that a lot of bases might be covered as a result of that network. However, they could not, they agreed, just sit back and wait in the hope that leads would trickle in. Both had a tremendous respect for the police, but both also realized they needed to be doing something on their own.

The meetings between the Butlers and the Montague-Sherry staff resulted in the creation of a "bulletin" or "flyer" replicated thousands of times at the agency for citywide distribution. The flyer contained a large picture of Joan, her physical description and the announcement that she was last seen in the early morning hours of Sunday, June 18. The flyer also showed a picture of the Chevrolet Corsica, along with description, license plate number CAF 734, and a partial vehicle-identification number. The staff at Montague-Sherry also created material for a billboard and paid for its posting on several boards throughout the city. The flyers also mentioned a reward offered through the Tips Hot Line.

The Butlers, other family members, Joan's friends and nearly the entire Montague-Sherry staff joined forces to distribute the "missing person" notices by the armload. Ralph Butler and others even traveled outside the metro area to post and distribute bulletins at turnpike and interstate truck stops and rest areas. They talked to people by the dozens everywhere they went. Joan's friends and family mounted flyers on shop windows at malls and shopping centers. Bulletins were tacked on lampposts and doors to office buildings and area arenas.

Beth Mura, John's daughter and Joan's close friend, also gave her all to the ever-expanding search. To Beth, Joan was like a sister, and her sudden and unexplained disappearance left Beth severely depressed. Beth's family made every effort to keep her busy, occupying her with tasks on Joan's behalf or on behalf of the Butler family. Among Beth's activities was a tireless effort to distribute flyers. Her efforts eventually would lead to an understanding of what happened to Joan Butler.

Among the many flyers Beth handed out was one she gave a close friend, Rae Ann Thompson. Rae Ann was a striking, young woman with sandy-blonde hair and blue eyes. She had received the flyer from Beth late in the week after Joan's disappearance and carried it everywhere. She even took it home with her during a weekend visit to her parent's house in Leavenworth, Kansas.

Rae Ann and her mother discussed the Joan Butler case in the kitchen as they prepared food for a family barbecue. Just as their conversation shifted to the Corsica leased by Joan Butler, Rae Ann's brother Eric joined them.

Eric was a student at Kansas University and living in an apartment in Lawrence. He was an all-American looking man standing just under six feet with broad shoulders and a well-developed upper body. Eric was also a car buff who paid close attention to the introduction each year of manufacturers' newest models. Eric was keenly aware that Chevrolet had just introduced the Corsica and its sister model, the Beretta, the previous year. "What's that you said about a Chevy Corsica?" Eric asked his sister. "Somebody missing one?"

"I was telling mom more about Joan Butler, the girl who has been missing in Kansas City. She's very close to my friend Beth, and she just vanished without a trace last weekend. Her family and friends are sick with worry."

Eric approached the kitchen table and sat down across from Rae Ann. "I remember seeing bits and pieces of that on the news," he said. "Wasn't she fairly young, like early twenties, and no one has a clue about what happened?"

"Exactly," replied Rae Ann. "She was just gone one day. It's got everyone baffled and her family is going crazy. It's really affected my friend Beth."

"What about the car?" Eric asked, his interest still piqued. "You mentioned a Corsica when I walked in. Is that what she had? It's a fairly new model," he added.

"It wasn't her personal car," offered Rae Ann. "The week before she disappeared, her own car was totaled in an accident. The Corsica was a rental, and it's missing too. They put a picture of the car next to Joan's on the flyer."

Eric moved his chair closer. "Do you have an extra flyer with you, or can you get me the information on the car?" he asked excitedly.

"I've got one in my purse," Rae Ann replied. She looked at her brother inquisitively. Returning with a flyer in hand, she asked, "Do you know something about the car?" Rae Ann placed the flyer in front of Eric.

"It's a burgundy or dark red," Eric said, reading from the flyer. "I suppose it would be too much of a coincidence, but a new Corsica, this same color, has been parked off and on in the parking lot of my apartment complex in Lawrence. Of course, anyone in the complex could have purchased a new Corsica this past week. Come to think of it, the car only comes in a few color options," he added, still studying the flyer. "I didn't notice if the one I saw in Lawrence had a leasing company's sticker on it, and I couldn't tell you about the tag number."

"It's worth a close look if you see it again," said Rae Ann. "Take the flyer back with you and be sure to call me if you find anything."

"I'll check it out tonight when I get back to Lawrence." Eric said.

As coincidence would have it, a burgundy Corsica sat parked in a stall at the Trailridge Apartment complex in Lawrence when Eric arrived home from Leavenworth. He parked two spaces away from the Corsica. The sun was just setting, and plenty of daylight remained for him to give the car a once-over. Eric strolled past the car, and glanced down at the license plate. It matched the tag number on the flyer! His heart began to beat as if coiled on a spring and suddenly let loose. He wanted to sprint into the building, but Eric resisted. He continued to move steadily from the parking lot to his apartment.

Eric did not have to recheck the flyer. He knew the number backwards and forwards. The car belonging to the missing woman now sat parked in the lot just outside his apartment building. Eric Thompson was energized beyond belief.

First he dialed the Tips Hot Line number from the flyer. He was stunned when the hot line operator told Eric that Lawrence, Kansas, was not in their jurisdiction. He was told to call the Lawrence Police Department. Eric was smart enough to know the value of the information he had. He would not waste time trying to convince a lukewarm hot line operator that what he had was real and significant. While dialing the Lawrence Police, Eric wondered how the missing girl's family might respond if they knew that the operator was rejecting solid leads for reasons of geography.

Eric's frustration mounted when the Lawrence Police dispatcher informed him that she was not familiar with the case. Eric patiently told the dispatcher as much as he knew about the case and about his discovery, parked not fifty yards from where he was calling. The dispatcher finally acknowledged that Eric's tip was probably legitimate and agreed to send a patrol unit by to check it out.

Information on the disappearance of Joan Butler was not entered into the National Crime Information Center computer, nor was it placed in the intrastate law enforcement computer data banks for dissemination to other state agencies. Thus, officers at the Lawrence Police Department, just twenty-five miles west of Overland Park, were not aware of Joan Butler's disappearance or the search for her car.

It was close to 9:00 P.M., with daylight giving way rapidly to darkness, when Lawrence Police Officer Brian Edwards pulled into the parking lot at the Trailridge complex at 2500 West Sixth Street. Spotting the suspect car with license plate CAF 734 as relayed by his dispatcher, Officer Edwards drove away from the immediate vicinity, not wanting to draw attention with his marked vehicle. He repositioned his unit about fifty yards from the Corsica at the opposite end of the parking lot.

Officer Edwards was a cop with an intimidating presence. He stood more than six feet; it was clear he was a weight lifter. Physical appearance aside, Edwards was soft-spoken, bright and experienced. He had been a cop since 1978, with all but three of those years served with the Lawrence Police Department. He had passed on several opportunities for promotion, opting instead to remain on patrol. He loved the streets and involved himself in programs designed to help troubled youth.

Edwards wasn't parked long before Eric Thompson, having circled the lot on the perimeter, approached the police car and identified himself. Edwards asked him to fill him in on what he knew about the car and the Overland Park case.

Eric pulled the flyer from his pocket and showed it to the officer. While Edwards looked it over, Eric told him about the massive search for Joan Butler taking place around Kansas City. Eric offered to walk by the Corsica and have a quick look around. He pointed out his own truck, parked just a couple of spaces away from the Corsica, and suggested that he could pretend to be getting something from it. He told the officer that if anyone questioned him, he would simply tell them he was admiring the new car.

The officer agreed to let Eric take a look, but asked that he not linger at the car and then head straight to his apartment. Eric got out of the patrol car and crossed the lot to his truck. He did not get the chance to get any closer to the Corsica.

Edwards watched from his police unit as a young, well-built black man approached the burgundy car. The man fingered through a set of keys and opened the trunk. Edwards stepped from his car, secured his nightstick through a loop in his belt and approached the subject. The cop kept his eyes on both the man at the Corsica and Eric, who remained seated in his truck waiting to see what would happen. As Edwards approached, he noticed that the black man was light skinned and muscular. The subject wore cut-off shorts, a tank top and sneakers.

The subject raised up from the trunk and spun around quickly at the sound of the cop approaching. Edwards was not surprised by the reaction. He had seen it hundreds of times, the reaction of suspects all too familiar with the sounds made by "the man." The suspect's next response did not surprise the veteran cop either. Without taking his eyes off Edwards, the black man raised his arm up behind him, caught the edge of the trunk lid, and slammed it shut. Edwards was certain the move was intentional, designed to ensure that the trunk was closed as Edwards approached.

"Do you have some identification on you sir?" Edwards asked.

The suspect paused, eyeing the policeman before responding. "No, I don't have any ID on me. It's inside the building," he said, motioning toward the apartment building. "It's in apartment 531 of that building right there."

Detecting a slight nervousness in the suspect's voice, Edwards cut to the chase. "Do you know who the owner of this car is?"

"My ID is in the house," the suspect replied, somewhat flustered and avoiding the question altogether.

The officer would not tolerate the evasiveness. "I didn't ask you that. The question is how did you come to be in possession of the keys to this car? Who's car is this?" Edwards insisted.

"Someone inside," said the suspect, his voice cracking. The suspect's eyes darted about. He wouldn't make direct eye contact with the officer. He looked to the ground, then toward the building. "Somebody inside gave me the keys."

The officer held out his hand toward the suspect. "Give me the keys to the car," he ordered. Too many things could happen before he got to the bottom of who had possession of the car and why. In the interim, he would ensure that the keys rested securely with him. The suspect complied, dropping the keys into the officer's hand. "Now, let's go inside and get some ID and see about this car," ordered Edwards, motioning for the suspect to lead the way up the walk toward the apartment.

In the parking lot, Eric Thompson watched the officer and the suspect move toward the apartment building. He couldn't wait to get inside and call his sister. He suspected that things had gone well and that

Edwards' suspect would shed some light on the car and, hopefully, on what had happened to Joan Butler.

The suspect was leading Edwards by a couple of feet as he arrived at the outer door of the apartment building. The door led into an open hallway leading to lower-floor apartments and a staircase to a second floor. The suspect was just inside the main door when he broke from Edwards in an all-out sprint down the hallway. Startled, Edwards took off after him. At apartment number 531, the suspect blew open the door and slammed it shut behind him.

Not knowing what awaited him on the other side, Edwards, with a hand on his holstered gun, opened the door and entered with a rush. Five pairs of eyes stared back at him from the center of the room. Two black men and three Hispanic men were sitting in the center of the small studio apartment. They were on the floor eating pizza. The suspect was not among them. Edwards spoke into his shoulder microphone calling for backup. The officer ordered the men to remain seated as he took a few steps toward the kitchen at the back of the apartment. Halfway there, he noticed that the screen from a side window had been knocked out. He moved toward the window. The screen lay bent and torn on the ground just below. Turning back toward the group in the center of the room, the officer asked if the man he was chasing had gone through the window. Several heads nodded. Still Edwards checked the kitchen.

The suspect was not in the apartment. Edwards kept an eye on the group as he went back to the open window and once again looked outside. He came face to face with fellow officer Terry Haak. "Did you see a suspect flee through this window?" Edwards asked. "He just blew through here seconds ago!"

"I ran up from the parking lot," answered Haak. "I didn't see anyone come out this way or run away from the building."

Edwards found it incredible that the suspect had, in a matter of seconds, eluded them. The fact that he got away would haunt him for some time.

7

It had been around 9:30 P.M. when the suspect escaped through the apartment window in Lawrence. By midnight, with the police processing of the Corsica under way, and early interviews completed, the suspect had been positively identified. His name was Richard Grissom Jr. His aliases were numerous.

Lt. Mike Hall, Chief of Detectives and a seventeen-year veteran of the Lawrence Police Department, responded to the Trailridge complex shortly after the suspect escaped. Hall also called out all detectives under his command, as well as all available support personnel. Police officers covered every foot of the Trailridge complex searching inside buildings and throughout the grounds. Flashlights in hand, they checked every car parked around the complex in case the suspect had chosen one for a temporary hiding place.

The Lawrence Police eventually called in tracking dogs that picked up a scent near the side window of number 531 and followed it around the building and down a few back streets until the scent faded a few blocks away. What the officers did not know was that long before their extensive searches were concluded, the suspect was well on his way out of Lawrence.

Locating Joan Butler's Corsica and identifying Richard Grissom as a primary suspect was a good-news-bad-news scenario. To officers in Overland Park, recovering her car was good news. To those same officers, and to the family and friends of Joan Butler, not finding Joan with the car was bad news. And, the only person who might have known anything about what happened to Joan had vanished into the night.

The police, however, had recovered a primary piece of evidence, the kind that readily would produce new leads. Arriving to help develop those leads were ranking officers and forensic specialists from Overland Park and Lawrence plus the Johnson County sheriff's lab.

Detective Sergeant Jeff Dysart, a fourteen-year member of the Overland Park force, knew that only the exterior of the Corsica would be processed by the crime-lab officers that night. His team would opt for a more controlled environment to process the car's interior. The location eventually would be the sally port at the Johnson County Sheriff's Department in Olathe, Kansas. Getting the car to the Sheriff's sally port would require towing it the twenty-mile distance, a process which might obliterate any trace evidence or latent fingerprints on the car's exterior. Avoiding that possibility required processing the exterior while the car remained at the Trailridge complex.

Crime-lab officers photographed the car from every angle, covered it front-to-back with fingerprint powder, and tape-lifted several latent prints of sufficient quality for comparison. Investigators made note of scratches found on the lower left-front fender and wheel hub, and on the left-side rear-view mirror. It appeared the car had been scraped by thick brush or small tree limbs. A thin coating of light-colored dust covered much of the lower exterior. It was the kind of fine dust that accumulates after a car has been driven through loose gravel. The investigators also noted that the rental company logo, once attached to the rear bumper of the car, had been removed.

When processing was completed, officers wrapped the car in evidence tape and crime scene stickers, making sure the doors, trunk, windows and hood openings all were sealed. The process was performed to ensure the preservation of any evidence inside. Officers followed the Corsica as it was towed to the Johnson County Sheriff's sally port where it was unloaded.

At the Trailridge apartments, several officers interviewed the five men left behind in apartment 531. The men recounted five varying, but not dissimilar versions of events leading up to the chase. According to the men, they were part of a painting crew hired by Grissom, who they said, owned his own paint-contracting and general-labor company he called Apex Painting and Maintenance.

With one exception, the men on his crew were day-workers, some homeless, who Grissom or his foreman, a black man named Marcelais Thibodo, picked up each morning from area shelters. During some periods, laborers from prison work-release or halfway house programs were hired. Hiring these men was not part of a good Samaritan approach to life by Grissom. To him, they were nothing more than cheap labor whom he could pay in cash, to avoid keeping tax and payroll records. A few of the men had been with Grissom off and on for a while and knew he had painting contracts at several apartment complexes in Kansas City.

The painters were brought to Lawrence by either Grissom or his foreman, Thibodo, who liked to be called "French" or "Frenchy." None of the five knew Grissom by his true name. In fact, most knew him simply as Rick or Ricky. To others, the boss was Richard. A couple knew him as Mr. Cho. A quick check of the Kansas State Law Enforcement computer, which stored the known aliases of felons or wanted suspects, revealed that all names mentioned were aliases for Richard Grissom.

When asked about their work foreman, Frenchy, the workers all told the same story. Frenchy had been at the Trailridge complex with them for most of that day and had left around 8:30 P.M. to go to his girlfriend's house. No, they did not know exactly where she lived, but they knew it was in Lawrence. Frenchy had told a couple of them that he was spending the night in Lawrence.

When questioned about the Corsica, the crew's answers were varied but made sense. Those who had been with Grissom for more than a week remembered their boss's small brown car, but also noted that recently he'd been driving the newer red one. Those who had been part of the crew only a few days knew only the red car.

The five workers were, in short order, eliminated as suspects in the disappearance of Joan Butler. The same however, could not be said for Grissom's foreman, whose good timing had momentarily helped him avoid the disturbance and early interviews at Trailridge. From what police learned about Thibodo, they could draw reasonable conclusions about his relationship with

Grissom. They suspected he might have more answers to their questions.

Police officers from Overland Park and Lawrence were waiting at Trailridge early the next morning when Thibodo arrived for work. Thibodo already knew a lot more about the activities of the previous night than the police might have guessed. He had not been at his girlfriend's house the entire night. He had, in fact, been with Grissom for part of the night but did not know why Grissom had fled Lawrence in such a hurry. He did know the police had been at Trailridge and that they were looking for Grissom. He considered two options that morning. He could hide out until the dust settled. Or, not really knowing the full extent of Grissom's activities, he could simply go in and face the police. He opted for the latter.

When detectives first grabbed Thibodo, he was not to be interviewed in the corner of an apartment like his five day-workers. He was a suspect for the moment and would not be handled casually. Thibodo immediately was taken to the Lawrence Police headquarters. Within hours, he began giving police his account of who he was and what he knew about Richard Grissom.

8

Marcelais Thibodo was a twenty-nine-year-old black man whose roots could be traced to ancestry in Louisiana, which accounted for the nickname "Frenchy." His mother and father had separated when he was young and he was raised, along with several brothers, by his father who owned and operated an auto-salvage yard in the Kansas City area. Thibodo worked on and off for his father in the salvage yard throughout his school years and intermittently after leaving home.

He was tall and muscular. He had, in fact, been a high school gymnast and a champion wrestler. His chances for an athletic career were cut short, however, when a truck pinned his leg against a post, crushing it and altering his life. Following several surgeries, his injured leg remained much shorter than his other one, forcing him to walk with a permanent limp.

During his interrogation, Thibodo admitted helping Richard Grissom escape from Lawrence. Under intense questioning by detectives from Overland Park and Lawrence, Thibodo insisted he did not know why Grissom had run, and could form an opinion only based on what Grissom had told him. He then provided his version of events the night before.

According to Thibodo, Grissom had hidden less than a mile from the Trailridge complex as the search for him intensified. From Trailridge, he had run to a nearby strip-shopping center on Sixth Avenue, to a pay phone outside the Dillon's market. From there, he had called Thibodo. In anxious, out-of-breath spurts, he'd ordered Thibodo to get his ass over to the strip center and pick him up. Thibodo dropped everything and ran.

Though darkness had settled over Lawrence, the strip center was well-lighted by both overhead street lights and the bright fluorescent light from the market. Grissom had hidden between parked cars in the lot.

Thibodo studied the parking lot as he drove his silver Nissan pickup toward the supermarket. No sign of Grissom. He slowed down as he passed the bank of pay phones near the market. He looked out over the parking lot. He did not see Grissom anywhere. Passing the market, he decided to loop the parking lot a second time.

Grissom watched from his hiding place between parked cars as Thibodo approached the market again. He looked around for police cars. When he thought it was safe, Grissom stepped from his crouched position and into the lane of the approaching truck. Thibodo spotted him and slowed just enough for Grissom to jump in. Grissom's first command was for him to drive back down Sixth Avenue and past the Trailridge complex.

As the pickup approached the complex, Grissom ordered, "Slow down, slow down. I want to see what's happening."

Thibodo stared into the parking lot. Flashing blue and red lights from police cars bounced off the building. Officers were scattered around the building's perimeter. Thibodo saw what he thought was Grissom's "rented" car with two cops standing near the trunk, looking it over. "What is this, man!" he asked excitedly. "What the fuck is going on? What happened, man?"

"You should have seen me, dog! I was like Jessie fucking Owens, man!" Grissom said, boasting about his narrow escape from the police and avoiding the real issue. "No one could have caught me, man!"

Grissom did not have to think long and hard for answers to Thibodo's questions. He could rattle off blatant lies as if reading from a cue card, and someone like Thibodo was easily convinced. "The cops found out I'd been ripping off a few bank accounts," Grissom said. "One account belonged to the girl who rented the car for me. She must have ratted me out to the cops."

Before Grissom could elaborate further, Thibodo held up his hand. "I don't want to hear any more man," he said. As the truck rolled past the complex, Thibodo turned for a quick look and then watched the scene fade in his rear-view mirror. "The less I know about this shit the better, man," he said. "Whatever you've been doing with someone else's shit is your business. I don't need to know about it."

"It's no big deal," Grissom shot back. "It's just a couple of ripped-off bank accounts." Grissom knew that Thibodo was not the smartest guy around, but he also knew he was street wise. Thibodo would know the difference between a major crime scene and a routine police investigation. What they had just passed was far from routine. Grissom sensed that his partner suspected there was more than ripped-off bank accounts. Grissom made another attempt at a smoke screen. "Listen man. The reason there's so much shit going on back there is because I got away man. The cops are pissed. A cop had his hands on me, man. I beat him. I got away. So they brought out the cavalry to try and find me."

"Where do you want to go?" Thibodo asked, ignoring Grissom's explanations. He really didn't know what to believe, and at that moment, he didn't care. Grissom ordered Thibodo to take him to his apartment in Lenexa, about twenty-five miles away. The two made the balance of the trip in near silence.

Richard Grissom's Lenexa apartment was a small, one-bedroom in the Chesapeake Estates complex just east of the interstate on Ninety-fifth Street. It was ample space for someone who spent little time at home. Grissom's lifestyle, his business, and the momentum of his ever-growing criminal agenda kept him away from home.

Thibodo followed Grissom through the front door of his apartment, and watched while Grissom hurried from room to room. To Thibodo, Grissom resembled someone without a plan but in a hurry to accomplish it. Grissom emerged from the bedroom with an arm full of clothes, and Thibodo stared in amazement as he carried the bundle into the kitchen to load it in the washing machine. Then Grissom began tearing clothes from hangers in the hall and bedroom closets, tossing hangars to the floor and clothes into a pile on the sofa. He emptied drawers of clothes and personal belongings into the same pile.

Thibodo stood by, unable to comprehend why anyone running from the cops, would take the time to do wash. He watched as Grissom stuffed the clothes and articles into plastic bags. Thibodo's apprehension was growing by the minute. His mind suddenly began registering the extent of his own involvement in Grissom's escape. He grew increasingly angry as he watched a cocky and bold Grissom bounce from room to room making jokes as he packed. Thibodo worried about the cops tracking Grissom to his apartment. In a panic, and wanting out of there, he grabbed an armful of plastic bags. "Where do you want these?" he asked Grissom angrily.

"Throw that stuff and the rest of this shit in your truck," Grissom ordered. "We'll load up your truck, and you can meet me somewhere else. It's quicker that way. We'll transfer the shit to my car at the other place."

Thibodo did not like the order but didn't refuse. He didn't like the sound of a plan requiring his continued presence. He did, however, think getting away as quickly as possible was a good idea. He hurried to complete his assignment.

The truck loaded, Grissom stood in the apartment lot telling Thibodo where he would meet him. Thibodo pulled away from the apartment and watched Grissom head back inside. Thibodo sensed there were other things Grissom wanted to get out of the apartment— things he didn't want him to see. He would not preoccupy himself with that, however. His main concern was getting away from Grissom. He headed toward the parking lot of Trafalgar Square, another apartment complex a short distance from Grissom's apartment. If Grissom did not show up there, the instructions were for Thibodo to meet him in the parking lot of a Motel 6, which bordered the interstate a few hundred yards from Trafalgar Square.

Thibodo waited anxiously at the apartment complex before moving on to the Motel 6, where again, he waited. Finally, Grissom arrived. He stuffed clothes and loose articles into his car. Before driving off, Grissom turned to his pal and said, "I left the apartment open, man. Whatever you want, take it. It's yours. I won't be coming back for any of it."

"What about the business, man?" Thibodo asked anxiously. "What do you want to do about the business?"

"It's yours, man. You take it over and run it. You'll do a good job. It's your cookie." Then Grissom squeezed himself into the packed Toyota, his possessions closed in around him. He turned one last time to Thibodo. "Yo, dog!" he yelled. "If they ask you, tell them I'm headed for California. I can get real lost out there." Grissom knew the cops would get to Thibodo. He also knew he'd tell them whatever he knew. He had to plant the last smoke-screen before he left.

After Grissom took off, Thibodo returned to his girlfriend's house in Lawrence. He spent most of the night's remaining hours awake, wishing the evening's earlier events had never happened. He reassured himself he had no knowledge of Grissom's crimes, whatever their nature and extent. But he also knew he had helped him escape, and he would have to answer for that.

Responding to questions about his long-term association with Grissom, Thibodo told investigators he met Grissom four years before, when both had attended a party at a Kansas City modeling agency. They had talked and got along but did not extend their association beyond that night. It was a year before they ran into each other again, this time at a bar in the Westport district. For another year, they ran into each other at various bars and clubs around Kansas City.

It wasn't until spring 1989, that Grissom approached Thibodo and asked him to join him in the paint-contracting business. Grissom now owned his own business, Apex, and wanted others to believe he was enjoying a measure of success. At first Thibodo resisted the offer, preferring to keep his current job. He had been employed at National Medical Care as a technician, setting up in-home oxygen-supply systems. After years of working with his father in the salvage yard, Thibodo was fairly content to be employed at NMC and saw no benefit in another change.

Thibodo would not admit to investigators whether Grissom made certain promises to lure him into his business. Investigators suspected substantial promises were made, but could only guess at their nature. No doubt Grissom exaggerated the size, success and value of his company. Maybe the offer included more money than Thibodo had made at NMC, or the promise of owning a piece of the business. It was possible that the thought of greater independence and being his own boss pushed him over the edge. He did try the job for a two-week trial run and apparently liked what he saw in Grissom's camp. He left his steady job at NMC and pitched his tent with Grissom.

Grissom was quick to take advantage of Thibodo. Shortly after Thibodo began working at Apex, Grissom enlisted his help in buying a car. Grissom poured on the excuses, which included cash-flow problems, temporary bad credit and the hardships of having to use borrowed cars to transport the day-workers and supplies. Why Thibodo missed such obvious clues regarding the state of the business, baffled police. To them, observations about the Grissom enterprise would have sent the greatest of optimists packing. Yet, Thibodo not only stayed with Grissom, he put his credit and his name on the bottom line for Grissom to secure his brown Toyota. Grissom made the low monthly payments, and Thibodo's name remained on the registration.

When questioned about the Corsica, Thibodo appeared less hesitant to talk. He admitted he first saw

Grissom with the new car on Tuesday morning the previous week. Grissom had told him a girlfriend rented it for him, and he was going to use it for the business. Thibodo admitted that on the day after Grissom first appeared with the new car, he ordered Thibodo to get lunch for the workers. Thibodo asked if he could take the Corsica to a nearby McDonald's. At first Grissom refused, telling Thibodo only he was authorized to drive the rental, and if Thibodo should have an accident, it would not be covered by insurance. Thibodo told the police he persisted, emphasizing to Grissom that he was only going a short distance and nothing would happen to the car. According to Thibodo, Grissom let him take the car but not before handing down a few instructions. Thibodo was told not to snoop around in the car. He was not to look in the trunk or in the glove box. Thibodo told police he drove the car to get the lunches and complied with Grissom's orders.

Regardless of what Thibodo told police in Lawrence, the primary investigators maintained that Richard Grissom was their prime suspect in the Joan Butler disappearance. If, during the course of the investigation, Thibodo landed in the category of co-conspirator, they hoped that he could lead them to Grissom. At the end of Thibodo's first interrogation, investigators remained divided in their opinions about the extent of his knowledge or participation in Grissom's criminal activities. Most were convinced, however, that Thibodo had not been involved in the abduction of Joan Butler.

The first priority of those heading up the investigation was to find Grissom and, if possible, Joan Butler. They were not concerned about the possession of a stolen car, or the lesser charge of resisting arrest. A young woman was missing, and the man believed responsible for her abduction stilled roamed the streets. Experience told them that Joan Butler was probably not alive. But, on the chance that she was, Grissom's timely capture was paramount. They had to ask themselves what Grissom might be capable of while in flight as a desperate fugitive. They soon would learn.

At the same time Marcelais Thibodo was being interviewed at Lawrence Police headquarters, the recovered Corsica was undergoing a thorough processing just twenty miles to the east at the Johnson County Sheriff's Department. Forensic Specialists Rick Fahy and Bill Chapin of the Johnson County Crime Lab were assigned the processing duty, which began at the sally port around 9:30 A.M. on the June 26.

Officer Fahy, a twenty-two-year police veteran and forensic examiner, was responsible for the inventory of all items found in the car's interior and trunk and for dusting the interior for latent fingerprints. Fahy, an easygoing man, referred to by a few area waitresses as "Cuddles," liked his work and took it seriously. A husky man, he stood around five-feet-nine and admitted only to being "heavyset." He was around fifty, balding slightly and wore bifocals.

Bill Chapin, usually paired with Fahy when processing crime scenes, had sixteen years with the crime lab. He was a bit shorter than Fahy, and his brown hair, though thinning, was still there. He also sported a thick mustache.

Chapin assumed responsibility for tape-rolling the Corsica's interior for hairs, fibers and other trace evidence. The tape-rolling procedure was conducted first in an effort to reduce contamination. The initial lifting of any hairs, fibers, small glass particles, sand or dirt particles, or dried blood would permit conclusion that the evidence came from an uncontaminated crime scene. The idea was to gather and protect those traces of evidence likely relating to a victim or suspect.

The car's interior also was checked for any spots or soiled areas that could prove to be blood or semen. If such spots were found, a Benzedrine test would be performed. During this presumptive test for blood, the Benzedrine reagent produced a bright blue or blue-green color if blood was present.

Once Grissom's painting supplies had been removed from the car's trunk, Chapin conducted a Benzedrine test of that area. He first ran test swabs over the trunk carpet and noticed that specks of blood reacted to the test. He then rolled up the carpet to be taken back to the lab for additional testing. With the carpet out of the trunk, Chapin noticed that only about half of the trunk's original sub-matting was still in place. The padding on the underside of the mat had also been torn away. Additional tests revealed more blood specks and one larger, two-and-a-half inch section of dried blood under the wire leading to the left tail light.

Following Chapin's trace evidence processing of the interior, Fahy applied fingerprint dusting powder throughout. When finished, he had recovered a single print of sufficient ridge detail for comparison. The print was found on the driver's side seat buckle.

A secondary search and cataloging of the articles found inside the car revealed an empty soda can, a pair of Reebok tennis shoes, a pair of athletic socks, a bottle of prescription pills, a digital pager, and a black leather wallet. The wallet's contents would help investigators add to their ever-revealing picture of Richard Grissom. Grissom had amassed a sizable collection of phony identification documents. In addition to several club memberships, three separate bank cards in different names were found. Also recovered were two Kansas driver's licenses, with photos of Grissom, in the names of Richard Grissom and Yoon Cho. State of Kansas photo ID's were found with the names Richard Grissom and Yoon C. Cho. Another bank card, airline tickets and telephone credit cards in names other than Richard Grissom Jr. were recovered as well.

In the glove box of the Corsica, Deputy Chapin discovered a Crossman air pistol. Also found were a supply of pellets, two pellet holders and two CO_2 cartridges.

9

The case officer assigned the Joan Butler investigation was Overland Park Detective Bill Batt. The detective was just under fifty years of age and had given better than seventeen years to the department. Batt was an imposing figure, standing six-feet-four and weighing over 200 pounds. He had a full head of dark hair, flecked with gray, and a thick mustache. The detective was well-known and well-liked by other officers and community leaders.

Batt's introduction to law enforcement while in his early twenties was indeed unique. Batt had been an eyewitness to an attempted bank robbery involving hostages. His timely reporting of the incident foiled the attempt and his identification of the suspects led to their successful prosecution.

The Police Chief at Overland Park at the time approached Batt and said, "If you ever want to become a police officer, you just let me know." Batt signed on.

Batt and his team at Overland Park were not optimistic about finding Joan Butler alive. She had been missing for more than a week, and until the discovery of her Corsica, not a trace of evidence had turned up. The Corsica offered clues about their prime suspect, but nothing about Joan. Batt had worked this kind of case before. Abduction and foul play were presumed, and the passage of better than a week did not speak well for the victim's chances. The team also faced the grim reality they had a madman on their hands, one very much on the loose.

Batt was quick to get to Grissom's apartment in Chesapeake Estates. Because the apartment was located in Lenexa, Batt coordinated his initial trip there with a Lenexa police officer and close friend, Pat Hinkle.

Hinkle had been with the Lenexa Department for nearly twelve years and a detective for three of those. A single word used to describe Pat Hinkle was "sharp." He was sharp in both appearance and ability. He was also athletic. His lean, muscular frame spoke for his of daily workouts. In the local haunts around the Johnson County Courthouse, where nicknames are doled out with regularity, Hinkle was known as "sexy." He stood over six feet tall, maintained his weight at around 175 pounds, and was blessed with thick, wavy, black hair and a boyish face. But, if anything, Hinkle was a solid, hard-working cop whose dedication and drive made him a favorite for placement on any crime-solving team.

Hinkle and Batt were let into Grissom's apartment by the management at Chesapeake. The detectives searched each room, the closets, under the bed and even the kitchen cabinets but found no one. The search team made note of the condition of the apartment, but could find nothing suggestive of foul play or indications that a victim might have been brought here. The apartment was in general disarray, with clothes and hangers scattered on the floor throughout the apartment. By law, this search did not permit a more thorough inspection, and the two detectives left without discovering much more than their suspect had left in a big hurry.

In the parking lot just outside Grissom's apartment, Batt and Hinkle discussed setting up a surveillance on Grissom's place. The manager at Chesapeake had informed them the unit directly opposite Grissom's was empty; it would be perfect for a stake out. However, Batt knew the department was undergoing budget and manpower constraints and such a surveillance likely would not be authorized.

Hinkle explained if Overland Park could not swing the surveillance, he would talk to his superiors at Lenexa about lending equipment and manpower. Before the day was over, Hinkle called Batt to say Lenexa was offering cars, manpower, and technical monitoring equipment if Overland Park wanted to set up a joint-surveillance on Grissom's apartment.

Batt was embarrassed to tell Hinkle that Overland Park would not authorize Lenexa officers to conduct the surveillance. Batt did not have to spell out the politics of the decision to his fellow officer. The top brass at Overland Park was extremely protective of its cases. Receiving full credit for the success in a major case was paramount and seemingly took on an importance greater than the case itself. Discovery of the Corsica in Lawrence had brought the Butler disappearance to the front page, and Overland Park had jurisdiction.

Hinkle knew his department could not set up its own surveillance. It was not their case and his own superiors would not authorize it without permission from Overland Park. Hinkle also knew if he pursued the issue, Batt would be caught in the middle. The surveillance issue was dropped. It was an unfortunate decision, the detectives would later learn, since Grissom would come back to his apartment. Hinkle, however, would not have to wait long before Lenexa received its own jurisdiction in a case involving Richard Grissom.

Batt's initial background investigations on Grissom revealed that he was no stranger to criminal activity or the inside of a prison cell. Grissom had a rap sheet, though not a multi-page document, and nothing in his criminal history revealed any activity more serious than burglary, theft or fraud. To Batt, something didn't fit. They realized that the theft of the Corsica was not a stretch for Grissom. But a con who survived for the most part by stealing and passing bad checks, did not generally graduate to kidnapping and possible murder. Ironically, Batt soon learned that the very law designed to protect citizens also had hidden part of Grissom's criminal past.

In Leavenworth County, Kansas, Batt found a protected case file that had been ordered sealed by the court. The reason? The subject in the case was a sixteen-year-old juvenile. His crime? The mutilation and murder of a seventy-two-year-old woman. His name? Richard Grissom. The file also contained psychological evaluations, profile and background summaries, and a final judicial decision handed down in the case.

A thorough review of the file allowed Batt and his team to close a major gap in their attempt to link Grissom to more serious crimes. Descriptions of the crime scene allowed Batt to conclude that a young monster had snapped his chains and unhooked his wires. Clearly he was capable of sinister and violent acts. Batt read that the crime had been classified as deviant behavior by a juvenile. The boy was given a one-to-five-year sentence which was served at a youth correctional facility. To the detective, the monster was off the table and out the door with little standing in his way.

Batt sipped his third cup of coffee and stroked his mustache as he read the details of Grissom's first murder. According to the case file, Grissom entered the home of seventy-two-year-old Hazel Meeker through a basement window. Meeker lived not far from Grissom's own home. He entered the elderly grandmother's house with the intent of robbing her, but was surprised by Meeker after she decided to check out a noise in her basement. Grissom easily could have escaped from her basement, Batt thought to himself. The slight woman could not have stopped the quick, muscular sixteen-year-old. He could have subdued her with ease. But that didn't happen. For reasons known only to him, Grissom chose a different path.

What really unnerved Batt was that Grissom was not contented by only killing the elderly woman. He had tortured her—he tied her to a chair and sliced and punctured her frail body with a long, rusty, railroad spike. Even after she was dead he continued to stab her bloodstained, lifeless body. When he finished, Grissom strolled casually away from the house as if walking away from a candy store. The police tracked him by following bloody footprints he left in the snow. He eventually was caught sitting on a snowbank less than two miles from Hazel Meeker's house.

Reading over the data, Batt's team quickly concluded that Grissom, now a twenty-eight-year-old man, was capable of anything. They also wondered how many others he might have murdered, and worse, how many more he might kill if not captured right away. If Grissom was indeed the one responsible for Joan Butler's sudden disappearance, the likelihood she would be found alive was very slim.

Reading on, Batt discovered facts about Richard Grissom's birth and earliest years. The most consistent accounts revealed he was born to a Korean prostitute. His birth father was a black Army GI, who may or may not have been part of his mother's life for more than a night. His mother kept him for at least the first two years of his life and then gave him up for adoption. Another GI named Richard Grissom and his wife, Fredonia, adopted the child at age two. The birth records showed that the child was born November 10, 1960. The new parents named the child Richard Grissom Jr., brought him to the United States and settled for a period in California. During the next several years, the Grissoms were transferred frequently but eventually resided at the military base in Leavenworth, Kansas. Even after retirement, they chose to stay in the Leavenworth.

Reviewing the early psychological profiles on his prime suspect, Batt learned that Grissom may have been adversely affected knowing his birth mother was a prostitute who abandoned him. Throughout his youth, Grissom lacked close, long-term ties and spent considerable time alone. The profiles characterized the suspect as distant and lacking emotional attachment.

Batt also learned that Grissom's ideas about discipline and those of his parents were not the same. The younger Grissom considered his parents' standards of discipline excessive. He viewed his parents' ideas about religion, dress, speech and school grades unreasonable. He resented what he considered their demands for perfection.

According to school records, Richard Jr. was an A and B student who did his best to participate in class and function according to the wishes of his parents and teachers. He was, in fact, liked by most of his teachers

teachers. He was, in fact, liked by most of his teachers and coaches. During one grading period, however, the sixteen-year-old Grissom let a grade slip from a B to a C. He decided he could not go home to face his parents. Instead, he wandered down a road in nearby Lansing, Kansas, and broke into a house—Hazel Meeker's house. A police officer at the scene in Meeker's basement was heard to ask, "How could anyone do this to another human being?" Batt learned that Grissom, in later discussions with psychiatrists and police, had more than once been heard to comment, "If I was going to kill anyone, I'd kill my parents." Hazel Meeker may have simply been a convenient substitute, the detective thought to himself.

Batt learned that Grissom was discharged from the Kansas Juvenile Detention Facility in 1980. He had served three years for the murder. He had been a model inmate who appeared to have learned from his "mistakes." He took courses and received his high school equivalency diploma while incarcerated. The law said it was OK to release him. Batt saw that the counselors and psychologists had added their stamp of approval.

A few days after discovering the protected file, Batt and his team dug up additional information about Grissom's life following his release from the juvenile facility. They learned that after his release, Grissom did not move back home. He enrolled at Kansas State University in Manhattan, Kansas, and declared his major in engineering.

College for Richard Grissom was a smooth ride, for at least a few semesters. He lived comfortably in an off-campus basement apartment, applied for and received student loans, and worked part-time at an Arby's restaurant near campus. He wasn't dating a lot but seemed to have surrounded himself with more friends than in high school. Grissom's landlord described him as "just an average college kid," and reported that he had people at the apartment all the time. The landlord found him polite, considerate, soft-spoken and "not a problem at all." The only thing that concerned him was Grissom's taste for quality material things. Grissom would not settle for cheap or used items like most college kids. Batt learned that to Grissom, appearances were everything.

In time, Grissom attempted college athletics, trying out for the Kansas State track team. He made the team, but not before questions arose about his past. In the offices of the university's track coach, Mike Ross, Grissom filled out the required application but left blank a few potentially revealing sections and falsely completed others. During an interview, Grissom told Ross he graduated from high school in Topeka. He admitted to having limited track experience, but was convinced of his natural athletic ability.

A basic background check told Ross that Grissom had not gone to high school in Topeka and had not been truthful about other details. When confronted by the coach, Grissom remained unruffled and casually replied, "I've had some trouble in the past." He did not specify what that "trouble" was. He added, "that's behind me now. You won't have any trouble out of me."

Coach Ross was not one to hold an individual's past against him. Everyone deserved a chance. Ross didn't pry or insist that Grissom reveal the exact nature of his "trouble." He reasoned that the school had admitted him, and if he could qualify for the track team, he could compete.

Grissom's tenure on the track team was short-lived. He tried hard, attended regular practices and even put in a lot of extra time. But, he just wasn't good enough. Coach Ross didn't dismiss Grissom from the team. He didn't have to. Grissom's fear of failure or of being somehow inadequate, forced him to walk off the team. Most team members were not sorry to see him go. No matter how much they tried to befriend or encourage him, Grissom remained distant, antisocial. It was not an unusual sight after practice sessions to see Grissom heading off alone in one direction while his teammates departed in another.

Grissom realized early on that many team members were superior to him in running and leaping ability. He knew he would never be the top dog on the team. If he couldn't be first, or at least one of the best, Grissom wouldn't participate. Walking away was safer. It was the surest way to avoid self-discovery and admitting failure.

While still on campus, however, Grissom did pursue an activity that brought him a little notoriety. He was good at racquetball. He first learned the sport while confined in juvenile detention. Grissom was probably more suited to racquetball than to any other sport since he was not a team player. The more he played, the better he became. Victory over others not only stroked his ego, but made him feel superior.

Those who knew and remembered Grissom during his few semesters at KSU recalled the same personality traits and habits. He was not a bar-scene personality. He spent much of his free time playing racquetball. He dated, but not often and with no one girl for any length of time. If Grissom had a character flaw, most would say it was his desire for status. If he made a solid effort to befriend someone, it was for reasons other than friendship. Grissom made a deliberate effort to surround himself with "friends" who had money, expensive cars and status on campus. Many expensive, late-model cars could be spotted regularly in front of Grissom's place. The kids coming in and out were usually

wearing the latest fashions. Grissom equated having
money and nice things with success. He hid his past
from others, afraid of exposing his prison record or his
crime, but also his parents who, to him, were insignifi-
cant. He would continue in his quest to prove he was
not in the same league with mediocrity. And, he knew
what he needed to set him on the "right" course. He
needed money.

A month before the fall finals and semester break of
1982, Grissom was arrested in Manhattan, Kansas, and
charged with stealing money from a local resume service. He was also suspected of having stolen money
from other businesses, as well as from individuals
around campus. With the word out about his crime,
Grissom did not re-enroll at KSU for the spring semester. However, the pending criminal conviction for the
robbery of the resume service did not present a large
enough obstacle to keep Grissom from pursuing other
criminal endeavors. He wanted money. He was arrested again in 1983 and charged with felony theft in
Manhattan. That charge, was dismissed in early March,
but did show up on Grissom's rap sheet.

Weeks later, Grissom stood before a Riley County
Judge and pleaded "no contest" to the charge of robbing the resume service. The judge, for whatever reason, demonstrated leniency and sentenced him to two-
to-five years which then was reduced to three years
probation. The judge also ordered that Grissom receive
regular psychological counseling during his probation-
ary period.

Before the end of March, 1983, another warrant was
issued for Grissom's arrest. This time, however, the
State of Texas was demanding his appearance to answer charges of credit card theft. Grissom had made a
trip or two to Austin, Texas, while attending KSU and
took liberties with credit cards belonging to other peo-

ple. For some reason, his probation officer did not become aware of the warrant, and Grissom was never made to appear in Texas.

By the summer of 1983, Grissom had moved to Kansas City. What he failed to leave behind in Manhattan, however, was his insatiable desire for the good life. If anything, the new trappings of the big city created more opportunities for criminal behavior. The pursuit of a steady job or career was not "instant" enough for Grissom. There would be no nine to five regimen for him. Before summer's end, he once again was arrested and charged with theft and the unlawful use of a credit card stolen from a Johnson County resident. In the Fall of 1983, it happened again, this time for misdemeanor theft and interference with a police officer. Grissom served ten days in jail and had another year added to his probation from Riley County.

Over the next few months a few who knew Grissom said he was involved in various entrepreneurial endeavors. He was claiming to be in business for himself, although no one knew what the business might have been.

By October 1984, Grissom once again appeared on the police charts when arrested for stealing a Mazda RX7 sports car in Johnson County. He was able to secure a bond and his release from jail with the assistance of a bonding agency. He had become just cocky enough to ignore the bonding agency and failed to appear in court for a scheduled proceeding. Grissom was street-smart, but in this instance he underestimated the bonding agency. It went after him.

The Sharpe Bonding Agency of Olathe, Kansas, dispatched two of their best men to find and arrest Richard Grissom. The two agents were large, muscular men who wasted little time finding their man. Within days they located Grissom, cornering him in the parking lot of a popular Westport bar named "Fanny's." When the two bounty hunters approached Grissom, he was playing the wealthy yuppie, sporting an expensive jogging outfit, a headband and designer sunglasses.

Grissom spotted the men approaching and pulled a large Buck knife from his pants. He waved the knife in short strokes through the air between himself and the two men. The agents looked at each other and smirked. They had seen the act before. Nearly on top of Grissom, they simultaneously pulled matching Colt 45 semi-automatics from their belts and pointed them directly at Grissom's chest. Each secretly was hoping for the opportunity to put a hole in the new sweatsuit. Unfortunately for several Kansas women, it was not meant to be. Grissom dropped his knife faster than he had drawn it and surrendered peacefully.

Later that night, following transport to the Johnson County Jail, Grissom suddenly snapped. He exploded from his cell bench, and running full speed, slammed his head into the wall repeatedly. The officers looked on in amazement.

"I'm not talking about gently tapping his head," said one of the officers, recounting the event. "He jumped up and just started slamming his head as hard as he could. I mean slamming it! Bam! Bam! Bam!"

In early 1985, with the stolen 1984 Mazda RX7 case still pending, Grissom stole another RX7, this time a 1982 model. He had already started using a variety of false ID's for much of his criminal activity. He gave the arresting officer a phony name and supported it with a fake ID.

By March of 1985, the cases and criminal counts against Richard Grissom had mounted. He now faced two counts of grand theft and two counts of burglary.

The case of the second stolen Mazda was somehow dismissed a month later.

Earlier that same year, Grissom had stolen a set of keys and entered a small, private office in Mission, Kansas, from which he took blank checks and cash. By the end of March he had pleaded guilty to the two counts of burglary, the theft of the original Mazda, and additional minor-theft charges. On the lesser charges he was sentenced to two-to-seven-years and the sentence was modified to one-to-two-years. On the more significant felony charges, Grissom was sentenced in May of that year to one-to-five-years and ordered to pay $12,000 in restitution. The sentences were combined by the courts to two-to-seven-years which was once again modified to one-to-seven-years. Grissom would serve time in a state penal institution but was eligible for release after one year.

Detective Batt knew that the sentences imposed on a career criminal like Grissom were only a slap on the wrist. Prison had only temporarily altered Grissom's course.

10

June 1989. Christine Rusch and Theresa Brown had been roommates for less than a year when they decided to throw a big party at their apartment. It was a farewell of sorts for Theresa, who had decided to go back to school and was planning to move in with her aunt to save money. The two women shared an upper-floor apartment in building 12909 at the Trafalgar Square complex, located just off of Ninety-fifth Street near I-35 in Lenexa.

Life was good for both women, and they wanted to celebrate. The date chosen for the party was June 24, the first Saturday of the summer. The roommates divided responsibilities for the preparations. Christine compiled lists of refreshments which included two kegs of beer. She could pick up the kegs with the help of her friend, Jim Grooms, who owned a pickup. Theresa's responsibilities was to make up flyers, announcing the time, place and date of the party.

Christine and Theresa had known each other briefly before moving in together. They had been introduced by a mutual friend. Theresa already was living at Trafalgar, and when a former roommate got married and moved out, Christine moved in. Theresa occupied the master bedroom with its own bath and Christine took the second bedroom. The Trafalgar complex was a convenient arrangement for both. It was situated just off one of the busiest streets in Lenexa, and close to malls, theaters, restaurants, the interstate and the junior college. The monthly rent was reasonable, and parking was provided directly in front of the units.

Unlike her roommate, Theresa did not begin her life in the Kansas City area. She was born and raised 150 miles to the southeast in the Lake of The Ozarks in Missouri. Her parents, Harold and Bobby Brown, had raised three girls and two boys in Camdenton, Missouri, the heart of the lake country. Theresa, one of the youngest children, graduated in 1985, from Camdenton High where she had been a model student, star cheerleader and Prom Queen. Throughout her teen years Theresa watched as each of her siblings graduated and migrated toward Kansas City in pursuit of careers and higher education. After high school and a year at Southern Missouri College, Theresa also followed the well-charted path and joined her brothers and sisters in Kansas City. Not long after Theresa's migration, her parents followed, relocating to the Kansas City suburb of Raymore, Missouri. They wanted to be close to their children.

Theresa was an attractive young woman. She was five-feet-six-inches tall, and kept herself in good physical shape. She had big, brown eyes and thick brown hair. In spite of her attractiveness, however, Theresa was extremely self-conscious about her appearance. She thought her complexion was too rough, and she was rarely happy with her hair, which she frequently attempted to modify through frosting and tinting. In the eyes of many who knew her, Theresa and her curling iron were nearly inseparable.

Theresa was popular with friends and co-workers. She was open and caring. Her boyfriend was a Johnson County Sheriff's Deputy, Mike Raunig. The two had dated for a year.

Theresa had always wanted to pursue a career in dentistry. After moving to the metropolitan area, she started work at a dental clinic. She planned to work at the clinic until she had enough money to enroll in a full-time college program. Just before the summer of 1989, she had accumulated enough of a nest egg to take the next big step. She enrolled in the dental-hygienist program at Johnson County Community College. The growing school was located just a few miles from her aunt's house, and she was to begin classes in the fall. Life was taking shape for Theresa.

Coincidentally, both Theresa Brown and Christine Rusch were born on the same day. They shared other traits as well. Christine, twenty-two, was as easygoing and lighthearted as her roommate. She stood five-feet-eight-inches, and had brown hair and brown eyes. Christine had the look of the all-American girl next door.

Christine was the older of two children born to Judy and David Rusch. She had been raised in the safe and solid surroundings of Overland Park, Kansas, was a graduate of Shawnee Mission High School and later enrolled for a brief period in the local community college. Christine never drifted far from her family or her friends.

After deciding that college was not her ticket to the future, Christine went to work for her father. David Rusch owned and managed Firestone Optics, a successful optical company in North Kansas City. He and his daughter had a close relationship, and upon hearing of Christine's desire to get to know the business, David Rusch welcomed her on board with open arms. In the summer of 1989, things were rolling along smoothly for Christine. She loved her work. She had a caring, supportive family and an active social life. In a nutshell, she had everything to live for.

Although they did not include him in their circle of friends, Christine and Theresa were familiar with Richard Grissom. They knew him only as a passing acquaintance, having met him out by the pool behind the girls' apartment. The management at Trafalgar had thrown a get-acquainted party for the residents one Saturday afternoon, and Grissom was there. So was Marcelais Thibodo. Surprisingly, Grissom did not hide the fact that he was a contract worker at the complex. He was, however, quick to point out to Christine that he "owned" the company responsible for the painting and maintenance at Trafalgar. The two women found Grissom friendly but nothing more.

Christine had additional encounters with Grissom around the complex between late May and mid-June. Grissom staged the meetings, always making them seem coincidental. He disguised his approaches, each one appearing to be a gesture of friendship. He occasionally would take newspapers from the doorsteps of other tenants at Trafalgar and place them at the front door of Christine's apartment. He later would approach her and ask how she was enjoying the papers, implying that he wanted to share them with her. Grissom's gift-giving pursuits continued, graduating to magazines and other items stolen from other tenants.

One evening in early June, Christine had just arrived home from work when she responded to a knock at her door. She opened it to find Grissom standing next to a barbecue grill—another "gift" said to have been abandoned by a nearby tenant.

Theresa was aware of Grissom's gestures of friendship toward her roommate, but like Christine, she was trusting and thought nothing of his actions. To her, his actions seemed to reflect his personality, which she interpreted as polite and unassuming.

Grissom, however, purposely stayed away from Theresa. He had done his homework. He knew that her boyfriend was a cop. He also figured that since Christine did not have a steady boyfriend, she would be the most approachable target. It was just a matter of timing and approach. Playing the stalking and luring game was part of his excitement.

Saturday, June 24, the day of the party, rolled around. Christine and Theresa spent the day getting ready for the party. The happy duo went with Jim Grooms to pick up the kegs of beer. That accomplished and the beer iced down on the deck, the three friends took a breather, grabbed a sandwich and waited for their party to take on its first signs of life.

The flyer, which Theresa had dutifully posted and handed out the week before, announced that the party would begin around 9:00 P.M. By 10:30 that Saturday night, throngs of people, many not invited but hearing of free beer, invaded the two-bedroom apartment. By midnight, moving through the apartment meant negotiating a sea of people in every room. The outside balcony was near collapse from the weight of too many partygoers. Some had even found their way onto the roof. There was a long wait for anyone wanting a refill of beer, and those arriving late were hard pressed to get even a first glass.

Christine and Theresa were having fun, but were spending a lot of time trying to maintain some measure of control. There were so many uninvited people at the party that Christine was not surprised when Richard Grissom wormed his way up next to her to say hello.

Christine chatted briefly with Grissom, then moved on to talk to other friends. She never noticed how he was casing the apartment.

And, little did Christine realize that this was not the first time Grissom had been in the girls' apartment. He had checked it once before, when they were not home. Now, Grissom roamed from bedroom to bedroom, thinking about a time when he would return—a time when he would be the sole visitor.

11

The next morning, Margaret Kelly was sipping her first cup of coffee as she answered the phone at Firestone Optics. "Christine, is that you?" Margaret asked, "What's wrong?"

Christine took a while to clear her throat. "I'm having some stomach problems, Margaret," she answered, her voice breaking slightly.

Kelly couldn't believe the caller was actually Christine. Her voice did not sound the same. "What's the matter? You don't sound good at all."

"I've had some problems all weekend, and I think I'm going to try to see a doctor today." Christine took a deep breath before continuing. "Please tell my dad that I'll be here later if he wants to talk to me."

"OK, I'll tell him first thing?" Margaret assured. "You just take care of yourself and let us know if we can do anything." That girl sounds really sick, Margaret thought. She left a message for Christine's father and would check on Christine later in the day.

Just prior to calling Margaret Kelly, that Monday morning, Christine called Dr. Cox's office at the Hickman Mills Dental Clinic. She told the receptionist she was calling for her roommate, Theresa, who was sick, and would not be coming in.

The phone call made for Theresa may have satisfied the staff at the dental clinic, but the same could not be said for Theresa's older sister, Joyce Greenstreet. Theresa and Joyce had always been close and stayed in constant contact with each other. Joyce lived near the Hickman Mills Clinic where Theresa worked, and it was a rare occasion when Theresa did not take her lunch breaks at Joyce's. When Theresa didn't make it, it was usually because the clinic staff was running late with a patient. Even though Theresa always called if she wasn't coming by for lunch. By noon, when Theresa had not called, Joyce phoned the clinic.

"Theresa won't be in today." the receptionist announced. "Her roommate called and said that Theresa was ill."

Joyce paused. "OK, thank you." she said. That's strange, Joyce thought to herself. Surely Theresa would have called to tell me what was wrong. The fact that Christine had called for her sister bothered Joyce even more.

Joyce's trepidation mounted when her calls to Theresa's apartment were consistently intercepted by the answering machine. She decided to call the management at Trafalgar Square. Joyce could not remember the name of Christine's father's business and asked the apartment manager if she could give her the number at Christine's workplace. They would not, but did offer to call Christine and have her call Joyce at home.

Minutes later when the phone rang, Joyce answered it quickly, hoping to hear either her sister's or Christine's voice on the line. Instead, it was the manager at Trafalgar. The manager told Joyce she had tried to reach Christine at Firestone Optics, but learned that she had called in sick and was not expected at all that day.

A large knot began forming in the pit of Joyce's stomach. She immediately dialed her brother Jim who was living at home with their parents. "Jim, have you heard from Theresa?" Joyce asked. "People at the clinic told me she was out sick, and she hasn't called me yet today. I thought she might have gone home to Mom and Dad's."

"No?" Jim replied. "Theresa hasn't been home. I would have been surprised if she came home because Mom and Dad went down to the lake for the week."

Joyce was becoming more uneasy with each passing minute.

Following a sleepless night, Joyce once again dialed her sister's apartment early the next morning. When the phone rang past the number of rings programmed to trigger the answering machine, Joyce breathed a sigh of relief. Thank God, she thought to herself. Someone is on the phone. Someone is finally home. But after several more tries without an answer. She realized no one was on the phone. The answering machine was full and not receiving any more calls. Her sister was not at home.

Joyce paced the floor until it was time for the dental clinic to open. She called the clinic only to learn that Theresa had not reported for work again, nor had she called. Joyce had a sickening feeling that something bad was unfolding.

Joyce placed a call to Theresa's boyfriend, Mike Raunig. "Mike, I haven't heard from Theresa since the weekend and I'm very concerned about her. Have you seen her or heard from her at all?" she asked.

"I'm glad you called," Mike answered. "I tried to call her at work yesterday and then at home last night but I couldn't reach her. I haven't seen her since Sunday. I stopped by the apartment last night after work but no one answered the door."

I'm scared Mike," Joyce said. "This is not like Theresa. She would never go this long without contacting either me or you. Christine can't be reached either. She also has been out sick according to the people at Firestone." Joyce and Mike agreed to contact each other immediately if either learned anything about Theresa or Christine.

Joyce called her siblings. They agreed to meet and discuss what to do. They decided not to talk to their parents about Theresa's disappearance until they had exhausted all attempts to find her. While waiting for her brother to pick her up, Joyce again called the manager at Trafalgar Square. She asked if they would let her in to Theresa's apartment so she could satisfy herself that Theresa was OK. The answer was no. Undeterred, Joyce and her brothers and sisters headed for the apartment.

When they pulled up just outside building 12909 at Trafalgar, Joyce noticed that Theresa's blue Toyota Tercel was parked in her space in front of the apartment. She held on to the hope that the car's presence meant something positive. Theresa could not be far away if her car was at the apartment. They proceeded up the stairs to apartment number four. They took turns pounding on the door and calling Theresa's name. They heard nothing from inside.

At the manager's office, Theresa's brothers and sisters learned that the management already had been in Christine's and Theresa's apartment that morning. No one was there and, from their observations, nothing appeared out of the ordinary. Joyce realized that the

management's views on missing tenants and her own
gut feelings about her missing sister were at opposite
ends of the emotional spectrum. Joyce wanted action—
answers. All she would accept was the sight of her
baby sister, alive and well, standing in front of her.
Anything short of that she did not want to consider. At
her wits end, Joyce knew it was time to call the police.

Meantime, for the Rusch family, the first realization
that something was amiss was starting to register.

When David Rusch first received word that
Christine was sick and not coming to work he tried to
call her. Her answering machine intercepted his call.
His first assumption was that his daughter was out
trying to see a doctor about her stomach problem. He
recalled the party she threw over the weekend. He
wondered whether her stomach irritation was a result
of that party.

David Rusch thought back to the previous Friday,
the last time he saw his daughter. She had stopped by
his office, as was her custom every day before leaving
work, to say good-bye. He remembered her saying that
she would see him on Sunday. Christine's mother was
due to have minor, outpatient surgery on Saturday, and
Christine had planned to come by on Sunday. They
had, in fact, heard from Christine that Sunday when she
called to see how her mother was doing; she mentioned then that she was having problems with her
stomach. Still, she had promised she would come over
Monday night and cook dinner for her. They just assumed they would be talking to Christine then.

David Rusch remained at work until around 7:30 P.M.
When he arrived home around 9:00 P.M., his wife was
anxious and upset. Judy told him she had not been
able to reach Christine, and that her answering ma-

chine was not accepting any more messages. David Rusch got back in his car and headed for Trafalgar Square.

David Rusch parked his car in the spot where he normally saw Christine's Dodge Colt. He looked up and down the rows of cars parked at the complex. He did not spot Christine's Colt. He thought for a moment about the Colt, and about the sheepskin seat covers he and his wife had given Christine the previous Christmas and how happy she had been to get them. David Rusch said a small prayer and went into building 12909 and up the stairs to number four.

He knocked, then pounded on the apartment door. "Christine! Christine!" he yelled. "Open up Christine. It's your father! Are you in there, honey?" He stood quiet in the hall for a moment. He considered breaking into the apartment, but just as quickly reconsidered. Surely Christine had gone out somewhere for the evening. He wondered whether her stomach problems had warranted a trip to the hospital. It would not have been the first time. Rusch thought that Christine might be in the hospital but had not wanted to worry her mother who had just undergone surgery. Maybe Theresa was with her, he reasoned.

A quick stop at the patient-registration desk at nearby Humana Hospital dashed Rusch's hopes of finding his daughter there. His head was now spinning. Where could she be? Rusch asked himself over and over again.

Back at home, David and Judy Rusch grew more desperate. The Rusches decided they would let the night pass. Maybe Christine and Theresa had gone someplace for the night and would be back the next morning. He would go back to Christine's apartment early the next day to see for himself that she was all right.

At Trafalgar Square the next morning, Rusch again pounded on the apartment door and called out his daughter's name. His cries drifted off and were absorbed by an unsettling silence. He looked around the landing and down toward the floor below. Neither that morning's noise nor the noise he created the night before had alarmed anyone from the surrounding apartments. Not a single person had come out to see who he was or what he wanted.

He studied the apartment door jam. The area where the metal bolt had slipped into its holder on the jam had been chipped slightly. It appeared that someone had chipped enough wood away to create a space wide enough to insert a credit card or thin tool to slip the lock. He pulled a credit card from his wallet and slid the card in. Having had no firsthand experience at opening a door by that method, Rusch was surprised when the bolt moved free and the door opened.

Rusch walked through the kitchen and living areas. He stopped near the sliding-glass doors and scanned the patio deck. He noticed two beer kegs and recalled the party of the previous weekend. That seemed like such a long time ago, he thought. Surely the girls would have returned the kegs by now. He called out Christine's name. Again, no answer. Rusch wandered through the rest of the apartment searching the bedrooms, bathrooms and closets. Not a clue as to where the girls might have gone.

He was surprised to see that both bedrooms were in disarray. He remembered the girls being neater, more concerned about their housekeeping. Beds were unmade, their clothes strewn about both bedrooms and closet floors. In Theresa's bedroom, the top sheets and bedspreads had been pulled half off the bed, as if torn from the bed in a single, jerking motion. In the master bath, the lights had been turned off, but Rusch noticed a small red light coming from the vanity. Theresa's curling iron had been left on. She had probably forgotten to turn it off, he thought. In Christine's room, sheets were at the foot of the bed, and a few articles of clothing lay on the bed and floor.

Rusch left the apartment more distressed than when he entered. Something wasn't right. The scene inside the apartment was askew. His mind curved around a variety of scenarios, most of which he did not want to consider. If ever a sense of foul play had invaded his mind, it was now. He was fighting hard to resist his intuition. His only daughter was missing. He drove straight to the police.

Meanwhile, Theresa Brown's brothers and sisters had resisted as long as they could before telling their parents that Theresa was missing. They had hoped it was only a matter of time before Theresa walked back into their lives. By Wednesday the twenty-eighth, they knew they had to tell their parents about Theresa's disappearance.

Joyce Greenstreet asked her two brothers to drive to the Ozarks and tell their parents that Theresa was missing and the worst was suspected. They had to be told in person. Joyce knew that her parents, once learning that Theresa had disappeared, would never be able to drive themselves back home.

12

Two missing person complaints were filed with the Lenexa Police at nearly the same time. The first was filed by Theresa's sister, Joyce Greenstreet, and her brother, Jim Brown. Less than two days had passed since they last talked to Theresa. After lodging the complaint, the two waited at Trafalgar Square for the police to conduct a search of their sister's apartment.

The second missing-person report was filed by David Rusch. He initially had gone to the Overland Park headquarters believing that the Trafalgar Square complex fell within their jurisdiction. He was sent to Lenexa, where an officer took his statement. The police reports included background and descriptive data on the missing women, information on family and close associates, vehicles, hangouts, and where the women had last been seen.

Lenexa Detective Tom Penhollow, accompanied by uniformed officers, responded to the Brown complaint. They were let into the missing womens' apartment by the manager at Trafalgar Square. The chance that the apartment could later be classified a crime scene required that members of the Brown family remain outside. Penhollow conducted an initial walk-through search. He was looking for bodies, signs of forced entry or any evidence of foul play. None was discovered. During the search, the apartment manager told Penhollow that she had checked the apartment earlier, but had touched nothing except the on-off switch of a curling iron which had been left on in the master bathroom.

Ordinarily, missing-person complaints filed with the Lenexa Police would have prompted the police to act routinely, but this case took on a sense of urgency for many reasons. First, the simultaneous complaints filed on behalf of two women missing from the same place at the same time were certainly rare. Second, family members and friends all could attest to the missing girls' responsible habits and lifestyles. The police could not ignore details like these. Last, with the media still focused on the mysterious disappearance of Joan Butler the week before, police in all surrounding areas were paying close attention to sudden, unexplained disappearances.

Lenexa Detective Pat Hinkle, already very familiar with Overland Park's case against Richard Grissom, was given the green light to investigate a possible link between Grissom and the women missing from Trafalgar Square. If a link could be established, it would propel the Lenexa Department into the Grissom investigation with full jurisdiction of its own. It was not a competition, nor was it a race for glory or recognition. To Hinkle and his team, it was a matter of getting Grissom behind bars as quickly as possible. The Grissom connection to the missing Lenexa women would be made very quickly through Marcelais Thibodo.

Detective Hinkle brought Thibodo in for another round of questioning and spent the better part of a day with him. Though he came willingly to the Lenexa Police headquarters, it was apparent to Hinkle that Thibodo was nervous about being there. Hinkle sat with Thibodo in an interview room and watched as his witness fidgeted, unable to sit still in his chair. He repeatedly rubbed his hands together and had difficulty completing sentences and expressing himself clearly.

"What's wrong with you?" the detective asked, unwilling to continue the interview until he understood the reasons for Thibodo's anxiety. "What are you so nervous about?"

"It's nothing, man," Thibodo answered. "You know, I just hate the pressure, man."

"No one is pressuring you, Frenchy. You're here as a witness, not a suspect. If I thought you were more than Grissom's business partner, you'd be in jail right now."

"I know, man," said Thibodo. "It's just that Richard was into so much shit, man, you know. I just don't know where I stand in all this. I worked with the guy. I hung out with him, you know, but I wasn't involved in any of his criminal shit, man. I don't know what he did, but I think you guys think I do."

"Just calm down, Frenchy. I asked you to come in and talk because I believe you can help us. There are a lot of things you know about Grissom that we don't know, and you can help us with that. We need to find him fast. We need to retrace his steps, learn about his habits, understand how he thinks. You can fill in a lot of blanks for us, Frenchy. And you know that as long as you're helping us, you're helping yourself."

Thibodo calmed and began answering Hinkle's questions about Grissom. Later, the two men drove around, checking out locations where Thibodo and

Grissom had either worked or hung out together. Hinkle treated Thibodo to lunch, during which he revealed even more information about his former friend. By the end of the day, each man had a much clearer understanding of the other.

After spending a full day with Thibodo, Hinkle realized that previous omissions by his witness were probably unintentional. Thibodo no doubt was nervous about how Grissom's actions might reflect on him, but he never tried to avoid the police. He was simply less candid at first. Hinkle recognized early on that Thibodo didn't always grasp the relevance of certain questions. He would answer the string of questions fired at him, but never see the value of linking pieces of information together to form the bigger picture.

Still, Thibodo's earlier omissions angered many of the officers involved in the investigation. For example, during his first interview in Lawrence, when asked about Grissom's painting contracts other than Trailridge, Thibodo mentioned Trafalgar Square as one of four or five other locations where contract work was performed. He failed to mention, however, that Grissom had a master key to the apartments and that Grissom had taken him into womens' apartments to look around when the women were not at home. One of the apartments Grissom enjoyed snooping around in had belonged to Christine and Theresa.

Thibodo told Hinkle that Grissom once said he had been asked by the management to check the Rusch-Brown apartment for water damage to the ceiling. Grissom had told Thibodo he needed his help. Once inside the apartment, Grissom had pretended to dutifully check the ceilings, but it wasn't long before he'd begun looking through the personal effects of the girls who lived there. Thibodo told Hinkle that on that occasion, Grissom roamed freely around the apartment, checking bedrooms, closets, jewelry boxes and dresser drawers. From one of the drawers, Grissom pulled a pair of panties, held them up toward Thibodo and said, "Yo man, check these out."

Thibodo also pointed out that both he and Grissom knew the two missing women and that Grissom had introduced him to them at a pool party. Thibodo told Hinkle that Grissom was always talking about one of the girls, the one named Christine. Thibodo admitted to being aware of Grissom's gift-giving tactics and his efforts to get close to Christine. Thibodo said he had not attended the party at the girls' apartment the previous weekend, but knew Grissom had gone. According to Thibodo, Grissom told him he wouldn't miss it for anything.

Based on Thibodo's statement that the Rusch-Brown apartment was not the only one Grissom entered unannounced, investigators turned up additional confirmation that other entries or attempted entries were made by their suspect at Trafalgar Square. A documented series of incidents occurred at the apartment of Brian and Jennifer Murphy-Dye who lived in building 12908, apartment one, on the same street as Christine and Theresa.

In late February, Jennifer was at home with her children when she heard a key unlock the front door and then heard the door close. She had been in the rear of the apartment; it was between 4:00 and 5:00 P.M. and she assumed her husband was returning home from work. When she heard no additional sounds, and her husband had not made an appearance, she went to the front and looked outside for Brian's car. It wasn't there. Suddenly, her heart began racing. Someone else had opened her apartment door and worse, might still be hiding somewhere inside. Jennifer got her children and took them outside the apartment. In a courageous follow-up move, she went back inside and checked throughout the unit, under beds, in closets, behind sofas, to see if anyone had hidden there. She found no one.

Two weeks later, Jennifer once again heard a key being inserted in her front door. The door opened and closed. This time, however, her husband was at home, so she knew it could not be him. Jennifer ran to the door in time to see Richard Grissom turning to enter apartment number two, directly across the hall. It was then that Jennifer realized that it was Grissom who had tried to enter her apartment two weeks before. Grissom of course, used the excuse that he mistook the apartments and simply entered the wrong one.

Brian and Jennifer Murphy-Dye sent a letter to the management at Trafalgar Square, registering complaints about Grissom's unannounced entries. They received only a letter of apology from the management. Grissom, in fact, boldly tried again. On his third attempt, he found Jennifer waiting at the front door for him. Grissom had no tools or painting equipment with him, and he did not announce himself when entering. He was caught in the act and surprised by a gutsy Jennifer Murphy-Dye. Grissom backed away, apologizing for having mistaken her apartment for the one across the hall.

It wasn't only his attempts to get into her apartment that bothered Jennifer. She also was concerned that Grissom had lingered for weeks painting the apartment directly above her. His crew had not worked with him, but to Jennifer, it was a job that any painter could have completed in less than a week. What she didn't realize, was that Grissom was lining up excuses to be around her. He was stalking her, taking a few early chances and waiting for the right time to strike. It appeared, however, that Grissom's interest in Jennifer had tapered

off around the time he had picked a more approachable target, Christine Rusch.

While riding around for most of the day with Detective Hinkle, Thibodo's pointing out an apartment
complex in Overland Park provided a significant link
between Grissom and the Joan Butler case. Thibodo
mentioned this apartment complex was where he had
dropped Grissom off during the same week that Grissom had the Corsica. It seemed Grissom needed a ride
to that complex to pick up his brown Toyota.

Hearing this, Hinkle's eyes lit up. The complex was
adjacent to the Comanche Place Apartments. Thibodo
said he had brought Grissom here to get his car on the
Tuesday or Wednesday after the disappearance of Joan
Butler. Thibodo also had pointed out exactly where
Grissom's car had been parked. It was a short walk
from there to the parking lot near Joan Butler's apartment. Hinkle knew it was where Grissom had parked
his car when he went back to pick up the Corsica. The
Butler case was the jurisdiction of Overland Park, so
later that day, Hinkle contacted Detective Bill Batt and
told him about his discovery.

Hinkle knew Grissom was somehow responsible
for Joan Butler's disappearance, and his suspicions
about his involvement in the disappearances of
Christine and Theresa were very strong. The young
detective also knew the two girls missing from Trafalgar might still be alive. It had been only two days since
anyone had seen or talked to Christine or Theresa. Just
maybe, the missing girls could be found, Hinkle reasoned.

In Leavenworth, Kansas, reporters and cameramen and a variety of curiosity seekers had camped in front of Grissom's parents' home. The media had been there since shortly after Richard Jr. had been declared a prime suspect in the Joan Butler case. Richard Grissom Sr. and his wife, Fredonia, were distressed over the sudden invasion by the press and angered by reporters repeated attempts to get them to say something, anything, about their son.

A knock at the front door that evening sent the senior Grissom exploding in rage to the front of the house. He was only slightly relieved to find that the knock was not made by the press. Grissom reluctantly let Detectives Hinkle and Burke into his home.

Grissom was visibly shaken by the unannounced visit by the police. He had certainly known they would be coming sooner or later, but had hoped for later. He nevertheless offered the detectives a seat.

The detectives studied the home's interior, hoping for a few insights into the Grissoms. Clearly they were simple people. From what the detectives saw, the house was modestly furnished and neatly kept. A few items in the room appeared to be of antique quality, but nothing jumped out as flashy or expensive. The entire house was dark except for the living room where they were seated. Mr. Grissom wore very plain clothes. The detectives officially announced they were looking for Richard Jr., but did not ask for permission to search the house for him. Not long into the interview, they realized there would be no need to search the house.

As Hinkle spoke to Grissom, the older man calmed a bit, but it was still apparent his anger had not dissipated. He was enraged by the actions of his adopted son. "I'm sorry I ever gave him my name," Grissom admitted. "I suppose we shouldn't be surprised. He's always been in some kind of trouble. Always!"

The detectives let him vent. They needed background data for an early, if only limited, profile, and Grissom could give them that. They did not press for information about where his son might be. They learned quickly that Grissom and his parents had lost touch by mutual consent.

The senior Grissom spoke at length about his son's troubles. He gave the detectives a chronology of Richard's sordid activities, at least those acted out while he still lived at home. The information provided a substantial base for the detailed profile they would eventually compile. It seemed that Richard Jr.'s trouble began before the family ever left California for Kansas.

From as early as age ten, Grissom's parents began finding expensive and unusual items hidden in his bedroom. They were things that neither of them had purchased for him and which he hadn't received from friends. The elder Grissom was quick to mention that whenever they confronted Richard, he confessed immediately, as if waiting for the opportunity to purge himself. Richard's early confessions initially revealed a pattern of shoplifting but, by the time they had settled in Kansas, that behavior had given way to burglary and other types of theft. Grissom Sr. shook his head as he detailed episode after episode of his son's criminal behavior. He mentioned a time when his son's baseball coach at Leavenworth High had confronted Richard about a burglary he was suspected of committing. The young player confessed immediately.

During the interview, details began to surface about Grissom's fascination with locks and his insatiable appetite for getting through locked doors and windows. He played with a variety of keys and had experimented with different locks long before the Hazel Meeker murder. At other times, the young Grissom had admitted to getting rid of his booty not long after a burglary to avoid getting caught. For Grissom, the greater thrill may have been the burglary itself, and not the booty. Richard Jr. had begun breaking into the homes of neighbors and friends of his parents when he knew they were at church or other community gatherings. He also continued shoplifting and had stolen from student lockers at school.

Hinkle asked the elder Grissom if his son was ever caught or interviewed by the police during the early escalation of his criminal behavior. The detective also wanted to know if Grissom Jr. had ever been interviewed by youth psychologists or counselors during that time. The answers would not surprise him.

"We're a quiet, God-fearing people," Grissom Sr. said. "This is a small community, and we're respected here. We handled our personal problems in our own way. If we found some stolen items in Richard's room, we confronted him. Most of the time he confessed to taking them, and we would march him back to where he got them and give them back. We made him apologize for what he had done," Grissom Sr. admitted.

The tactic, the elder Grissom explained, served their purposes until finally, an apology wasn't enough. During the burglary of a house located not far from his own, Grissom tortured and beat a family's pet cat, nearly crushing its skull. After much pleading, the Grissoms were able to convince the family not to call the police and agreed to pay the veterinary bills. Grissom Sr. admitted that incidents at school often were handled through Richard's coaches, who may have provided their own discipline, but who took no additional steps to refer Richard to school counselors or authorities.

During the interview, the detectives heard what they thought was whimpering coming from an adjacent room. In time they realized that Mrs. Grissom had been sitting within earshot of their conversation. The room where she sat was dark, and the detectives could barely make out her shoes and the lower part of her dress when caught by the light from the living room. Mr. Grissom had, in course, explained that his wife could not participate in the interview. She had been devastated and emotionally weakened by the recent accounts of what her son had done. Grissom's mother had given up on her son before his last trip to prison. She had refused to visit him in prison and had tried to avoid him on those occasions when, after his release in 1988, he returned home in the company of prostitutes and prison buddies demanding money from them. She had, for quite some time, been very ashamed of him.

Before the detectives left the Grissom house, Grissom Sr. made a promise. He told them he did not know where his son might be at that moment, but he would lead the police straight to him if the boy called or made contact with him.

Detectives Batt and Hinkle sifted through mounds of police hot line data records in an effort to piece together a profile of their suspect. They hoped that somewhere within the maze of data, there might just be a clue to where Grissom was or where he might be going. Every lead, manpower and time permitting, would be checked.

Further background checks showed that Richard Grissom had served part of his last sentence in the Kansas State Penitentiary in Lansing. In prison, he had moved from high to low security, an indication that he was not a problem prisoner. Grissom was a low-profile inmate who understood that in prison his usual, inflated view of himself would not serve him at all. He might have gained a modicum of respect on the prison racquetball courts, but his ego would be quickly returned to earth during all other facets of prison life.

In June of 1988, fresh out of prison and monitored on parole, Grissom set out to "get his life back together and make a new life for himself." At least that's what he told his parole board during his review hearing. It was, no doubt, what they wanted or needed to hear.

A long-time acquaintance, hearing of Grissom's release, offered to help him with his "fresh start," and invited him to live in a basement apartment in his home. The friend was Eric Pour; the room would be rent free until Grissom could get on his feet. Eric was of Middle Eastern descent and a man of small build. He owned and operated several small businesses in the Kansas City metro area and had done well for himself. He drove sports cars, was known to frequent many popular night spots around town and owned his home on Eastern Avenue in Kansas City, Missouri.

Pour's and Grissom's paths had crossed during the period of Grissom's entrepreneurial pursuits around Kansas City. A casual friendship had developed, and Grissom spent a lot of time picking Pour's brain for ideas and leads. Pour had been involved in a variety of businesses, including used-car dealerships and painting and maintenance contracting. Along his own course, Pour had seen a lot of personalities come and go and did not look down on Grissom for having drifted to the wrong side of the law.

Pour's home was a comfortable, multi-level contemporary, situated in the midst of large, older homes with sizable yards and established landscapes. It also had a swimming pool and other amenities. Grissom was given the finished lower basement area, as well as access to the kitchen, other living areas and the pool. But, Pour was not finished. He also offered Grissom a job.

The business in which Pour offered employment was called Metrotech Painting & Maintenance. Grissom would be a part of Pour's crew but was expected to be promoted to crew foreman in short order. Pour also talked with Grissom about the possibility of learning the business well enough to go out and solicit contracts on behalf of Metrotech. Pour's generosity was leaving Grissom no room for excuses. Pour was asking for nothing in return.

Just out of prison, Grissom's worldly possessions included a few sets of clothes, a small TV and a VCR. He moved his things into Pour's basement apartment. He had access to Pour's phones and other essentials, and Pour advanced him money as he began work with Metrotech. Unfortunately, Grissom did not feel grateful for Pour's generosity. Rather, he saw it as the golden opportunity, a holding pattern from which to re-establish his criminal pursuits.

It didn't take long for the relationship between Pour and Grissom to start unraveling. After just two months, Pour began receiving inquiries about past-due phone bills and unpaid accounts on credit cards which had, by then, become Grissom's responsibility. Pour discussed the problem with Grissom. Pour agreed to pay the balances on the fast-accumulating bills with the promise from Grissom that he would improve his financial responsibility and future bills would not go unpaid. During this period, when Grissom had convinced Pour that he was making every effort to improve, Pour often lent him his car and occasionally small amounts of cash.

Grissom again rewarded Pour's generosity in his own unique way. Pour received more inquiries over the following weeks. This time, however, they appeared to be of a more threatening nature. In addition to continued notices of unpaid balances on charge cards, accusations that bad checks written by someone using Pour's home address were received. The checks, Pour was informed, were being written by someone named Rikki Y.C. Cho. Pour realized what Grissom was doing and soon learned that his housemate was also using his basement to manufacture phony identifications for his check-passing spree.

Pour again confronted Grissom. A heated exchange took place in Pour's garage. Pour was considerably smaller than Grissom and would have been no match for him physically, but his anger blinded him to that contrast. When Grissom backed down and began his standard pretense at humility and embarrassment, Pour grew more enraged. He landed a few glancing blows off Grissom's head, as the full extent of Grissom's gambols finally registered.

Grissom did not challenge Pour or even attempt to keep Pour from hitting him. He merely cowered in a corner of the garage and listened as Pour berated him for his criminal activities and for his lack of gratitude. Grissom knew what he was doing by not fighting back. He was the one with the most to lose when the confrontation ended. He could not yet afford to fall completely out of favor with Pour. As he had hoped, he was given another chance.

An extra month of grace was all Grissom would get from Pour, but it was apparently all he needed. He continued to build his arsenal of supporting documents for the check-cashing schemes. He often was missing from contract sights and had all but abandoned his work responsibilities at Metrotech. Grissom's plans were never long term no matter what promise they presented. His needs seemed to require immediate gratification.

By the end of the month, Grissom had left Pour's house. He departed in the middle of the night. Before he left, Grissom forged Pour's signature on the title to his car then sold it to a young, unsuspecting buyer.

By the Spring of 1989, Grissom was staying a few paces ahead of the law, and had his own apartment in Lenexa. He also had his own painting and maintenance contracting business, which he named Apex. What he really had was a sufficient number of working aliases and bad checks to maintain them both. His apartment at 9202 Legler in the Chesapeake complex was sparsely furnished but held the basics for a moderate lifestyle, thanks to his ability to pass the checks. Even groceries were being paid for with bad paper. Grissom's criminal activity was gaining incredible momentum and reaching a point where nearly everything he did had at least some measure of criminality. He was cocky and confident and seemingly unconcerned that any of his activity would ever catch up to him.

The sprayers and generators needed for his painting business were leased under assumed names from towns in Missouri and as far away as Wichita and Topeka, Kansas, and were never returned when the leases expired. Grissom, of course, had the necessary quantity of mixed ID's to contract for the equipment. Grissom also leased storage lockers, which he used to store the stolen painting equipment, a variety of other stolen items and a key-duplicating machine.

From his tenure with Pour's operation, Grissom learned what he needed to know about the paint contracting business. It was enough for him to go out and scrape up a few contracts for himself. With the right equipment, the ability to hire cheap, unskilled labor and the ability to undercut other "legitimate" contractors, Grissom had locked into three or four sizable painting contracts before inviting Marcelais Thibodo into the fold. One of those contracts was of course, Trafalgar Square.

Before Grissom's sudden departure from Pour's home, he had amassed a criminal debt of several thousand dollars. By May of '89, those totals had climbed considerably and they were restricted to Johnson County, Kansas, alone. Additional checks passed by Grissom in Missouri and other parts of Kansas would take longer to surface, but eventually would be linked to him and the totals would grow even higher.

With little trouble writing bad checks or using someone else's credit cards, Grissom easily provided himself with what he needed. He was getting away with an incredible crime spree but, to him, it wasn't enough. Grissom believed he was only living day to day. Nothing he was doing would vault him into that next financial category he believed he needed or deserved. Most of all, nothing gave him the high, the deep-seated gratification he experienced when breaking into other peoples' homes and handling their possessions. Aligning himself with criminal networks, Grissom reentered the world of the burglar.

Something stirred deep within Grissom when he was inside someone else's home. Maybe it was the personal violation itself, the act of owning someone's space or controlling a part of their life and getting away with it. Usually, his trespass was frighteningly bold. It reflected the intensity of his focus, his absolute craving for satisfaction.

His original purpose, the burglary itself, was overshadowed by the deep pleasure derived from the act. Grissom broke into places, made keys, and later walked into peoples' homes because he knew how it would make him feel. The intensity of his pleasure was increasing with each new trespass. His needs were like those of a drug addict in need of a "hit" or a "fix." As with the addict, more "hits" in ever-increasing doses were required to achieve the same levels of satisfaction. Could Richard Grissom remain gratified by repetition of the same activity? Could he assuage his growing needs by increasing the number and frequency of his burglaries? No. Grissom would resort to greater evil to achieve his personal "highs."

13

Just before 9:30 P.M., Grissom drove his Toyota into the parking lot of the Stonybrook Apartment complex in Grandview, Missouri. Stonybrook was a large complex with a series of three-story buildings situated about 150 yards from the frontage road that bordered busy Highway 71 in Grandview. Grissom had been to the complex many times before. He knew it well from the days he painted there. Stonybrook was one of Grissom's first contracts following the creation of Apex and consequently one of the first places after Apple Creek that provided him with a master key. It was also a place where Grissom had targeted women. He simply had not taken the time to come back for them until now.

As he drove through the parking lot, however, Grissom knew it wouldn't take much to draw attention to himself. He was a wanted fugitive whose name and picture had been spread throughout Kansas City. One of his targets at Stonybrook might be his last shot at another victim before leaving town for good.

Grissom studied the lot before parking. His eyes darted from car to car. He zeroed in on a car belonging to Stephanie Foster, the manager at Stonybrook. The manager's office was closed for the night, but Grissom knew Stephanie lived at the complex. Her office and apartment were, in fact, right across the hall from one another on the lower floor of building number 1508. Grissom had been inside both the office and Stephanie's apartment and knew the layouts well.

Grissom parked his Toyota. He purposely selected a vacant spot next to a large trash dumpster; it would hide his car. The space was also close to the entrance of the building. Grissom focused, thinking several steps ahead. He sat behind the wheel and waited. Night had settled over the area. He sat motionless in the dark. Flies from the dumpster buzzed around his opened window. He waited about five minutes, mentally rehearsing his moves. Then, when he was ready, he got out and walked toward the apartment building.

Grissom headed toward the utility room at the end of the hallway on the lower level. He had a key to the room. He let himself in, located the electrical-control panel and cut off the hall lights at the opposite end—the end where Stephanie Foster's apartment was located. From the utility room, he headed back down the hall and stopped in front of Stephanie's apartment door, now darkened. He waited for a moment in the shadow, listening. The building was quiet, and he could hear nothing from inside the apartment. Grissom slipped the master key from his pocket and slid it into the door.

Suddenly, he heard the sound of keys rattling. Grissom stiffened and remained still. He wondered if the keys might belong to Stephanie. Should he duck inside and wait? The keys jingled again. The sound came from just outside the door at the far end of the hall. Not knowing what he might encounter inside the apartment, he could not risk going in with someone walking the hall just outside. Grissom crouched under the darkened staircase he had just descended. He braced himself against the back wall and listened as the door opened. Someone was entering the building.

The jingle of the keys grew louder. Grissom remained motionless. The noisy set of keys did not belong to Stephanie Foster. They were hanging from the waist of Stonybrook's maintenance man Bill Mayo, a young, trim Italian who had been employed there since shortly after Grissom completed his contract.

Mayo was checking to find out why the hall lights had gone off. He approached the manager's office intending to get another set of keys to the utility room. As Mayo entered the office, Grissom waited, with his back still pressed against the wall. Unfortunately for Grissom, he could not conceal himself.

When Mayo came out of the office and turned to lock the door behind him, he caught sight of the shadowed figure under the staircase. Mayo approached. "What are you doing there?" Mayo asked nervously, unable to make out Grissom's face. "What do you want? Are you looking for someone?" He popped his questions in rapid order, trying to sound in command.

"I'm looking for Michelle," Grissom replied tentatively. "I'm not sure I'm on the right floor." Grissom purposefully avoided using Stephanie's name. He could not risk Mayo's telling her he had been there. Stephanie probably knew he was a wanted man. His plan for her must remain a surprise.

"What's her last name?" Mayo asked, growing more suspicious.

"I can't remember her last name," Grissom answered. "It's been awhile since I've seen her. I just know she lives here in the complex somewhere." He made no effort to move from under the stairs.

Mayo did not like Grissom's reply. To him, everything about this man hiding in the dark was suspicious. Mayo asked Grissom to step out from under the stairs. He had had his share of problems with prowlers and thieves before and wanted to get a closer look at the man. Something about Grissom was vaguely familiar. He knew the face from somewhere. Mayo had performed maintenance duties at Apple Creek and wondered whether that was where he'd seen him. Whatever the case, Mayo was not about to let the man roam through the buildings. He questioned the intruder, "Oh, you mean Michelle from upstairs, kind of short, heavyset, with dark hair?"

"Yeah, that's her!" Grissom replied too rapidly. He realized immediately that Mayo had not described the Michelle he knew. Mayo had set him up. Grissom was angry at himself for having fallen for the stupid trap. Grissom and Mayo stared at each other. Each knew what the other was thinking. Grissom had to get out of there. Mayo wanted to call the police. Suddenly Mayo turned and moved toward the utility room, stopping at the base of the stairs.

"Well, good luck finding her," Mayo said, as he grabbed the banister. "I have to go and check on what happened to these lights." Mayo then headed up the stairs. He knew a trip back into the manager's office to use that phone would have been too obvious. His mother and sister shared an apartment on the main floor of the building. He would go there to call the police. At the top of the stairs near the main entrance, Mayo turned back to see Grissom striding toward the rear of the building. Mayo waited until he heard the sound of the door opening and closing.

Grissom panicked. His plan had gone up in smoke. Fearing the maintenance man was calling the police and, most probably, watching the front of the building, he couldn't risk trying to get back to his car. Grissom hid in a wooded area in the rear of the building. He waited to see if Mayo had indeed called the police. He had been in the woods about ten minutes when he spotted a police car as it entered the parking lot. As soon as the patrol unit disappeared from his view, Grissom took off running. He followed a path that led to the frontage road along Highway 71. He hurried across the highway, entered the woods again on the opposite side and disappeared. He knew the police would search the grounds around Stonybrook. He could not afford to be close by.

Bill Mayo had not seen the evening news, which was probably why he could not tell the responding officers from the Grandview Police who the prowler was. The officers took the complaint from Mayo and searched the grounds around the buildings and parking lots. Finding nothing, they left.

Stephanie Foster had been at Stonybrook the evening of Grissom's attempted "visit," but had gone to see her boyfriend who leased a unit in a nearby building. Coincidentally, Stephanie had been talking about Richard Grissom earlier that evening with Gina Kelly, the manager at Apple Creek. Gina had called Stephanie to report the latest news about Grissom whom they both knew. He had worked at Apple Creek when employed by Eric Pour. He, no doubt, came away from there with a master key. Gina warned Stephanie about the manhunt for Grissom and the search for his Toyota.

Within forty minutes of Grissom's attempt to get in to her apartment, Stephanie Foster returned to check her phone messages. On her way back to her boyfriend's apartment, she ran into Bill Mayo who was scouring the complex to make sure the "prowler" was not still there. Mayo told Stephanie what had happened in the hallway. He had not completed his description of the "prowler" when Stephanie interrupted.

"Oh my God!" she said, feeling her stomach turn to knots. She braced herself against Mayo's shoulder. Her knees weakened. "It's him! It has to be him!"

Mayo had no way of knowing what she was talking about, but saw she was deeply troubled. Stephanie told Mayo that the prowler was probably Richard Grissom, and that she was certain he had a key to her apartment. Grissom had come for her. There was no doubt in her mind. He had been discovered just feet from her apartment door. She squeezed Mayo's shoulder. "We've got to get the police back here," she said in near panic. "I know who the man was and I know what he wanted! The police are looking for him!"

"OK," said Mayo, trying to calm Stephanie. "I'll call them again. You come with me. I'll stay with you until they get here."

"Did you see what he was driving?" Stephanie asked, as she and Mayo descended the stairs to her office.

"No, I saw him leave out the back door. I don't know if he even had a car. If he did, I don't know if he tried to circle back around to the front to get it. I went back outside in the front to wait for the police right after I called them. But he had a few minutes. He could have made it to a car."

"The police are searching for his car, too," Stephanie said. "It's a brown Toyota hatchback, an early eighties model I believe."

"I'll keep looking around the complex if the police don't find anything in their own search," Mayo assured.

Once again, the Grandview police officers returned to Stonybrook. This time they met with Stephanie Foster, who insisted that the man they had searched for earlier was Richard Grissom. The officers recorded her statements, took down a more thorough description of the suspect and set out to have a second look around the grounds at Stonybrook. When their search once again proved unfruitful, the officers left.

Bill Mayo's diligence after the police left the second time paid off. He was concerned for Stephanie and was worried that a killer could be still hanging around. An additional search and patrol took him around the complex parking lot. Mayo figured that if Grissom had come for Stephanie, he had parked somewhere nearby. He also suspected that unless Grissom slipped back and retrieved his car, it should still be in or near the lot. Following a fifteen-minute search of the area, Mayo found a car matching the description Stephanie had given. It was parked next to the large trash dumpster in front of building 1508. Mayo wasted little time contacting Stephanie who, in turn, couldn't get the Grandview Police back there fast enough.

After the third call to the police, Mayo returned to wait by the Toyota until the officers got there. Using his flashlight, he looked through the windshield of the Toyota. On the dash he immediately noticed a large key ring filled with keys. One of the keys caught his eye. It had a rubber tip around its top and lettering read, "Apple Creek." Mayo knew right away that the key was a master to some of the units at the Apple Creek complex. He knew because he himself carried an identical key. He turned the flashlight to other areas of the car's interior. It was difficult to make out exactly what was there. The car windows were slightly tinted. The car was crammed, floor to ceiling, with bundles and bags. To Mayo, it looked like the car was being used to move someone's worldly possessions. Finally, he aimed the flashlight down toward the floor. There, he noticed two credit cards but could make out only a partial name on one of them. The name was Rusch.

The Grandview Police dispatcher directed the officers back to Stonybrook for a third time that night. When they pulled into the Stonybrook lot, they once again were met by Mayo and Stephanie Foster who were standing in front of building 1508. Stephanie Foster's earlier identification of Richard Grissom as the prowler at the complex had not registered as significant to the two Grandview officers. Their roll-call briefings that afternoon had made no mention of the fugitive, and they were not familiar with the Overland Park case.

Bill Mayo, however, now very aware of the history of the man he'd confronted, was bursting at the seams in an effort to tell the officers what he had spotted inside the Toyota. After listening to Mayo describe his discovery, one of the officers called his dispatcher and asked for any data available on a possible fugitive named Richard Grissom, as well as a check of Nebraska license plate 78A 947 found on the Toyota.

The dispatcher wasted little time informing the officer that the tag had been reported stolen. The date of the reported theft was sometime during the night of June 7, 1989, and the location of the theft was from an address in Wichita, Kansas, an address just a few blocks from where Terri Maness had been murdered.

The officers suddenly became excited when realizing the magnitude and value of the discovery in the Stonybrook lot. Word of their find traveled rapidly to Overland Park where Detective Bill Batt was immediately notified.

When the tow truck arrived to take the seized vehicle to the Grandview Police department, the driver was asked to slim-jim the driver-side door of the Toyota for the officers. They wanted to establish the identity of the car's owner. The stolen tag offered little help, but a cursory search of the inside, or a check of the VIN number might reveal the information they sought. It did. The car was legally registered to a Marcelais Thibodo. The name meant nothing to anyone at the scene. Before closing the door, an officer aimed his flashlight beam toward the car's floor just beneath the steering wheel. It was where Mayo had indicated he saw a card with the name of one of the missing women. A closer inspection gave the officer a good look at two credit cards lying on the floor. One of the cards did indeed have the name "Christine Rusch" written across its front. The name on the other card was "Theresa Brown."

The officer closed the door and then sealed the car in evidence tape. He also secured a sign to the side of the car. It read: "HANDS OFF — PROTECT FOR PRINTS." Before the officers completed taking their latest statements from Bill Mayo and Stephanie Foster, they asked members of the crowd of onlookers that had gathered if anyone had witnessed anything that night. The answer was no. The weary policemen followed the tow truck out of the Stonybrook lot and escorted it to the Grandview Police Department. It would be just a matter of time before the Johnson County Crime Lab team was swarming all over it.

14

There was little doubt in the minds of everyone tracking the criminal trail of Richard Grissom that, in addition to Joan Butler's disappearance, he was responsible for the disappearances of Christine Rusch and Theresa Brown. But how the women were taken and where they might be remained perplexing questions. How much evidence did Grissom leave behind? Enough, investigators hoped, to enable them to establish the irrefutable pattern they would need to prosecute him. To help answer these and other questions, forensic examiners and search teams were called in to process the missing women's apartments.

Forensic Specialists Rick Fahy and Bill Chapin took charge of the crime-scene processing of Joan Butler's apartment. The lab team was accompanied by Overland Park Detective Dan Carney, who broke the crime scene seals that had been placed across the front door of the apartment nearly a week before.

Chapin and Fahy liked their work and were good at it. They were experienced technicians who had worked together for years on a variety of cases. The team brought to each investigation a shared sense of responsibility. They knew the importance of crime-scene processing and forensic investigation. They had long accepted that their type of police work would never attract the limelight, that their discipline was destined to remain in that unheralded and often anomalous background called science. But they understood that in most cases—even those where confessions are obtained—corroborating evidence can make or break the case.

For each search, Chapin and Fahy had a system. Chapin, for the most part, took the initial photographs at the scene. He "charted" the entire dwelling and conducted tape liftings from room to room. He labeled each hair, fiber or particle recovered, and gave each piece of evidence a chart designation according to where it was found. Fahy generally followed Chapin, dusting each area for latent prints. He then tape-lifted any prints of sufficient detail and quality, marking each and listing the room from which it was recovered. Fahy collected, marked and tagged additional pieces of evidence to be taken from the crime scene. In some cases, recovered pieces of evidence could stand on their own and be presented in court. In other cases, recovered items were subject to additional forensic processing in the more controlled environment of a lab. Every lift or piece of evidence was marked with the specialist's own identifiers.

The first step in the lab team's methodical approach to processing the crime scene was a slow and calculated walk-through of the premises. The three officers went from room to room, each making independent observations. The activity was referred to as "checking the natural state of a unit." The intent was to formulate an initial opinion about the condition of the dwelling. Did it appear normal? Were there obvious signs of a struggle or foul play? Were beds unmade or clothes and other articles scattered about? Had dresser drawers or jewelry boxes been left open?

Joan's apartment was a small, one-bedroom unit, and the walk-through was quickly concluded. The consensus of the three officers was that the apartment appeared normal. It was neat and orderly, and no signs of any activity that might be considered out of the ordinary were apparent. They noted the piece of partially eaten toast and half-smoked cigarette on the kitchen counter top. Though appearing "normal" to the three officers, it was also perplexing to know that Joan had made it home from a night of dancing, had something light to eat, and then, for reasons not yet established, she was suddenly gone.

While photographing the Butler apartment, Chapin came across a thin, gold chain-necklace lying balled up in the carpet just off the kitchen. The chain had settled into the fibers of the carpet and was not readily seen with a quick pass of the area. The chain blended with the caramel-colored carpet. Chapin photographed the chain and made a mental note to tell Fahy to retrieve it during his collection and bagging routine. Chapin, however, forgot to tell his partner about the chain, and Fahy did not notice it. Only later would the necklace emerge as an important clue.

In Joan's bedroom, Detective Carney took possession of the black dress Joan had worn the night before she disappeared. From inside the closet, he also recovered her black pumps. Carney made note of the fact that Joan's bed was unmade, but the room showed no signs of struggle.

Fahy and Chapin verified that the bed held no evidence of rape. There were no semen or bloodstains. Fahy tape-lifted the bedding for hairs and fibers while in the bedroom and collected Joan's pillowcases for further processing at the lab. In this type of case, certain items were collected in the hope that closer lab processing might reveal samples of blood, hair or saliva belonging to the victim. In missing-person cases, or cases where murder was suspected but the body had not been recovered, there were generally no blood or body fluid samples available for comparison with samples found at other locations. Any trace amounts found at a crime scene could provide investigators with what they called 'known' samples.

During the collection phase of his processing, Fahy noticed a pair of eyeglasses left behind on Joan's bedroom desk. He also recovered a contact-lens case which had been in the cabinet above the bathroom vanity. He collected used tissues, Q-Tips, a hairbrush, hairspray and cosmetics belonging to the victim. He also collected the partially smoked cigarette from the ashtray in the kitchen. Prior to their search, interviews with those close to Joan provided conflicting opinions about whether or not she smoked. Her parents could not be certain that she did. The cigarette might belong to someone else who was there just before Joan disappeared. No purse was found in the apartment. None of the officers could find Joan's driver's license, her checkbook, credit cards, any form of ID, or anything with a signature.

The searchers realized before entering Joan's apartment that they were operating at a disadvantage. Unless a specific piece of evidence could be undeniably linked or matched to a suspect, most of what was found in the dwelling would have to be considered tainted. In a case such as this, the search did not begin with the police. It began with friends, associates, or family members going through the residence. The residence, when considered for purposes of crime-scene processing, would be far from the pristine or untainted condition preferred by investigators. In the Butler case, investigators were forced to deal with the fact that seven to eight people had gone through Joan's apartment before the police were called in. It could never be argued in court that the apartment was processed in the exact condition it had been in when Joan was suddenly taken from it.

Later that day, Chapin and Fahy began processing the Rusch-Brown apartment at Trafalgar Square. From the previous day's investigation, Lenexa Detective Tom Penhollow was able to tell the lab team that at least three people besides the police-response team had been in the apartment before them. The detective also told Chapin and Fahy that he had removed an address book and other items containing names and addresses as probable sources for tracing the girls.

He also mentioned that Theresa's boyfriend, Mike Raunig, had been in the unit with him. Then, he broke the really bad news that there had been a party at the apartment the previous Saturday, and it was reported that the apartment had been given a thorough cleaning the day after. The specialists were thorough in the search and processing routine, once again taking into consideration what had happened before their arrival.

Their initial walk-through revealed no obvious signs of foul play. The bedrooms were messy but nothing indicating a struggle or an injury to anyone. Detective Penhollow had told the forensic team about the KU T-shirt which was found lying on the floor in Theresa's bedroom. Mike Raunig had pointed out that it was the shirt Theresa had been wearing when she left his place on the morning of the twenty-sixth. It was proof that Theresa had made it home before disappearing. The remainder of the apartment appeared clean and orderly.

Joan Butler, as a 20-year-old student at Kansas University. This photo was taken near her sorority house on campus during Father's Weekend.

Joan, at 23, Thanksgiving 1988, waving good-bye to her family in Wichita as she leaves for Kansas City.

Theresa Brown, age 19, at graduation from dental hygienist school.

Christine, left, and Theresa at a party at their Trafalgar Square apartment, Spring '89.

Christine Rusch was 22 when she had this portrait taken as a gift for her mother's birthday.

Theresa and Christine were sharing this upper-floor apartment at Trafalgar Square Apartments in Lenexa, when they disappeared in June '89.

Christine, left, and Theresa, at Christine's parents' home in Overland Park, just weeks before they were abducted.

Richard Grissom is returned to Kansas to face murder charges in November 1989. Flanked by Kansas State Troopers, he's escorted to a waiting plane in Dallas.
Scott Smith, Olathe Daily News

Richard Grissom lived alone in this lower-level apartment at Chesapeake Estates in Lenexa.

Lenexa Detective Pat Hinkle, left, and Overland Park Detective Bill Batt, right, during a land search for Joan Butler in a Kansas City, KS wooded area.

Wichita Police Lt. Kenneth Landwehr led the Maness homicide investigation and traveled to Kansas City to help with the Johnson County investigations.

Officers dig at a possible grave site near an apartment where Grissom once lived in Kansas City, KS. Left to right, Lenexa officers Calvin Smith, Jeff Hartzler and Pat Hinkle.

Michelle Katf, during Grissom's trial, identifies the pellet gun Grissom used during his attack on her during the early morning hours of July 12, 1989. She narrowly escaped being abducted from her Kansas City, Missouri, apartment. At right, Johnson County District Attorney Paul Morrison. *Dave Kaup/Olathe Daily News*

Grissom on trial for murder in Johnson County Court in Olathe, Kansas. Public defender, Andrew Warren, at right. *Dave Kaup/ Olathe Daily News*

Grissom expressed little emotion and never took the witness stand during his two-week trial. Tom Erker, right, was one of his two court-appointed attorneys.
Scott Smith, Olathe Daily News

Richard Grissom was convicted of the murders of the three missing Johnson County women in November 1990. Three weeks later, he was sentenced to prison for four life terms, plus an additional 361 years. Defense Attorney Kevin Moriarty, at left. *Scott Smith, Olathe Daily News*

Following their walk-through, Chapin and Fahy once again divided up their forensic and processing responsibilities. As with the Butler apartment, no Benzedrine testing was performed since no obvious traces of blood were found in the apartment. Unlike the Butler processing, however, the bedding from both bedrooms was bagged for processing at the lab. An on-scene determination was made that the bedding was too bulky to be processed carefully inside the apartment. The lab would provide a larger space and a more controlled environment.

Fahy discovered a contact lens case containing both lenses in Christine's bathroom. He also recovered hairbrushes from the bathrooms of both women. Fahy dusted everything in the apartment that looked like it might hold a print, including the beer kegs on the deck. Like the Butler search, this one did not yield purses, wallets or any forms of ID belonging to either of the missing women.

While Chapin and Fahy processed the inside of the apartment, Officer Burke, assigned by Lenexa to assist with the processing, supervised the removal of the front door locks. The locks not only were being replaced for security reasons, the police were taking the locks as evidence. Burke was in the hall just outside the front door when he received a call over his radio. It advised them that Christine Rusch's missing Dodge Colt had been recovered in the parking lot of a Motel 6, just a few hundred yards from his location. Door locks in hand, Burke went back inside the apartment to inform Chapin and Fahy. Burke found the two lab men standing on the deck near the beer kegs. When Burke broke the news, Fahy and Chapin stared at each other. Their day was just starting. Their next processing duty awaited them just a few hundred yards away.

It wasn't long after the discovery of Christine's Dodge Colt at the Motel 6 that the car was towed, under police escort, to the Lenexa Police Department. An alert officer had found the car during a routine pass through the motel parking lot. Theresa Brown's blue Toyota Tercel, which had been identified by her family and by her boyfriend Mike Raunig, was towed in as well. Her Toyota had remained untouched where she left it the morning she returned from Raunig's, but it nevertheless was brought in for processing.

Chapin and Fahy made quick work of their searches of the two cars. The cars were nearly empty except for a pair of sunglasses, a paper cup and a few pieces of paper found inside the Colt. Everyone involved in the investigation believed the Colt had been used, possibly exclusively, during the abductions of Christine and Theresa. But it held little evidence. Grissom had probably cleaned out the car before leaving it at the motel lot.

While Chapin was photographing the Colt, he noticed a long scratch along the car's exterior on the driver's side. The scratch was wide, as if made by the car scraping against a rough surface. The striations appeared to be smeared with blue paint, and the marks ran the length of the cream-colored Colt.

From his tape-liftings inside the Colt, Chapin recovered two small hairs believed, at first glance by the experienced officer, to be of Negroid origin. A single hair was found on each of the sheepskin seat covers near the headrests. A dusting for prints turned up a latent of sufficient quality on the passenger-side seat buckle. No traces of blood were found inside the Colt. Nothing indicated that a struggle had taken place in the car.

By the time Richard Grissom was identified in Lawrence, Kansas, Detective Ken Landwehr of Wichita had chiseled away at the mountain of leads in the Terri Maness murder, which had occurred approximately three weeks earlier. Detectives and support officers dug into the three-page list of names compiled early on in the investigation. Most of those on the list checked out as having a reasonable and legitimate association with the victim. Those getting a careful look were ex-boyfriends, and male acquaintances who socialized with the victim. Alibis were checked and rechecked.

Door-to-door interviews with residents living within a multi-block radius of Terri's town house had been painstakingly conducted from morning until night over the course of several days. Police reports of any burglaries or thefts reported in the area around the time of the murder were reviewed. Some reports dated weeks before the murder also were studied. The report of the stolen license plate taken just blocks from Terri's town house on the night of her murder was linked almost immediately to her case. The victim's car had, after all, been taken from the scene, driven just a few short blocks and ditched near the car from which the license plate was stolen.

Additionally, checks of burglary and theft reports occurring at commercial establishments around the time of the murder also were ordered by Detective Landwehr. He concentrated on commercial establishments within specific geographic areas around Wichita. It wasn't long before Landwehr's team had isolated at least two theft reports from two separate equipment-supply outfits. They were felony complaints involving the theft of hundreds of dollars worth of equipment, commercial paint sprayers and generators that had been leased and not returned. The name on the rental contracts made the detective sit up and take notice. The name was Rikki Cho. It had been at the bottom of the list compiled in the Terri Maness case. Landwehr also learned from Detective Batt at Overland Park that it was a known alias of Richard Grissom.

The eventual discovery of the stolen license tag on Grissom's Toyota and recovery of phony ID's in the name of Rikki Cho from the Corsica were the icing on the cake for Landwehr and his Wichita team. The link between Grissom and both the Wichita and Johnson County investigations brought Detective Landwehr to Kansas City as a participant in the hunt for Grissom.

Detectives Hinkle and Batt immediately recognized Landwehr as a valuable asset. In fact, they recommended his inclusion on the investigative team, known as the metro squad, which had been assembled within a week of the Rusch-Brown abductions. However, a "formal" invitation from the brass had not been extended. Landwehr continued on his own, however, to do his part in the Grissom investigation. Batt and Hinkle, recognizing Landwehr's talents in serial-killing investigations, were instrumental in getting the detective to address the investigative squad during its early stages. To most of the squad, the lecture was an eye-opener.

Landwehr began his talk by providing a brief history of the documentation and tracking of multiple, or serial, murders in the United States. He reported that the FBI began compiling its own records in the early 1970's, and had advanced its documentation and analyses to include not only the methods, variations and unique features of these crimes, but had developed complete psycho-sexual profiles on such killers and rapists. The Wichita detective explained that the majority of serial killers were sociopaths who preyed on the vulnerable, whether man, woman or child. He also noted that at any given time in the country, roughly 5,000 serial killers were actively pursuing their prey.

The primary targets were women and young girls. The primary motive was sex. But a serial killer could strike to obtain money or property which, at any given time, may be as important as sex. The vast majority were males who traveled and committed their acts alone, but the years had produced pairs of killers, including pairs of the opposite sex who acted together. Some serial killers traveled the freeways, streets and country roads in search of their next victims. Others kept to the cities where victims were easily stalked, and the act was planned well in advance. Some acted out reprisals for their own perverse reasons. The killing of prostitutes generally fell under this category. Others killed or raped just for the thrill of it.

Landwehr told his audience that the FBI had described the method of operation of a serial killer as a "one-man guerrilla strike force: locate victim, strike, kill or rape, retreat to safety." The detective advised that not many serial killers were ever caught. A primary reason was that their victims were usually strangers and generally the only witnesses. Most victims had absolutely no connection to the killer. Since the late 1980's, around 50,000 teens and children had turned up missing each year in the United States. It was probably a safe bet that a lot of them were victims of serial killers.

Landwehr emphasized that when some serial killers eventually were caught, items belonging to their victims were usually found in their possession. The detective referred to the items as "trophies." The serial killer kept an item or several as a reminder of both his victim and his accomplishment. It was, in fact, a rare case when a serial killer did not take trophies. If caught with them, the evidence went a long way toward assisting in the killer's prosecution. Landwehr emphasized that the Richard Grissom case would be no exception.

To focus on Grissom as a serial killer, Landwehr utilized both the available psycho-sexual profile on Grissom and his own firsthand data documented in the Terri Maness murder. Grissom was a loner with a questionable past. He first killed at a young age and the experience had not proved negative for him. His sexual preferences, the investigators had learned, were abnormal. He stalked his prey and fantasized about his eventual acts. He supported himself through the commission of other crimes, and some of his victims were killed before, during or after those crimes. He was deviously smart, but his boldness often got the better of him, forcing him into mistakes. He was a good thinker, but not good enough to think a scenario through from beginning to end with complete clarity.

A few individuals in the press and in the psychology and sociology professions initially had refused to label Grissom a serial killer. FBI profilers and Detective Landwehr disagreed. Landwehr asked that none of his fellow investigators jump to that wrong conclusion. "Make no mistake," he insisted before concluding his address, "Richard Grissom fits the profile perfectly."

15

At 7 A.M., a tired and groggy Bill Chapin received a phone call at home. He could not yet see the bottom of his first cup of coffee, so a call from his watch commander was not exactly a pleasant push he needed to start the day. It had been late the night before when Chapin and his partner finally finished recording evidence from their searches. Chapin knew the phone call would be ordering a repeat performance of yesterday's work. He was right. The watch commander was calling to remind Chapin that he and Fahy needed to be in Grandview, Missouri, first thing. Richard Grissom's packed Toyota awaited their personal touch.

"Detective Morgan will have the search warrant with him," the watch commander informed Chapin. "You'll need to meet with him at Overland Park before heading out to Grandview. He'll be going along with you."

Chapin gulped down another cup of coffee.

At the Grandview Police Department's back bay garage, a warrant was formally issued for the search of

Grissom's car. The lab officers broke the seals of evidence tape from around the car and began processing. Both officers knew much of the forensic processing of the car's interior could not take place until the car had been emptied. Fahy began calculating the extent of the work that would be required to remove and catalog every item in the car. Chapin began photographing the car's exterior to record its general condition and to record the stolen Nebraska tag still on the car. A few photos were taken of the interior.

The lab specialists then began the arduous process of unloading the car and taking inventory. In addition to suitcases full of clothes and gym bags filled with athletic gear, they removed several large plastic bags stuffed with more clothes. They removed two briefcases filled with papers. They discovered two cameras, a stereo boom box, a box of cassette tapes, photo albums containing mostly pictures of Grissom himself, several loose keys, in addition to the large ring of keys found on the dash, loose papers and litter scattered throughout the backseat and hatch areas. A ribbon from a word processor was found balled up on the front, passenger-side floor.

In the search for evidence that might be considered part of a serial killer's "kill kit," only a few items were recovered. A silver knife with an eight-inch blade was found under a pile of clothes on the front passenger seat. A pair of thin, dark-colored, leather gloves was found inside a cloth backpack on the rear seat. A section of rope, with what initially appeared to be a smearing of blood at one end, was recovered.

The recovered Toyota was a virtual treasure chest of evidence linking Grissom to the crimes under investigation. From the keys found all over the car, it was immediately obvious to Fahy and Chapin that Grissom had a thing for keys. The key ring recovered from the dash had numerous keys, some of which were marked with the names of apartment complexes and buildings.

The contents of the two briefcases clearly revealed the extent of Grissom's ability to fabricate false ID's. His efforts had been considerable and thorough, giving him enough falsified documentation to perpetuate his scams for a long time. In addition to birth certificates in several names, Grissom had compiled numerous Social Security cards and applications for several more. Cards were found with the names Yoon Chul Cho, Rikki Y.C. Cho, Richard Anthony Griffin, Richard Anthony Lee and Randy Rodriguez to name a few. Grissom also had three active drivers licenses with the Cho, Griffin and Grissom names.

Fahy picked up the two credit cards belonging to the missing girls. The first was a Chase Manhattan Visa card in the name of Christine Rusch. The other, a Citibank Mastercard in Theresa Brown's name. Inside the car's glove box were discovered three more valuable pieces of evidence: three women's rings, a diamond solitaire, an opal and a pearl.

When the car had been emptied, Chapin began the tape-lifting and his search for trace and particle evidence. When finished, he also removed the car's floor mats and seat covers and bagged them for processing at the lab. Fahy dusted the car throughout for latent prints. Several prints were lifted; they would be turned over to the crime lab's fingerprint expert for final comparisons against known prints. Before the specialists had finished, they had spent five hours processing Grissom's car.

Within thirty-six hours of the forensic examination of Grissom's Toyota, Chapin and Fahy began a similar procedure inside Grissom's Lenexa apartment. With a search warrant in hand, Detective Hinkle opened the door to number 377 at Chesapeake Estates.

Chapin's initial photographs inside Grissom's apartment supported Thibodo's contentions about what happened the night of the twenty-fifth when Grissom was on the run. The place looked like it. Clothes and hangers were still strewn about the floor of every room. Drawers were pulled half opened with clothes hanging out. Trash had been piled high in the kitchen and laundry areas. Towels, clothes, hangers and papers had been scattered across the bed, the sofa, the kitchen counter and a computer desk.

Fahy recovered a word processor from the middle of the living room floor. The machine and the ribbon, found earlier inside Grissom's car, would prove significant in linking Grissom to the creation of the fraudulent documents he used for check-writing schemes and other thefts. From the bedroom closet, Fahy recovered a plastic container for a Crossman Air Pistol 357. The package also contained a receipt for the pistol, indicating it had been purchased on April 11, 1989, from a K-mart store less than two miles from Grissom's apartment. Used CO_2 cartridges and packets of pellets also were discovered.

Only a handful of latent prints found in Grissom's apartment were of the quality to warrant lifting. Fahy lifted them and stored them for comparison. No blood smearings or fluid spots were found during the search. A few hairs, again believed to be of Negroid origin, were tape-lifted from the bedroom and bath areas of the apartment.

It was late morning when Joseph Hetzel awoke from a sound sleep in the bedroom of his ground floor apartment. He was a traveling salesman who had returned home late the night before from a long road trip. Hetzel lived in the Briarwood Apartments, a sizable complex just off the frontage road to Highway 71, in Grandview. Briarwood was located just across the highway from the Stonybrook complex.

Hetzel thought he heard a noise in the living room or kitchen area of his apartment. He got out of bed and, still half asleep, stumbled out of the bedroom. He immediately noticed that his sliding-glass door, leading out to a patio at the back of the unit, was open. A thin curtain that covered the window was swaying in the breeze. Hetzel tried to recall events of the previous night. He remembered watching a little TV, but tired quickly and went to bed. He was certain the sliding-glass door had been closed. He guessed that someone had opened the door during the night or earlier that morning; he wondered if they had entered the apartment or had taken anything. As he looked around the living room and kitchen, he could find nothing missing or out of place.

After his shower, Hetzel dressed and had a quick bite to eat while watching the noon news. As he approached the TV for his remote, he noticed that a candy dish usually kept on a table next to the TV was missing. He could not remember moving it. Then it hit him—some of his buddies at the complex had pulled a prank on him. They opened the door and took the candy dish. Hetzel laughed it off, decided to forget lunch and get on the road. He locked the sliding-glass door and grabbed his briefcase. Once outside, Hetzel stopped dead in his tracks. His car was not where he had left it the night before. His first thought was that his friends had taken their joke a little too far. Then he remembered. He had left a spare set of car keys in the candy dish. He went back inside to call the police.

Members of the Grandview police department had spent a frenzied night investigating Grissom's appearance and getaway at the Stonybrook complex. Unsure about whether Grissom might have stayed in the area, the police were paying close attention to any suspicious activity reported from surrounding areas during the night. The Overland Park and Lenexa teams also were monitoring reported activity in Grandview and along routes they suspected Grissom might have chosen for his escape. Consequently, when Joseph Hetzel called to report the theft of his Pontiac Grand Am, from an area just across the highway from where Grissom was last seen, they knew Grissom had Hetzel's car.

Late in the day on the twenty-eighth, Detective Landwehr drove up from Wichita to lend a hand in the Grissom investigation. By early the next morning he was out covering leads everyone knew were significant but, for reasons of manpower constraints, could not get to right away. Landwehr knew Grissom's type, and he knew that time was their enemy. The Terri Maness crime scene remained fresh in his mind and he knew that unless stopped, Grissom would strike again. Landwehr wanted him caught, and he would do his part to see that happen.

Following a lengthy debriefing from Hinkle and Batt and a review of file materials, Landwehr drove to Lawrence, Kansas. He focused his attention on some of the information already provided by Marcelais Thibodo which included details of the painting contract at Trailridge and the fact that both he and Grissom had girlfriends in Lawrence. Landwehr noticed no one had interviewed Grissom's girlfriend, Cathy Arenal. He wanted to cover that lead right away.

When Landwehr first approached Cathy Arenal at her home in Lawrence, the young coed did not want to talk to him, or anyone, about Richard Grissom. Several minutes into his attempts to persuade Arenal, and her reluctance still resolute, Landwehr began to understand why. Arenal's hesitation to talk had nothing to do with any attempt to protect Grissom. In fact, the opposite was true. He was still on the loose, and she was deathly afraid that he was coming for her.

Arenal believed that Grissom thought she was the one who reported him to the police in Lawrence. She was so convinced, that on the night of Grissom's escape from Lawrence, which she had seen on news reports, she fled her own house. She had spent the entire night and much of the next day hiding out at the radio station where a friend worked. In fact, Cathy and her friend both were in a state of near panic when the receptionist at the radio station failed to show for work. Cathy feared Grissom had gotten to the receptionist in a desperate attempt to locate her. He hadn't. The receptionist eventually showed up for work.

Adding fuel to the fire were the subsequent news reports linking Grissom to the disappearance of two more women. It mattered little to Cathy Arenal that his victims lived in another city. Grissom had made the trip from Kansas City to Lawrence on numerous occasions and at all hours of the day and night. The distance was inconsequential to him and Arenal knew it. Landwehr had a very difficult time convincing Cathy Arenal that Grissom was long gone and would not be coming for her. He did, however, succeed.

The detective from Wichita was an experienced interviewer. Calm and soft-spoken, he had a tranquilizing effect on the apprehensive Cathy Arenal. He pointed out right away that if Grissom had paid attention to both the printed and broadcast reports about him, he would have known that it was someone else, and not Cathy, who had reported him. He also told her that every investigator working the case believed Grissom had fled the state and would not likely return. Landwehr emphasized that Grissom would assume the police were watching Arenal and her house. Before long, Cathy Arenal settled down and began telling the detective all she knew about Grissom.

Arenal's recollections of Grissom's possession of the Corsica during the week after Father's Day went a long way toward corroborating other witness testimony. Landwehr knew that if the case against Grissom ever made it to a trial stage, the more eyewitness testimony about his possession of the Corsica, the better. Cathy admitted that she not only saw Grissom with the car, she rode in it on one occasion when Grissom took her to a convenience store for cigarettes.

She also provided details of the Saturday night before Father's Day when she and a friend met Grissom at Pizazz in Lawrence. She told the detective that she danced with Grissom that night and they stayed at the club until closing. She had said good-bye to Grissom in the parking lot at Pizazz around 2:30 A.M., at which time he told her he was heading back to Kansas City.

Cathy pointed out that after the police reports linking Grissom to the Joan Butler disappearance, she began thinking about some of the things she had noticed in the week after Father's Day. She told Landwehr that when she next saw Grissom, it was Tuesday of the following week, and he looked horrible. His eyes were red and puffy, and his hair was unkempt which was not like him. Cathy said that she asked Grissom about his haggard appearance, and he told her he had not slept at all since he last saw her the previous Saturday.

Landwehr's last series of questions had as much to do with the Terri Maness murder as with the case of the three missing women. Landwehr knew that certain pieces of jewelry had been taken from Terri Maness the night of her murder. Without telling her exactly why he was asking, Landwehr asked Cathy if Grissom had ever given her any jewelry.

"Oh sure," she responded. "The same week he had the red car he gave me an early birthday present. At least that's what he called it." Having answered his question, Cathy hurried off to another part of her house to prove it to him. Moments later she came back into the room and held out her palm. "It's a chain and a coin pendant. He gave it to me on the second or third time I saw him with the new car," she said.

Landwehr studied the chain and gold coin-pendant. It was nothing he recalled from the Wichita reports, and nothing about missing jewelry had been reported in the Johnson County cases. Nevertheless, his gut told him the necklace was somehow important. If Grissom had given it to her, someone, somewhere was missing that piece of jewelry. "When exactly did he give this to you?" Landwehr asked.

"It was during that same week," she answered. "The same week he had the red car." Cathy paused for a moment. "It was on that Saturday, the twenty-fourth. We went out for a short while that night, and he gave it to me then."

"And he told you it was an early birthday present?"

"Yeah! He said he wanted me to have it, that he bought it for me and I should just consider it an early birthday present. I thought it was nice, but you know, I had no idea." She cut herself off, unable to voice the thoughts forming in her mind about where Grissom may have gotten the pendant and chain.

"When is your birthday?" Landwehr asked.

"July thirty-first."

"Pretty early present," Landwehr commented, shaking his head.

"Yeah, pretty early," she agreed.

Landwehr turned the chain and pendant over to detectives at Overland Park. A subsequent check with the Butler family determined they could not identify the jewelry as anything belonging to Joan. The pieces were then turned over to Dan Carney of the Property Crimes Division at Overland Park. Carney locked the jewelry away in a file cabinet to be checked against other cases at a later date. The chain and pendant would remain locked away for nearly a month before being brought out for inspection by witnesses. The jewelry eventually would provide an additional link between Grissom and the Joan Butler case.

16

A few days after first being interviewed, Marcelais Thibodo had more information he was eager to share with investigators. He agreed to meet Hinkle and Batt at Overland Park Police Headquarters. The two detectives were waiting at the front door of the headquarters building when Thibodo pulled his Nissan pickup into the lot. They went out to meet him.

"I found these in the locker," Thibodo reported, holding out a pair of sunglasses toward Hinkle. "I think they're women's glasses," he added.

"In what locker?" Hinkle asked studying the glasses. "What locker are you talking about?"

Thibodo answered his question matter-of-factly, as if it were acceptable that he had waited to reveal an incredible lead. He told them about Grissom's storage locker in Stanley, a rural area just south of Overland Park. Grissom leased the locker to store painting supplies and equipment. Thibodo added that Grissom also kept a key-duplicating machine in the locker but had removed it just before leaving town.

Hinkle was making every effort to calm himself. Why had Thibodo waited to tell them about the locker? Why hadn't he mentioned it when they were out together two days before? Why had he just now offered the sunglasses? How much more might be in the locker? "How long have you had these glasses?" Hinkle asked, glaring at Thibodo.

"About a week," came the casual reply. "I found them at the locker last Saturday."

"Is that the last time you were there?" Hinkle asked.

"Yeah, I was there last Saturday and I haven't been back since."

Hinkle and Batt wanted to believe Thibodo. They wanted to be sure he was telling the truth and telling them everything. His surprises, however, were making that difficult. Based on everything he had given them thus far, they knew Thibodo could be a valuable witness, but there were too many others involved in the investigation who believed that Thibodo was in some way criminally involved with Grissom. Batt and Hinkle and even Landwehr were making every effort to stay in Thibodo's corner. He was not making it easy for them, however.

"What do you think about giving us permission to search your truck?" Hinkle asked, catching Thibodo slightly off-guard. The detective knew he was walking on thin ice. He didn't want to risk alienating a witness, but he had to be very certain about him as well.

Thibodo paused and took a step back. He looked at Hinkle and Batt. He could see they were serious. He was confused, but he acquiesced. "OK," he said. "Go ahead. You can search it if you want, man."

The search was brief, confined to the cab of the truck. Nothing was recovered. "Thanks for letting us take a look," Hinkle said, attempting to limit any damage caused by their suspicion. "We just needed to be sure. You understand, right?"

"No problem, man. I guess it's OK." With that, Thibodo answered the detective's question about where they would find the storage locker.

The detectives left immediately, traveled south to Metcalf Avenue in Stanley, Kansas, and located the Metcalf South Storage Facility. Thibodo had told them about locker number eighteen, a five by ten feet unit leased by Grissom. Thibodo also had told them that the lock had been removed from the locker door, and a lot of the equipment and supplies had been cleaned out.

Inside the locker, detectives found the bucket in which Thibodo had discovered the sunglasses. The glasses had been resting on top of some rags inside the five-gallon bucket. The detectives studied the shag carpet that covered most of the floor of the locker. It was a dirty-brown or rust-colored carpet that, Thibodo had also casually mentioned, came from an apartment at Trafalgar Square, though not the Rusch-Brown apartment. The detectives made a note to have the lab team collect the carpet during their processing of the locker. The big question remaining in the minds of both Batt and Hinkle was whether Grissom had held any of the missing women in this locker. They would make every effort to find out.

On Saturday, July 1, eighteen-year-old Scott Hendricks was on his bike heading south on Metcalf Avenue toward work. He had just started a summer job with the district office for Johnson County Schools, located around Metcalf and 150th Street. Near the intersection of Metcalf and 139th, he noticed some personal items—maybe things that had fallen from a car—scattered about in a ditch.

Upon closer examination, he noticed credit cards, an eyeglasses case, receipts, papers, a checkbook holder and a white T-shirt. Scott studied the scene. He reasoned a car must have swerved off the road for the items to have fallen where they did. A couple of tire tracks through the gravel made him feel his assumption was correct. He reached down and picked up the T-shirt and immediately noticed a yellowish-brown stain on the front. He dropped it back where it had been and did not pick up any other items. He figured that whomever dropped them probably did so earlier that morning and would return for them. If they were still there that afternoon when he passed back, he would pick them up.

That afternoon, Scott retraced his path home from work, having all but forgotten his discovery of that morning. When he approached the intersection at 139th, the items he had seen earlier were still there. He had with him a large envelope containing some papers from work and decided to use it to carry the items from the road. He didn't take the soiled T-shirt or the eyeglass case, leaving them, instead, where he first spotted them.

At home that evening, Scott showed the items to his parents who instructed him to conduct his own minor investigation to find the owner of the property. Weighted by other distractions of a busy summer schedule, Scott procrastinated. He did not get back around to tracking the woman, whose name was written on the property, until later that week. By Saturday morning, news reports gave him the answers he needed. Scott and his parents noticed the name on many of the discovered items was the same as one of the missing women being talked about on the news. The items belonged to Christine Rusch. They called the police hot line.

Officer Jennifer Watkins, Overland Park Police, responded, listened to Scott's story and retrieved the items he had found. Watkins asked Scott to ride along in the squad car to show her exactly where he had recovered the articles. Scott directed the officer back to the intersection of 139th and Metcalf. Some items remained where he left them—a few papers, the pink eyeglasses case. The T-shirt, however, was gone.

Deputy Bill Chapin immediately was dispatched to the location. In time, other officers from both Overland Park and Lenexa arrived. Chapin ordered a full search of the area, including both sides of Metcalf Avenue and areas well beyond. In the end, everything from more papers linked to Christine to McDonald's soda cups were picked up and placed in plastic evidence bags for the crime lab. The articles picked up by young Hendricks also would be taken to the crime lab for processing.

Late that afternoon, Chapin mopped his brow as he stared down at the ditch where the items had been recovered. Thoughts ran through his mind as to how Christine's things ended up on the side of the road. Had the suspect tossed them from the car on his way through the area? Had the items fallen out during a struggle or an attempt to escape? Did Christine throw them out herself, in an effort to let someone know where she had been, where she was going? Had the car been heading for the storage locker?

Toward the end of the search, a team member handed Chapin an envelope. As he opened it and examined its contents, he found a receipt and a small instruction sheet on how to tap and clean a keg of beer. He recalled his search of the women's apartment and the empty kegs left behind. He thought about the party the women had thrown the previous weekend.

He thought about the two young women's last happy days alive.

July 1, 1989. Efforts to apprehend Grissom were stepped up when the Kansas City Metro Squad was formed. The concept of a metro squad, though not used in many metropolitan areas of the United States, was well-established in Kansas City. It was designed to pull together detectives from jurisdictions around the metro area into one unit to conduct cross-jurisdiction investigations into major crimes. In addition to eliminating potential issues of interference between jurisdictions, the formation of the squad helped increase the supply of manpower. The formation of the metro squad usually guaranteed coverage of most leads developed within the first thirty-six to forty-eight hours.

The squad of detectives assembled to work the Grissom case numbered more than twenty-five. The primary jurisdictions of Overland Park and Lenexa, from where the three missing women were abducted, were considered the host agencies and were sufficiently represented. Johnson County placed detectives and crime-lab specialists on the squad.

Also assigned were detectives from the Kansas City, Missouri, and Kansas City, Kansas, and the Kansas Bureau of Investigation. The squad had four main divisions, with a detective heading each one. Leading the squad itself was Major John Round, a twenty-year veteran with Overland Park who had served on several other metro squads through the years. The lead officer was Detective Jeff Dysart, with Overland Park, whose primary responsibility was to check and prioritize incoming leads, coordinate "tips", and direct the flow of the investigation. A records officer was assigned to coordinate reports and ensure that leads were matched with follow-up reports. A press officer served as liaison to the news media.

The command center for the squad was located at Overland Park Headquarters, where separate squad rooms with desks, chairs, conference tables, wall maps, charts and chalk boards had been assembled in short order. Members of the squad knew that in this case, time was of the essence. Young women were rapidly disappearing without a trace and a prime suspect, who had attempted other abductions remained at large.

17

The first week of the metro squad's work on the Grissom case set a record for the most calls to the Tips Hot Line number in a single week. Over eleven hundred calls were received. The majority of the calls were from people who either wanted to report possible sightings of Grissom, or who seemed to know where the girls were, or what happened to them. Squad detectives did not ignore any leads, no matter how ludicrous they might have seemed.

Calls came from all over the metro area, from people who thought they'd spotted Grissom in bars, nightclubs, restaurants, convenience stores or someone's house or apartment building. One caller, using a pay phone at a restaurant, told the hot line operator that Grissom was standing at a salad bar fixing himself a salad at that very moment. The detectives thought it was a stretch, but they checked it out. It wasn't him. Another bar-restaurant sighting resulted in detaining a man. The man did look like Grissom; it turned out that he was a businessman in town for a day.

Calls from individuals, mostly women, claiming to know Grissom well, surprised many detectives for a couple of reasons. The sheer number of calls was indicative of how many women Grissom knew. They also were taken aback by the number of calls from women who expressed opinions about why Richard Grissom could not have committed the crimes. The women insisted that Grissom was of a quiet nature and friendly disposition and was inclined to help, not hurt, other people. Many women reported it was impossible for Grissom to have committed a sex crime. He was rarely active sexually, they said. Some reported they practically had to beg him to sleep with them; some had dated him for weeks before he ever touched them.

A number of calls the first week were related to sightings of the missing women, or locations where they were believed buried. Reports of mysterious odors or unusual activity in remote areas received immediate responses from investigators. Still other calls were from purported psychics, who claimed to be receiving information from the missing women themselves.

One early call, believed to be of significance to investigators, was from a woman who had seen a young black man with a white woman in the vicinity of Longview Lake. The lake was just off Highway 71 and south of Grandview, where numerous sightings of Grissom already had been reported. The caller said the woman looked exactly like Joan Butler, and the man appeared to be leading her by the arm. Tracking dogs were called in, and overhead infrared scanning to detect heat from a decomposing body was used. The teams spent hours dragging the bottom of the lake. The land and water searches turned up nothing.

Psychics and visionaries from Kansas City, as well as others from around the country, called the hot line. Many of them were judged to be kooks, following the wave of publicity generated by the case. One man claimed to be able to find bodies by the divining technique, not unlike the method for locating water. He naturally offered his services to police.

Other callers reported dreams and visions of the girls and where they were buried or being kept. Some of those claimed to have left note pads and pens by their beds at night and when the visions came, they'd awakened to write down the information. Still others claimed that spirits themselves came and wrote on their pads. A number of accounts mentioned that the bodies would be found near certain landmarks—grain silos, billboards, farm out-buildings, abandoned quarries and caves. Other visionaries reported they were not dead and that the girls had been sold into prostitution in places as close as Las Vegas or New York, and as far away as the Middle East or South America.

By July 3, with the hot line still lighting up, many of the leads were put on hold. Although, two leads sounded as though they had the potential to lead detectives to Grissom. The calls followed each other closely, both indicating that Grissom was making contact with at least two women from wherever he was hiding.

The first call came from a very concerned father of one of the women. He told detectives that his daughter had heard from Grissom at least twice between July 1 and 3. He did not know where Grissom was, and his daughter was not saying. The man told detectives his daughter, Sherry Cash, had been seeing Grissom romantically for several months and was planning to marry him. The distraught father said that his daughter did not believe a word of what was being reported about Grissom, and she remained very much in love with him. The caller feared that his daughter was preparing to join Grissom when he called for her.

The other call was from a young woman who lived in Kansas City. She had known Grissom and recently had received a phone call from her girlfriend who claimed to have just heard from him. The caller said her friend, Karen Marshall, was now living in Chicago. The caller explained that both of them had known Grissom. According to the caller, Grissom became fairly serious about Karen, and the two began seeing more of each other. The caller told detectives, however, that Karen did not know where Grissom was calling from.

No less than ten metro squad detectives investigated the two leads. Hinkle worked with Dan Carney to cover one lead, and Batt teamed with detective Burke to cover the second.

Detectives Hinkle and Carney got a short-notice warning from Cash's father that Sherry had suddenly piled her things into her car and had left for Nashville. The detectives had known in advance that Sherry was contemplating a move there. Her father had the address of the house in Nashville where she would be staying.

Given Sherry Cash's unwillingness to cooperate with the police, Hinkle and Carney knew the trail to Grissom through Sherry would be a dead end if they didn't catch up to her in Nashville. Before flying out, Hinkle contacted the Nashville Police and requested a surveillance on the house where Sherry was due to arrive. He asked that she be followed if she left before Hinkle and Carney got there.

Hinkle had been in the Nashville airport terminal for about five minutes when he learned Sherry had arrived at the house, and one of Nashville's finest drug-surveillance units was watching her. The bad news, however, was that Sherry wasn't staying put. She was packing to leave again. The surveillance team's jurisdiction was confined to the Nashville city limits.

Hinkle was in a minor panic. He sensed that Sherry Cash was going to Grissom. He begged the Nashville detective to arrange for a rental car and, if possible, to have it in the vicinity of the surveillance. Hinkle and Carney would take a fast cab to that location. They could tail her if only they could get there in time. If Cash left the city limits or crossed the state line, they could follow her.

Hinkle and Carney did get to the surveillance location on time. In fact, they had just enough time to throw their bags into the Nissan Sentra rental car before Sherry Cash decided to take off. She was driving a small, green, Japanese import and headed straight out of town.

Hinkle and Carney were on her, making sure to keep several car lengths away. Watching her without getting "burned" was easy as long as she stayed on the interstate. A one-car surveillance could get tricky on city streets and isolated back roads. When Sherry reached a point about ten miles outside of Nashville, she pulled off the interstate and into a roadside service area where she parked. She didn't get out of her car.

"Counter-surveillance!" exclaimed Hinkle. "She knows we're on her!"

Carney pulled the rental around to the far side of the service area and out of view. After a five-minute wait, Sherry pulled out once again but headed back toward Nashville. She was "dry cleaning" herself, a surveillance term, used to indicate when a target was trying to make sure they were not being followed.

Sherry pulled the counter-surveillance stunts several more times, pulling off the interstate over a ten to fifteen mile stretch outside of Nashville. Throughout it all, the detectives felt reasonably certain they had not been burned, but as long as she continued to play games, they could not be certain. They finally decided they were safe when Sherry headed out of town and kept on going. She drove from Nashville to Bowling Green, Kentucky, and then on to Louisville. Just outside of Louisville, she started playing games again. Sherry began taking rural exits, only to turn around and get back on the highway.

The one-unit surveillance team had to improvise. Often when she exited, they simply waited until she came back around. Their options were limited. They could not do much more than they were doing. As it was, the risk of being burned was great. Whenever she exited, they stopped somewhere within sight of the exit, changed shirts and positions and waited for her to reappear. Often Hinkle sank down in the seat while Carney drove, and Carney would do the same when Hinkle was at the wheel. The two-person-to-one-person switch seemed to be working.

Finally, heading out of Louisville toward Cincinnati, the detectives thought for a moment they might once again enjoy a stretch of smooth sailing along the interstate. They were wrong. There was no end to Sherry Cash's paranoia. She took an exit outside of Louisville but didn't stop. She got back on the interstate heading in the opposite direction.

Hinkle and Carney, irritated by this time, began arguing about what to do. They could not afford to let her get back into Louisville without them. They finally agreed to go after her, but only after a brief wait to let several cars get between them. They had gone only about three miles, when they were forced to speed right by Sherry, who had stopped her car on the highway median. By the time the detectives found the next exit, turned around and headed back, Sherry Cash was long gone.

Hinkle stepped on the gas, reaching speeds between seventy-five and eighty miles per hour and headed toward Cincinnati. If Sherry was going that way, they eventually would catch her. They did, only to lose her again in downtown Cincinnati. Sherry had been circling a popular shopping district in downtown Cincinnati and then suddenly disappeared.

The detectives were at a loss to explain how Sherry had eluded them. Hinkle made a loop around the district one more time but could not find her. He pulled into a parking lot of a small strip center and parked. Hinkle glanced over Carney's shoulder, and parked just two cars away was the green import. Sherry, however, was not in it.

Looking around the shopping center, Carney spotted her. She was standing near a bank of phones talking with two men. One of the men left with Sherry and rode with her to an apartment house not far away. Hinkle and Carney watched as Sherry parked her car, and she and her companion carried suitcases into the apartment building. Sherry, to the delight of the exhausted, two-man surveillance team, remained there for the night.

While Carney watched the apartment, Hinkle called the local FBI office, identified himself, and described the metro-squad case being worked out of Kansas City. He asked for help with the surveillance on Sherry Cash. The FBI sent a surveillance team to watch the apartment.

The next day, July 4, Sherry spent most of the day alone, driving around the city. She stopped several times at pay phones and made calls but did not meet with anyone or appear to be waiting to meet with anyone. By early evening she was back at her friend's apartment and apparently in for the night.

At 3:00 A.M., Hinkle was awakened from a deep sleep by the telephone ringing in his hotel room. It was the FBI calling. Sherry Cash had left the apartment earlier that evening, and the surveillance team lost her.

Hinkle and Carney were exasperated and ready to climb the wall. They had tailed this woman for several hundred miles, through several states, using one car and a lot of ingenuity. Then, they turned her over to a surveillance team with a host of agents working a familiar city and they lost her! The two detectives stared at each other in disbelief.

Hinkle and Carney decided to find out if the man with whom Sherry had been staying could tell them where she was. Before dawn, on the fifth, with the assistance of the Cincinnati Police, the detectives rousted him out of bed. Their intent was to shake him up enough to find out where Sherry had gone. That would not be necessary. Sherry never had left the apartment. She had been asleep until the detectives knocked on the door.

The detectives were surprised to learn that Sherry had no idea she was still under surveillance. She admitted she had suspected it in Nashville but hadn't noticed it while traveling north. She had purposely avoided contact with her family and had not told anyone back home in Kansas City where she was. Sherry remained uncooperative on the subject of Richard Grissom, but she admitted that she had been driving around trying to make up her mind about whether to go to him. In the opinion of the two detectives, her hesitation had probably kept her alive.

Hinkle and Carney took Sherry to the Cincinnati Police Department. They wanted to question her more before arranging to have her transported back to Kansas City. They knew they had lost her as a conduit to Grissom but hoped that talking with her might help her realize that Grissom wasn't who she thought he was— that she was jeopardizing her life by trying to see him again. In time, Sherry would see things more clearly and would speak with the detectives at length about

Grissom. She would reveal many of his habits, his peculiarities and his sexual preferences. Her revelations would prove extremely valuable when the time came to assemble a more complete psycho-sexual profile on their fugitive.

In Chicago, while their fellow detectives had chased Sherry Cash across several states, Detectives Batt and Penhollow had camped out in the home of a very cooperative Karen Marshall. She had been completely candid about her association with Richard Grissom. She had gone out with him and had liked him as a friend, but that was the extent of it. More important, Karen believed what the police and her friends in Kansas City had told her about Grissom. She allowed the detectives to set up a trap-trace on her phone and gave them permission to monitor her calls. By July 6, the Chicago team had a bead on Grissom and were preparing to cast the bait that, hopefully, would lure him out of hiding.

The trap-trace on the phone line allowed the detectives to pinpoint where a call was coming from. Although, an exact determination generally was not made with a single call unless the call was lengthy. The success of the trap-trace depended on progressively narrowing the geographical field with each call until an exact location was determined. Over the July 4 holiday, Grissom made at least four calls to Karen Marshall. He had also placed a few calls to Sherry Cash's place in Nashville where a trap-trace was in place. From Grissom's first calls to Chicago and Nashville, the detectives knew he was in Texas. His subsequent calls to Chicago narrowed the field to Corpus Christi.

By the end of the day on the fourth, Metro Squad Detectives Joe Langer and Tom Robinson were on their way to Corpus Christi. At the same time, the Chicago team of Batt and Penhollow had successfully guided Karen Marshall through her conversations with Grissom. The detectives were careful to take things slowly and let the situation play itself out. They made certain that Karen asked Grissom nothing about his location or how to contact him. He would be easily spooked. Karen initiated none of the calls and allowed Grissom to volunteer whatever he wanted. Her responsibility was to make him feel comfortable and talk to him as if knowing nothing of his being wanted. Karen was calm, collected and played her role well, the detectives thought. She also helped secure the opportunity to take the performance to the next step.

Before his last call, Grissom had asked Karen to join him in Texas. Once she agreed, Grissom said he would meet her flight at the Dallas-Ft. Worth Airport on the morning of July 7. There wasn't a detective on the metro squad who didn't believe the setup was too good to be true.

Batt and Penhollow followed through with every detail of the plan. They were not just going to have Karen give Grissom a flight number and a time of arrival and see if he showed up to meet her. They were putting a gutsy Karen Marshall on the plane to Dallas. She would be surrounded by cops, they assured her. In the event that Grissom had her watched, either in the Chicago terminal or on the plane, it would be made to appear that Karen was traveling alone.

Reinforcements were sent to Chicago from the metro squad. There would be a detective near Karen at all times during the trip. She told Grissom that she would be coming in on American Airlines. He was given the flight number and time of her arrival. All he had to do was show up.

As Karen's flight departed Chicago for Dallas, another American Airlines flight was departing Kansas City for that same destination. On board was FBI Agent Mike Napier. He stood six-feet tall and was of slight build. Napier did not fit the stereotyped image of a streetwise, crime-busting FBI agent, but he was a crack polygraph examiner, hostage negotiator and interview specialist. The agent had been invited into the Grissom case by the metro squad. In the event that Grissom was captured in Dallas, Napier had been asked to conduct the early, post-arrest interviews.

The two American flights were scheduled to arrive within twenty minutes of each other. They were, however, parking at separate terminals at the Dallas Airport.

Karen grew more nervous with each passing minute. As the plane touched down, she took several deep breaths. She could feel her heart pounding. Did she look nervous, she wondered? Would Grissom show up? Would he notice her anxiety? She tried to hold back any thoughts about whether she could pull this off.

Inside the terminal, police officers of the Dallas Tactical Unit were in place around the terminal. Metro squad detectives Joe Langer and Tom Robinson had traveled from Corpus Christi to take positions near the arrival gate for Karen's flight. By the time Karen's flight had landed and taxied toward the gate, every police officer in the terminal was poised and ready to pounce. They were also nervous and very uncertain. Grissom had not been spotted anywhere in the terminal and he had not given Karen instructions for meeting him elsewhere.

He was there, however. He had shown up to meet Karen, but had gone to the wrong American terminal.

18

Shortly after 10:30 A.M., Grissom pulled his stolen Pontiac Grand Am in front of one of two American Airlines terminals at the Dallas-Ft. Worth Airport. The signs along the curb indicated the area was for passenger pick up and drop off only. Cars were not to be left parked and unoccupied. Grissom, dressed in a T-shirt, shorts and a pair of thongs, jumped from the Grand Am and hurried inside the terminal. He intended to leave his car at the curb just long enough to find out at which terminal and gate Karen would be arriving. Then, he would park the car and return for her.

While Grissom casually checked the bank of arrival monitors located just inside the terminal, FBI Agent Mike Napier was entering the same terminal from the other direction. Napier was just coming off his flight from Kansas City. The agent walked casually down the concourse. He knew, that if Grissom showed up for Karen Marshall, the commotion would be happening at another terminal. Napier planned to call the Airport Public Safety Department for an update and make his plans according to its report.

Then, as Napier reached the center of the terminal, he saw him. Out of the blue, it was Grissom—Kansas City's most wanted fugitive—standing there reading a screen of arrival times. Puzzled, Napier scanned the terminal. There were no cops anywhere around Grissom. For a split second, the agent wondered whether Karen Marshall's flight had been routed to another terminal, but seeing Grissom at the monitor told him the suspect was probably in the wrong place.

His mind racing, Napier slowed his pace but continued to move toward Grissom. Suddenly, Grissom turned toward Napier, and for a brief moment, the two were staring at each other. Fortunately, Grissom did not make Napier for a cop. To him, he was just another businessman carrying a briefcase. Calmly, the agent passed by his suspect and once again studied the terminal for the presence of detectives or any suitable backup. He noticed two uniformed officers standing at the far end of the terminal. He stopped and turned slightly, trying not to appear conspicuous. He checked his watch and looked around as if searching for someone.

Then, he saw Grissom moving toward the terminal doors and heading outside. Napier quickly identified himself to a ticket agent and asked her to summon the two uniformed officers he had seen. "Tell the officers I have an emergency just outside those doors over there, and tell them I need backup right away!" He spun around and followed Grissom outside. Napier could not predict what Grissom would do next, but he couldn't just let him walk away. Grissom may or may not go to meet Karen, Napier thought. He had to take him.

His adrenaline pumping, Napier hurried down the sidewalk toward Grissom. When he was close enough he dropped his briefcase and moved his hand to his

gun. "FBI, Grissom!" the agent shouted. "Get up against
that wall!" he ordered. Grissom came to a halt and
turned back toward him. He knew Grissom had superior speed and could escape him on foot. The agent
moved in on him quickly, making him believe his
opportunity for escape had been lost. To his surprise,
Grissom faced the building and took a half-step toward
it. Napier quickly placed a hand between Grissom's
shoulder blades and nudged him the rest of the way to
the wall. "Let's have your name," said the agent, already well aware of exactly who it was standing in
front of him.

"Richard," replied Grissom, in a soft, unhurried
voice.

"Your full name Richard. What's your full name?"
the agent pressed. When Grissom hesitated Napier
pressed. "Well, what is it?" he asked, giving Grissom a
slight nudge. "What's your full name Richard?" Napier
was stalling for time, waiting for the backup he hoped
was coming. He was trying to keep his suspect off
balance.

"Grissom, Richard Grissom Jr.," replied the suspect.
As he spoke, Grissom took a step or two back from the
wall.

Napier knew what Grissom was planning. The fugitive would bolt as soon as he realized that Napier was
alone. Napier could not let that happen. He stuck his
gun in the back of Grissom's neck just above his shoulders. "Stay against the wall," he ordered. "Stay put and
don't make any sudden moves." The experienced agent
placed his foot between Grissom's legs and ordered
him to spread them. "Put your hands behind your
back," he commanded, stepping away enough to allow
Grissom to obey. Then, to Napier's relief, he saw the
two public-safety officers running down the sidewalk
toward them.

Grissom did not turn to look. He knew that sound. Seconds later he could feel the cold handcuffs placed around his wrists and the officers patting him down. Any chance to escape had passed. The three men led Grissom back inside the terminal. For Mike Napier, the ordeal was over, but only a small part of his job had been completed.

At the other American terminal, detectives and officers maintaining the surveillance on Karen Marshall were notified. Grissom had been arrested next door by the FBI and was being held in the public-safety office nearby. The teams gathered around Karen Marshall, who had been isolated and waiting for Grissom to show up.

Her biggest hope had been that Grissom would be spotted by the detectives and arrested long before he got to her. Things didn't go exactly as planned at her terminal, but her prayers had been answered. Batt and Penhollow stayed with Karen and made arrangements for her return trip to Chicago. Batt had promised Karen's father that he would personally ensure that Karen was escorted safely back to Chicago. Batt also called metro squad headquarters in Overland Park to let them know the good news.

When the news of Grissom's arrest reached the metro squad, cheers echoed throughout the building. Detectives exchanged handshakes and broad smiles. At least one of their two greatest concerns had been resolved. Richard Grissom was off the street and unable to hurt anyone else. The celebration, however, was tempered by the unanswered questions about Grissom's victims. Except for a stream of questionable phone leads and doubtful sightings, the metro squad detectives had no hard, factual information that might lead them to the locations of the three missing women. They would wait anxiously for more details from Dallas. They knew Grissom would be questioned at length. They hoped for a second round of good news.

After his arrest, Grissom spent the next eight hours across a table from his interrogators at a public safety sub-station at the Dallas Airport. He was alone with Agent Napier for the first forty minutes until joined by Metro Squad Detective Joe Langer.

Langer had served nine years with the Leawood, Kansas, Police Department. He stood well over six-feet tall; the way his shirt molded to his body revealed his muscular frame. Langer's square jaw and close-cropped, sandy colored hair gave him the look of an able ex-Marine. Langer was not there to intimidate Grissom, but if Grissom was a person easily intimidated, he would surely have been reduced by the presence of Joe Langer.

Napier decided early on not to record any of Grissom's interview. He would also not disrupt the flow of the conversation by taking notes on everything Grissom said. Two important elements of the interrogation were gaining the trust of the suspect, and preserving the flow and tempo of the interview. Napier knew that the very presence of a tape recorder could reduce the potential for cooperation. Suspects often were intimidated by the permanence implied by a recording. The agent wanted nothing to diminish the chance for a complete confession from Grissom. The downside, of course, was that the multi-hour affair would have to be reproduced from memory and committed to reports after the fact. It was another good reason to have two officers present. If Grissom's case went to trial, the two could corroborate each other's statements.

Before Langer had arrived, Napier had formally advised Grissom of his constitutional rights, advising him that he had the right to an attorney and to protect himself from self-incrimination. Because Napier was alone with Grissom, the suspect remained handcuffed when the agent showed him the "Advice Of Rights" and "Waiver Of Rights" forms and asked him to read them carefully. Grissom read from the forms and told Napier he understood his rights. He had, after all, been down this road before. Napier did not ask for Grissom's signature, but accepted his verbal acknowledgment that he did not need an attorney and that he would talk with the agent. Once Langer arrived, the handcuffs were removed.

Napier opened the interrogation with questions about why Grissom was at the airport. Grissom replied that he was picking up a friend. The question was designed to make Grissom believe that his being discovered in the terminal was a fluke, that the agent really didn't know why Grissom was there. It was also a test to see if Grissom suspected that Karen Marshall had set him up. He didn't.

Napier next moved to questions designed to determine if Grissom still had possession of the stolen Grand Am. During the arrest, Napier had not looked for the car outside the terminal.

Grissom decided to play a cat-and-mouse game, offering only that he had hitched a ride to the airport. If his friend showed up that morning, he was planning to call another friend to pick them up. Grissom's hitch-hiking story did not hold up for long. The search of his person during the arrest produced a set of General Motors car keys. The officers believed the stolen car was parked somewhere at the airport.

Later in the interview, when he seemed to relax a little, Grissom finally admitted to some of his activities following his flight from Stonybrook the night of June 27. He admitted to having spent the entire night in the woods just beyond Highway 71 in Grandview, and to entering the ground-floor apartment the next morning and finding a set of car keys in a candy dish near the door. Eventually he told Napier and Langer that he had stolen the Pontiac and that it was parked in a short-term passenger pickup area near where they had arrested him.

Surprisingly, Grissom also admitted to having driven the stolen car back to his Lenexa apartment the night of the twenty-eighth, when he picked up a tent, some other camping gear and more clothes. He also stole a Colorado license plate from another Grand Am and put it on the car he took from Grandview. During the next bathroom break, Langer got word of the car and its Colorado tag to Detective Robinson and a public safety officer, who immediately set out to locate the car.

When Napier began questioning Grissom about the more serious accusations of murder and abduction, the investigator started not with questions about the three missing Johnson County women, but about the Terri Maness murder in Wichita. It immediately was obvious that Grissom wanted nothing to do with discussions about that incident. He insisted he had no idea what Napier was talking about. The FBI Agent dug in with the obvious evidence against Grissom. The police knew he was in Wichita that night. They knew he was acquainted with Maness and had told some of his friends that he was going to see her that night.

As Napier spoke, the color drained from Grissom's face. Then, Napier added the obvious, Grissom's possession of the Nebraska license plate stolen from where he had abandoned Terri's car just blocks from her house. He pointed out they knew Grissom had hung around Wichita the morning after the killing of Terri Maness, and that he had leased expensive painting equipment from local contractors.

Grissom shook his head violently from side to side, indicating none of what Napier said was true. The agent told Grissom that the Wichita Police had found his pubic hairs at the scene and could make a positive match to him. It would only be a matter of collecting samples from Grissom.

When Napier thought he had Grissom on the edge, he took a few of the Maness crime scene photos and laid them on the table in front of him. Grissom looked away. Sweat was already forming in beads across his forehead. He would not look down at the pictures, despite prodding from his interrogators. Suddenly, Grissom balled his hands into fists and began rubbing his eyes intensely. Napier sensed that Grissom was trying to block out the memory of anything he had done to Terri Maness. Napier coaxed Grissom. He talked to him softly and put his hand on his shoulder while telling him that nothing short of revealing exactly what happened would help him purge the memory of that night.

"I didn't do that! I didn't do that!" was all that Grissom would say. He repeated the same words several times, still rubbing his eyes. He didn't stop until Napier removed the Maness photos and asked Grissom if he wanted to take a break for a soda. Napier had plenty of time left. He also wanted to talk to Grissom about the other women and did not want him to withdraw at this early stage. They took a break.

After getting Grissom a soda, Napier and Langer involved him in small talk. Napier knew how important it was to keep him relaxed. They wanted Grissom to trust them and when they could, they asked him questions about his everyday life and talked a little about themselves as well. For a brief period, they avoided discussion or questions about Grissom's victims. When they sensed he was calm and more inclined to answer questions about the women, the interrogators moved back to that subject.

The early focus of Napier's questions about the missing women was on Joan Butler. The agent once again removed some photos from his briefcase and set them on the table in front of Grissom. "Do you know this girl?" the agent asked.

Grissom glanced down at the photos of his victim and just as quickly turned his head away. He was still staring at the bare, white wall to his side when he replied. "No, I don't know her," he said. Grissom was instantly uneasy again.

Now, Napier persisted. There was always the chance that if they walked him into it gradually, he would weaken steadily and eventually cave in. "You don't know her?" asked Napier. "You've had no contact with this woman? None at all?"

"No, none at all," came the quick but nervous reply from Grissom.

Napier was far from backing off. "Are you sure, Richard?" Napier asked calmly, then continued. "Maybe you've seen her out somewhere, maybe dancing at a club or something? Or maybe you've been to where she lives? You can remember that, can't you?"

"No!" Grissom fired back, without looking at either man across from him. "I haven't seen her anywhere, and I haven't been to her apartment. I don't know where she lives."

The agent and the detective shot knowing glances at each other. Neither had mentioned the word apartment in that line of questioning. But Grissom seemed to know that Joan Butler lived in an apartment.

Letting Grissom's slip go for the time being, Napier moved on to Joan Butler's rented Corsica. It would be a subject Grissom would have difficulty dancing around. Napier pointed out that Grissom had been seen driving the car around for nearly a week and that other witnesses had actually ridden in the car with him. Then there was his obvious flight from Officer Brian Edwards in Lawrence. "Why on earth would you run from the scene, Richard, if it wasn't because you had possession of Joan Butler's car and you would be linked to her disappearance?" Napier asked.

Grissom fabricated a tale around his possession of the Corsica. He didn't deny having it or driving it, but insisted it came from Frenchy, that Frenchy had rented it for the business. The officers knew the unliklihood of that scenario. The interrogators also had access to both Thibodo's and Cathy Arenal's accounts of the events involving Grissom's possession of the Corsica.

Grissom, however, would not admit to anything more than having the car and driving a few girls around in it over the course of a few days. He attempted to cover anything Thibodo might have said by telling Napier and Langer that he first saw the car when Frenchy asked him to meet him at a Cap-Fed Bank in Overland Park and that Frenchy was driving the Corsica at that time. Grissom originally said that they met at the bank on the morning of the June 16, but when questioned about that date, he thought for a while and changed it to the eighteenth. Grissom continued to embellish, adding that on the front seat of the Corsica, which Frenchy was driving, there was a woman's purse. He did admit, however, to going through the purse "for items I could use." Napier and Langer let Grissom tell his version of events without interrupting.

"Yeah!" Grissom continued. "Frenchy showed up at the bank with the car and the purse. He asked me to meet him there because he needed my help. He found a bank card in the purse, but he knew I was the one who could figure out the code and get some cash with it. I have a system for figuring out codes and PIN numbers that the owners use. French didn't know the formula, so he needed me there."

"Did you make a withdrawal from Joan Butler's account that morning at the Cap-Fed?" Napier asked.

"Yeah, but Frenchy was with me for that one," Grissom answered confidently.

"Was Joan Butler with you?" Napier asked, catching Grissom slightly off guard.

"No!"

Joe Langer was aware that the metro squad investigation had turned up evidence of three withdrawals from Joan Butler's account on consecutive days beginning the morning of June 18. "Who made the other withdrawals from the account?" the detective asked, hoping to get an admission from Grissom about the timing and sequence of events. Grissom seemed convinced that any admissions to lesser crimes, such as theft or bank larceny, would never be a sufficient link to Joan Butler's murder; he admitted only that he depleted the account, but that he was asked to do so by Frenchy, who agreed to a sixty-forty split of the money.

Napier decided to cut back his questions while Grissom was talkative. They knew his scenarios were complete fabrications, but they let him talk. Along the way he would trip himself. He would forget important details and eventually contradict himself. The back-pedaling would produce more lies, and his problems would mushroom. Napier changed the focus of the questioning to Christine Rusch. He replaced the Butler photos with a few of Christine. "How about this girl?" Napier asked. "Do you know her?"

"Yeah, I know her. She lives at Trafalgar Square Apartments where I paint. I've seen her around over there."

"How do you know her though?" asked Napier. "You admitted you knew her. How?"

Grissom's facial expression changed. He hesitated, unable to figure out where the agent might be going with his question. "Well, I don't actually know her," he said. "I just see her around the apartments, that's all. I think she's cute, but I never really had any contact with her."

"You never gave her any gifts?" asked Langer. "You never brought stuff to her apartment and talked to her there?"

"No!"

"How about some newspapers and magazines? Didn't you bring her a charcoal grill at one time?" Langer pressed.

"No!" Grissom answered, avoiding eye contact with Langer. "I never gave her anything."

"You didn't go to a party at her apartment, Richard?" Napier asked. "You never showed up at a party at her place? Think about it, it would have been the Saturday night before you were spotted with the Corsica in Lawrence."

Grissom denied he had gone to a party at Christine's place. When asked about Theresa Brown, Grissom told them he knew Christine had a roommate, but didn't know her last name. Grissom said that he found Christine very attractive but that "I wasn't attracted to her roommate."

When Napier dropped a picture of Theresa Brown on the table, Grissom turned away and began once again rubbing his eyes with his fists. Napier removed the picture and moved on.

Not long into the questioning about Christine Rusch and Theresa Brown, Napier confronted his suspect with the girls' credit cards which were found in his Toyota after he abandoned it in Grandview. How did he explain that?

Grissom, once again, concocted a series of unrealistic events, offering excuses and once again introducing Frenchy as the scapegoat. He began retracing the events that began with his flight from Lawrence. Frenchy had driven him out of town that Saturday night, but according to Grissom, Frenchy did not drive him to his apartment in Lenexa. He drove him to Trafalgar Square where, believe it or not, he found a compact Dodge in the parking lot with its engine running and a purse on the front seat. Grissom described how, upon finding the Dodge, he jumped out of Frenchy's truck and into the car and sped off with it.

When asked for details about the car's year, model, or color, Grissom's recollection suddenly escaped him. Grissom reported that he and Frenchy were to meet again at a Motel 6, just a few hundred yards from where he took the car. He could not, however, recall exactly when and how that meeting had been arranged.

Grissom initially told Langer and Napier that Frenchy had indeed joined him at the Motel 6 parking lot about fifteen minutes after leaving Trafalgar Square. After thinking awhile about that admission, Grissom changed it. Realizing he had not given his only scapegoat enough time to commit a sinister act, Grissom revised his account, saying he waited at the motel for well over an hour before Frenchy showed up. He was careful to add that when he was pulling the stolen Dodge away from Trafalgar Square, he noticed that Frenchy had gotten out of his truck and was heading into the apartment building where Christine lived.

Napier asked "Why would you mention that, Richard? Why mention that you remembered seeing Frenchy heading for the girls' apartment?"

Grissom hesitated. He knew the two men knew he was creating the story. There was absolutely no reason to bring up anything he saw Frenchy doing unless it was to cover what he himself had done. He stammered. "Well, you know, we both had keys to those apartments. We had been saving them for future use. I just figured Frenchy was going into the apartment to rip it off," Grissom answered. Grissom picked up a napkin and wiped the sweat from his forehead and neck. Even the air-conditioned interview room was getting sticky for him.

"What do you mean by keeping the keys for future use?" Napier asked.

Grissom would not explain what he meant in any greater detail. He would add only that he left the Dodge in the Motel 6 lot, never driving it anywhere after that night. The only thing he took was the purse he had found in the car.

"What time of day was it when you took the car from Trafalgar?" the agent continued.

"Oh, it was late, or very early in the morning, I mean. It was still dark out," Grissom answered, correcting himself.

"Where did you go from the Motel 6 parking lot?"

"Well, from there I got back in Frenchy's truck, and he took me to my apartment where we finished dividing up the stuff from the purse," Grissom said. "I took a couple of the credit cards and one bank card, and Frenchy took the rest of the stuff." Grissom went on to detail his activities for the balance of those early hours on June 26.

Langer knew that by eight o'clock Monday morning on the twenty-sixth, Grissom already had abducted Christine Rusch and Theresa Brown. But in nearly every scenario Grissom created, he attempted to place Thibodo in the criminal role and himself in a more passive, secondary role. The most he would commit to was that he left his apartment that morning and drove to the South Metcalf storage locker. He did so in his own Toyota, and he took a nap while waiting for Frenchy to meet him there.

"What was Frenchy supposed to be doing at this time?" asked Langer, hoping that Grissom would offer at least some details of the abductions while trying to shift the blame to Frenchy.

"I don't know, man. I guess he was just out there doing his own thing," Grissom replied. "But after a couple of hours he met me at the warehouse and wakes me up."

"You're sleeping at the warehouse, and Frenchy wakes you up?" Napier asked.

"Yeah, only now he's driving another car, and he's got another purse."

"Whose purse does he have, Richard?" Napier inquired.

"It was Theresa Brown's. This time it was Theresa Brown's purse." Grissom was suddenly very casual in the use of the girl's name he had previously admitted he never knew.

"So the first purse, which you found on the front seat of the Dodge, a car which had been left running in the parking lot at Trafalgar, that purse belonged to Christine Rusch?" Napier asked. "And the second purse, belonging to Theresa Brown, was brought to you by Frenchy at the Metcalf Storage locker while you were taking a nap? Is that what you're telling us?"

"Yeah, that's it!" Grissom replied, as if pleased with himself at having successfully convinced his interrogators. He went on to spin more tales about being allowed to keep only one credit card and one bank card from Theresa Brown's purse. According to Grissom, by the time Frenchy had stolen Theresa's purse, he had learned the formula for the code and PIN numbers himself. He no longer needed Grissom for that. That was why Frenchy kept most of the contents from Theresa's purse, giving him only the two cards. There was also supposed to be a split of the profits from that theft as well, but, according to Grissom, Frenchy left the warehouse that morning and never came back with Grissom's share. Grissom also said that he never saw Frenchy again after that.

While piecing together the sequence of his fabrications, Grissom was sure to keep all of the episodes occurring immediately after his flight from Lawrence under the dark blanket of "early morning hours." He didn't really know what happened to Frenchy after they had taken the possessions from his apartment and said good-bye at the Motel 6. He could only guess that if Frenchy went back to work at Trailridge the next morning, the cops grabbed him. If that were the case, he reasoned, then the cops would have talked to him for a while on the morning of June 26. He could not implicate Frenchy during the actual times when he abducted Christine and Theresa from Trafalgar. He therefore ensured that his scenario fell within a time frame prior to sunrise on June 26.

Napier and Langer moved on to questions concerning Grissom's movements after meeting Frenchy at the storage locker. Grissom told them that for the balance of the twenty-sixth, he drove to visit a friend near St. Louis. He added that when he got there, he felt the trip had been a mistake. He turned around and came back to Kansas City. When asked about the identity of the friend he went to see, Grissom replied he'd rather not say. Langer knew the trip he described was the one where he got as far as Colombia, Missouri, made a series of phone calls using a credit card, and then, turned around. Langer knew that Grissom simply was changing the dates of the trip to cover his activities.

Napier suggested a break for something to eat and to let Grissom relax. Napier stayed in the room with the suspect and engaged him in small talk. Langer left to check with Tom Robinson on the status of the stolen Grand Am. When Langer returned and Grissom had finished eating, Napier refocused his line of questioning, targeting other aspects of the abduction-murder cases.

"We have your car, Richard. You know that don't you?" Napier asked, leaning across the table toward Grissom. "We have all the stuff from your car, Richard. And in that stuff are lots of things that belong to those missing girls. How do you explain that?"

Grissom didn't blink. He glared at the agent. "I'm not surprised you found the credit cards, but you shouldn't have found any other personal items in my car!" Then, suddenly flustered again, Grissom went on without thinking. "When I headed north on I-35 from Ninety-fifth Street, I threw everything out the car windows. If something was in there, it must have blown back inside the car." Grissom was stumbling all over himself. North on I-35 was nowhere near the Metcalf South locker.

"Tell me this, Richard," Napier asked. "If you were throwing stuff out of the car while going north on I-35, how did most of Christine's stuff end up on the side of the road at Metcalf and 139th?"

Napier watched Grissom. He knew he had touched a button. He was forcing him to relive the events leading to Christine's possessions being thrown out near 139th Street.

Grissom hesitated, then offered another lame excuse. "Well, if I threw some things out going north, I could have just as easily tossed a few things out on my way to the locker."

The interrogators had Grissom flustered. They needed to keep him off balance. Langer knew the metro squad had uncovered information about a couple of transactions in Missouri involving Theresa Brown's bank account. He also knew that the transactions had been captured by bank cameras, covering the ATMs. "What about all the bank transactions, Richard?" Langer asked. "Those ATMs have cameras you know."

Before Langer could add another word, Grissom cut him off. "You go ahead and check the film up at any of those ATMs!" Grissom insisted. "You won't find a picture of me! I won't be in any of those pictures!" Grissom answered confidently.

Langer could have beaten the issue to death. Grissom would not be tripped up on this one. He knew that if there were, in fact, photos, he would not be found on any of them.

While Grissom's interrogation continued at the Department of Public Safety's main station at the airport, the stolen Grand Am he had brought to the terminal was recovered and towed. The Colorado license plate found on the car was checked and found to have been stolen from the Kansas City area sometime between June 28 and 29. The car's original Missouri plate, registered to Joe Hetzel, was found in the trunk. The search of the car's interior revealed an ice chest with ice and several cans of soda, a bamboo sleeping mat, a sleeping bag, a rolled-up tent, a green sports bag, some food and additional camping gear. Also recovered were a motel key from a motel in Corpus Christi, Texas, a pair of thongs, a few combs and a bottle of sun block. From the glove box, officers recovered a package of Crossman pellets and a package of CO_2 cartridges for a Crossman Air Pistol.

The most disturbing find, however, was the contents of the green sports bag found on the backseat. The bag contained the ingredients for another so-called "kill kit." The "kit" contained a Crossman CO_2 Air Pistol, a claw hammer with a reddish-brown stain on the claws, a pair of black leather gloves, a box knife with retractable blade, two stainless hunting knives with sheaths for both, a roll of silver duct tape, a one-hundred-foot coil of yellow, nylon rope, and a large container of wet-wipes. Upon discovery of the items assembled for the "kill kit," Detective Robinson thought about Karen Marshall and was forced to wonder how her day might have gone had she arrived in Dallas to meet Grissom by herself.

Photographs of the items found in the car were immediately taken and processed to assist Napier and Langer with their interrogation. The newly completed prints were passed on to Joe Langer during one of the breaks in the interview session.

Back in the interview room after the break, Detective Langer wasted little time dropping the latest props, one picture at a time, on the table in front of Grissom. He studied Grissom's face as he watched each picture take its place on the table. First, a photo of the claw hammer was lowered, followed by one of the duct tape and rope and razor knives, until finally even a shot of the wet-wipes fell among the others.

Grissom kept his head lowered, looking at the photographs. He was no doubt forming his responses to forthcoming questions. Napier let him sit for a while. He wanted to allow time for the message to sink in. He wanted Grissom to know that they knew what he was all about. After a few moments, Napier broke the silence. "If we subject that claw hammer to a thorough examination, will the lab find that the stain on it is blood?"

"If it is blood, it's my blood because I cut myself in the storage shed when I was duplicating some keys," Grissom answered defensively.

"You duplicated keys in the storage locker, Richard? Why would you do that?" Napier asked.

Grissom hesitated before responding. "I needed extra keys for my work, OK?" Grissom grew more defensive as each response dug him a little deeper. "That's all there is! There's nothing more to it than that!" he added.

Detective Langer jumped in. "That storage locker was checked, Richard. There was no duplicating machine in there."

Grissom looked away from Langer. He paused. "I got rid of the machine," was all he would say.

"But what about all this stuff, Richard?" Napier asked, pointing a finger at the photos on the table. "What about all these tools and accessories you carry around with you all the time?"

Grissom fired back with increased intensity. "There's nothing that I carry in my bag that I don't use for camping! Where are the pictures of my tent and sleeping bag? All of the stuff I have is for camping!"

Napier backed off. He picked up the photos and stacked them at one side of the table. Grissom's sensitivity to his weapons of assault was apparent. The agent perceived that a confrontation right then would get him nowhere. He changed the subject. "What about your temper, Richard?" Napier asked, a bit softer with his approach. "We've heard some things about your temper. What kind of person are you? How do you see yourself?"

Grissom looked at Napier and then back down at the table. He focused on the question and appeared to relax a bit. "I have a temper that can explode once in awhile. It can sometimes be beyond my control," he admitted in a tone seemingly designed to evoke sympathy. "It's a problem I've had all my life. I recognize it though, and I work hard to keep it in bounds, keep it under control. Some stress situations I handle by just backing away from them. I have to try and isolate myself from whatever is stressing me out."

"Sounds to me like a good formula," Napier said. "Does it work for you?"

"Well, I still keep a lot bottled up inside, you know. And sometimes, even something real small can set me off. When it does, I explode. You know, sometimes it's not a big deal, but I keep so much stuff jammed up inside me that it all has to come out. The little stuff can trigger it. I just let go. It can happen when I'm with friends or with strangers. It just happens." Grissom continued and his interrogators just let him talk. "Sometimes I have blackouts," Grissom admitted, as if suddenly recalling a problem. "Sometimes its just for a minute or so and other times, I don't know how long I'm out for."

The suspect looked anxiously back and forth at the two men across from him, searching their expressions, as he detailed his episodes of sudden bouts of amnesia as if, truth or not, he had stumbled onto a justification for many of his sinister activities. Grissom held his left hand out across the table demonstrating a significant knot where the bone had protruded upward on his ring finger. "I went to the doctor for this, but I couldn't tell him how I got it. I just blacked out during the time when it happened. I can't remember what I do during those times when it happens. I can remember up to the time of the blackout, and from the time after it, but nothing during it."

Recognizing that Grissom might be running out of defenses, Napier took advantage with a point-blank question. "Could you have had one of your blackouts when you confronted Joan Butler?"

"It's possible," announced Grissom, more convinced that his blackout story was affording good cover.

As the interrogation progressed, Grissom was asked directly on several occasions if he had killed the three missing women. Prior to the blackout excuse, he had emphatically denied his involvement. Now, responses were, "I don't think I could do that," and "I'm not capable of something like that." To Napier's surprise, on one occasion Grissom said, "If I was going to kill anyone, I would have killed my parents."

Napier could sense that he was breaking through Grissom's icy emotions a layer at a time. He persisted with the direct line of questioning about Grissom's involvement in the missing girls' deaths. The agent suggested that it might have been possible for Grissom to have killed the girls, given his admitted outbursts of temper and periods of blackout.

Grissom fought off the agent's approach by straddling the line between flat objection and the more pliant denials. Then Grissom tried another tactic. "I could not have killed those girls because I believe they're still alive," he advised, quite sure of himself.

Napier was angered by the response. "Let me ask you something, Richard. Why is it that you think the girls' deaths are so unlikely? Why are you the only one out of everyone looking at this case, who believes those girls are still alive?

Grissom only shrugged his shoulders in response.

"Let me tell you a little something about likelihood and probability, Richard," said the frustrated Napier. "All three of those missing girls come from loving, caring, giving families. They were surrounded by people who loved them and worried about them every day. Surrounded by people who knew their bright per-

sonalities, their habits, their likes and dislikes, knew all
about what was happening in their lives. All of those
girls had very close ties to family and to many friends.
They had plans for the future, and those plans were
structured and solid. They did not include running off
or disappearing without telling anyone. Do you want to
know what the likelihood is of all three of those girls
just taking off and not telling anyone? It's zero, Richard.
It's a big zero! So why don't you tell me why it is that
you, and nobody else, thinks they're still alive."

Grissom did not respond. He had grown progressively nervous during Napier's grilling. Grissom once
again balled up his fists and began rubbing them into
his eyes. He suddenly turned away, unwilling to face
his accusers.

Napier was not about to let it go. "You know
what's happening to you, Richard?" he asked, leaning
over the table toward Grissom. "You're seeing them.
Isn't that it, Richard? You're seeing those girls. You see
yourself with them, don't you? You're seeing what you
did to them. What you did to those girls is playing in
front of your eyes like it was on a TV screen. Only you
can't turn it off, Richard. Can you? You can't! It just
won't go away. You're rubbing your eyes trying to
erase it all, but it won't go away! The image is pretty
clear, isn't it? You're with them! You're with those girls!
It's all flashing back now and you can't get rid of it!
Listen to me, Richard. You can't change what you did
to them no matter what you do."

Grissom shook his head, digging his fists into his
eyes.

Napier continued, but in a slightly different tone.
"Why don't you just relax now and tell us about it,
Richard. It's the only way you're going to make those
images go away. They'll leave you alone if you come
clean and put this all behind you. You can get help if

that's what you need, but first, you have to open up, let it all out and admit what happened. It's the first big step, Richard. But once you take it, everything else after that becomes easier. Once you talk to us about it, the rest will be easier to handle."

"No!" Grissom shouted, still covering his eyes. "No! They're just not dead!"

"You don't want them to be dead, Richard," Napier broke in. "You want them to still be alive. All of us want that, Richard, but it's not going to happen. We can't change what happened, not now. You can only try and make up for it by helping the families and helping us. We all need to put this behind us. You and I both know what happened. We know the girls are dead. The only question left is what are we going to do about it now?"

Silence fell over the room. The officers waited. Grissom said nothing. Napier breathed a sigh of frustration. They had been at the edge and they knew it. Langer sat back in his chair. His arms dangled at his sides. His shirt had long been ringed in circles of sweat. He watched as Grissom took his clenched fists slowly away from his eyes.

With his head still turned away from his accusers, Grissom finally spoke. "Well, they're probably dead by now."

Langer's eyes met Napier's. Both men stirred in their chairs. Langer sat up straight and moved his arms as if to re-energize. Napier went back to work on Grissom, pressing him for an explanation to his comment. He offered none. Napier continued, doing everything but begging Grissom for an elaboration. When the questions and entreaties stopped, both agents believed that Grissom would not acquiesce. Napier backed off. He and Langer settled back in their chairs in obvious frustration.

No sooner had they relaxed, when Grissom spoke again, in a softer tone. "You'll dig them up some day." It was all he would say.

19

The Grissom interrogation did not end as Napier and Langer had hoped it would. Nor was the result to the satisfaction of the victims' families, or members of the metro squad waiting for word back in Kansas City. Everyone close to the case knew Grissom had abducted and probably killed the three missing women. All had hoped for a firsthand confession, but short of that they would have settled for knowledge of where he had left the bodies. Coming away without at least that much after a long and fatiguing effort was, to Napier and Langer, tantamount to failure. Certainly, some of Grissom's admissions were revealing and would be considered incriminating should the case against him go to trial. But they didn't get the information they wanted.

Napier and Langer knew they were running out of time with Grissom. The length of the interrogation had drawn dangerously close to a critical legal stage. Grissom still had to be taken before a magistrate. Even before that, arrangements would have to be made for an attorney to be present for him during his court appearance. They could not jeopardize their arrest with a legal technicality. Still, Napier estimated that enough time remained for one more shot at Grissom. He realized that Grissom had offered nothing additional after his "you'll dig them up" disclosure, but Napier felt he had one hand left to play. He had not talked to Grissom about the possibility of a deal.

Napier began speaking to Grissom in terms of how he could really be his own best asset. He spoke of a bottom line and about the two-way street of confession. As the agent spelled things out, Grissom's interest in his words was obvious. Napier's line, "You tell us what we want to know in exchange for something that will be of help to you," made Grissom sit up straight in his chair.

When Grissom admitted that he might "possibly" be open to a "deal," Napier began outlining the specifics. "The most important ingredient here, Richard, is recovering the bodies. And not just for the sake of the investigation but for the sake of the families. Those people left behind are victims too, Richard, and they need to know what happened to their girls. They're entitled to know what happened. They just want to get their girls back and bury them properly," Napier continued, trying to touch on even a molecule of sympathy if any existed in this suspect.

Grissom listened to the agent, occasionally nodding his head as if in agreement. Grissom offered no objections. Napier was clearly talking in terms of the girls being dead, and Grissom offered no resistance. It was a good start. With Grissom's complete attention, Napier continued. "Any deal also means that you have to clearly and explicitly represent your involvement in this matter here." Napier was careful to avoid the use of words like murder and abduction. "You'll have to give us details about each girl, what happened and how it happened."

The agent paused briefly to consider yet another tactic, another offer which might appear less threatening. "If you want, Richard, you can give us your version in sort of a third-person or what-if scenario. You know, like what if I told you this or that, or how would it sit for me if I told you such and such? You have to play your best hand, Richard. There's no question that this is the best way for you to go."

Napier sat back and waited for a response from Grissom. He looked over at Langer who raised his eyebrows as if to say, "let's see." The interrogation team could almost see the gears turning inside Grissom's head. Then suddenly they saw that the suspect's enthusiasm for a possible "deal," had tapered.

"But what would be in it for me?" Grissom asked, trying to measure what might be gained from confessing to three murders.

"Well, that depends," Napier replied, somewhat prepared for the response. "We can't make that call until we assess the value of what you've told us. A lot of conditions have to be met, Richard. You have to be completely candid and truthful with us. Whether the details are firsthand or even what-if, we need to know everything, and that means everything up front before we can evaluate it and present it to get you a deal. Don't forget that our primary interest is in recovering the bodies, Richard. That you committed the crimes is not at issue here. The prosecutors know you did it. No one is going to be able to hand you the world on a platter, but you can maybe get some concessions your way and help your own cause. It really is just a matter of tying up loose ends."

"Yeah, but I still don't see anything in it for me," Grissom said.

Napier went over his proposal a second time, emphasizing that Grissom needed to come clean first. He also told Grissom that time was on his side for now, but would not be for long. The agent used the analogy of a bunch of bananas sitting on a shelf. "When the bananas are first put there, all bright yellow and ripe, they have value, they're worth something to someone. If they're allowed to sit for a long time, however, they'll go bad, turn spotted and brown. When that happens, they're of no use to anyone. Right now, Richard, what you have to offer is valuable, but it may not be as valuable a week or two down the road." As a slight but added incentive, Napier told Grissom that with a full confession about the girls, he did not have to worry about being prosecuted for the lesser crimes of car theft, ATM theft and burglary. Napier concluded, baiting his hook with the revelation that in the state of Kansas, there existed the possibility that someone convicted of murder can become eligible for parole in fifteen years.

Grissom jumped all over Napier's last remark. "Oh, everything happened in Kansas," Grissom blurted. He had thought ahead, apparently less concerned about parole than with the more critical issue of the death penalty. "I know Missouri has the death penalty!" he told the officers. "Kansas doesn't! You won't find anything in Missouri!" Grissom half smiled with satisfaction.

When Grissom finally suggested that it would be better if he had an attorney to present a deal for him to the prosecutors, the day-long session was called to a halt. Grissom immediately was taken for an appearance before a local magistrate. Escorting him were members of the metro squad and officers of the Dallas Department of Public Safety. Agent Napier chose not to attend the court proceedings, opting instead to remain behind and commit the day's events to paper while still fresh in his mind. Detective Langer likewise remained behind making his own notations of the session as he recalled it.

Following his court appearance, Grissom was returned to a holding cell at the airport Public Safety office. Upon Grissom's return, Napier learned that, for reasons of time and availability, Grissom had not been appointed an attorney for the initial proceeding. Napier found Grissom in his holding cell and approached him for a final time. The agent took out a business card and handed it through the bars in the cell. "I can come back and talk with you anytime you want," Napier said. "We can talk about anything you want to talk about, Richard. The officers here know what hotel I'm in, and they can reach me any time."

Grissom reached up and took the business card. He read it and then looked through the bars at Napier. It was one of the few times that day that Grissom sustained eye contact. They stared at each other without speaking. Grissom's knowing stare conveyed that he understood that Napier knew everything that had happened, that he had seen through the cat-and-mouse antics, the embellishments and the outright lies.

Napier wondered if Grissom's gut was telling him to come clean, to tell all. Or was it that his mind was telling him to hold out for a deal, to get something out of this for himself.

"I can give them the whole thing, you know!" Grissom said, breaking the silence.

"I know you can, Richard. But you have to be talking about everything," Napier replied. "Are you? Are you talking about telling the whole thing?"

"Yes!" Grissom shot back emphatically. "I can give you everything. I want you to tell the prosecutor that if

I gave him the what-if story and told it all, that there would be two other people involved in this. Be sure to relay that piece of information when you tell him that I can give it all to him."

Napier assured Grissom his message would be conveyed. The agent then left the holding area and returned to the interview room where he had spent most of the day. He retrieved his notepad and made a few additional entries. After that, he sat back in his chair and ran his fingers through his hair. He rubbed his eyes and thought about the day's twists and turns. In the end he didn't have everything he came for, but he had a lot. Grissom was, at last, behind bars, and the experienced agent knew he had information that could be converted to solid, critical testimony during a trial. One of the many remaining questions was whether or not the case would ever get that far.

20

After Grissom's arrest, the metro squad continued covering leads at a feverish pace. One of the earlier leads that helped establish the sequence of Grissom's activity on the morning of June 26, came from Scott Hendricks' finding Christine Rusch's possessions on the side of the road. Among the recovered articles were Christine's checkbook and ledger. Detectives noticed four checks were missing from her checkbook that had no corresponding notations on the ledger. Detectives Jerry Burke and Tim Burnett obtained a subpoena and drove to the main records branch of the Metcalf State Bank in Overland Park. They requested the records pertaining to the Christine Rusch account and specifically to the four missing checks.

It wasn't long before Burke and Burnett had what they needed. The records indicated that Christine's money market account had been depleted in a span of less than an hour on the morning of June 26. The four checks in question were, in fact, the ones used to withdraw the funds. The first check, in the amount of

$500, was issued and cashed at the bank's main branch. The other three transactions occurred at different banks, all of which were situated along Metcalf Avenue in Overland Park. Two of the remaining three were withdrawals for $500 each. The last was for the balance which was $900. The four checks apparently bore Christine's signature.

Interviews with the four bank tellers handling the transactions revealed that, in each case, a young woman had issued the checks for cash; the transactions all occurred at drive-up stations, and the necessary ID had been produced. It would later be learned that Christine's phone call to Margaret Kelly at work took place between these transactions, and the call was made from a pay phone on Metcalf Avenue.

A supporting lead on Christine Rusch and her bank transactions came from Sam Mahoney, an Overland Park pharmacist whose business was located near the Metcalf State Bank. Mahoney told detectives that he had been at the main branch of the bank on the morning of the twenty-sixth. He remembered pulling into a drive-up teller station next to a cream-colored, compact Dodge. Mahoney reported that as he waited for his own transaction to process, he glanced over toward the Colt and saw a young, white woman in the car with a black man. He could not positively say that the woman was Christine Rusch, but he did emphasize that the woman looked disheveled. Her hair was tousled and she appeared weary. Mahoney said he remembered thinking that this poor woman's day was not starting out well.

When questioned about how he remembered the time and date of his appearance at the bank, Mahoney told detectives he was banking in preparation for a vacation that was to begin that week. Mahoney's observation, though not a positive ID, was at least eyewit-

ness testimony that probably placed Christine Rusch in
her car with Grissom the morning of her disappearance.

Having learned about the withdrawals from the
Christine Rusch account, detectives set out to determine
if there had also been similar activity on the accounts
of Theresa Brown and Joan Butler. For detectives, it
was a logical assumption that, following his near-cap-
ture in Lawrence, Grissom's motives were those of a
desperate fugitive. One of his reasons for abducting
Christine and Theresa might have been to get money to
support his continued flight.

Retracing the activity on Theresa Brown's account
at Boatman's Bank, detectives discovered that the last
check written on her account was for pizza, delivered
to her apartment on June 25, the day after her party.
Two transactions recorded by the bank's ATM machines. During the late evening hours of the twenty-
sixth, an unsuccessful attempt was made to withdraw
funds from Theresa's account at the American Bank in
Raytown, Missouri. An inquiry also was made for a
savings-account withdrawal, but Theresa's funds were
in checking. Within an hour of that attempt, a successful withdrawal was made from an ATM at a Boatman's
Bank in Belton, Missouri.

Given what the detectives could piece together
about the Butler abduction, however, Grissom had not
initially pursued Joan Butler to get money. Nor had he
had any links to her. He did not have a painting
contract at Comanche Place. Apparently, Joan was simply in the wrong place at the wrong time. Detectives
nevertheless checked Joan's bank records and learned
that Richard Grissom took advantage of everything his
victim had.

Joan Butler had banked at Capitol Federal Savings
& Loan. A review of the records showed activity on the

account early on the morning of her abduction. In fact, one ATM transaction occurred within two hours of the time she would have arrived home from her night out with Celeste Becker. The Cap-Fed banks had an ATM withdrawal policy that limited the amount an individual could withdraw within a single twenty-hour period. The maximum amount per day was $300. At 5:59 A.M. on Sunday, June 18, someone withdrew $300 from Joan Butler's account using an isolated ATM at the bank's College Boulevard branch. Within a minute of that withdrawal, the machine recorded an inquiry on the balance of funds in the account. Bank cameras had not been in place at the time.

Further probing revealed that two additional ATM withdrawals were made on Joan Butler's account. The two transactions took place in the early morning hours and on consecutive days. The first was recorded at 3:50 A.M. on June 19, and the second at 2:15 A.M. on the twentieth. Both were for the maximum limit of $300. All of the transactions took place at separate branches of the Cap-Fed system.

A reconstruction of probable events in the Butler case told detectives that Grissom depleted the accounts himself, without the help of his victim. It was possible that Joan Butler was with him during the first transaction on the morning of the eighteenth, but not likely. Detectives believed Grissom likely forced Joan Butler to reveal the PIN, or code numbers, on her account. Then he withdrew money as time and bank policy permitted. Detectives also believed Grissom had been driving her Corsica by the evening of June 19. He would have killed his victim by then.

Investigators were puzzled by the fact that transactions on the Rusch and Butler accounts all occurred within a specific area at banks or ATMs in Overland Park. However, transactions on Theresa Brown's account in the distant suburb of Belton, Missouri, was difficult to understand. The suspect's switch from the convenience of one area to the seemingly out-of-the-way location of the other, forced detectives to assume that Grissom was probably on his way out of town when he made the withdrawals. The detectives concluded that late on June 26, Grissom fled to Missouri and remained there throughout the twenty-seventh.

As they probed deeper into the banking transactions, investigators discovered a piece of startling evidence. Grissom was not the one actually making withdrawals from Theresa Brown's account at the two Missouri banks. Nor was it Theresa. It was her roommate, Christine Rusch. Security cameras of both the American Bank in Belton and the Boatman's Bank in Raytown recorded the transactions.

Lenexa Detective Allen Harris, assigned to the financial crimes unit, issued subpoenas and took possession of the film canisters that contained the recordings of the two ATM transactions. A review of the American Bank film revealed several frames of a battered, disheveled and frightened Christine Rusch, wearing a bandage on her forehead and dark sunglasses to cover marks around her eyes. The film registered the time and date—10:00 P.M., June 26, 1989.

The video was of tremendous evidentiary value to detectives as they pieced together collaborating evidence against Grissom. What remained unexplained, however, was why Grissom had risked taking Christine Rusch all the way to Raytown and Belton, Missouri. Apparently he kept her with him all day and for at least part of that night, driving her around to parts of the city. He could have locked her in his Metcalf storage locker for much of the day. It was, after all, near where Christine's belongings had been found. But where was Theresa Brown during this same period? Had he already killed her? Would he have kept both girls locked up in the same place all day? The missing pieces were not coming together fast enough for the detectives.

Back at metro squad headquarters a few days after Grissom's interrogation, detectives scrambled to build a solid case against him. Realizing that he was not going to confess or reveal the location of his victims, they knew that they had to amass enough evidence for a strong circumstantial case against him. It helped that they had linked Grissom to the Corsica, but that was for the Butler case only.

The other victims' credit cards and personal items were found in his car, but that would be far from enough to support a circumstantial case. Grissom had not been captured on film by the bank cameras, and he could not be positively linked to the other transactions. He had made a few admissions in Dallas, but they were broad and did not reveal anything detectives could substantiate. One of the primary witnesses, Marcelais Thibodo, was nearly a suspect himself. In short, the detectives had their work cut out for them.

Upon returning from Dallas after Grissom's arrest, Detective Batt wasted little time getting back into the flow of the investigation. He retrieved the key ring found in Grissom's Toyota from the crime lab. The ring had fourteen keys on it, and it was a safe bet that they were masters to several complexes. Even before Grissom's arrest, detectives had arranged for the locks from the apartment doors of all three missing women to be removed.

There were two locks from the Rusch-Brown apartment and one from Joan Butler's. The locks had been mounted on slabs of wood and detectives insured that the pins and tumblers were not altered in any way. Batt

was not surprised when one of the keys from the key
ring unlocked both locks from the Rusch-Brown apartment. None of the keys, however, was a match to the
lock from the Butler apartment, and none matched the
Wichita townhouse of Terri Maness.

Comparisons were made with some of the loose
keys found on the floor of Grissom's car; one key
opened the lock to Joan Butler's apartment. It was not
a master key, but one probably taken from her purse
by Grissom after her abduction. Joan Butler had probably been surprised and overpowered by Grissom after
opening her front door around 4:30 that fateful Sunday
morning. The loud crash heard by Joan's downstairs
neighbor was supporting evidence.

When Batt and Hinkle were unable to match any of
the remaining keys with known locks, they contacted
the other victims' families to see if any of the keys
looked familiar to them. Judy Rusch, Christine's mother,
picked out a key that she told detectives looked familiar. It should have. It was a key to the front door of her
house. Judy Rusch told the detectives that when the
locks to her house had been changed, she gave
Christine a new key to the front door. Christine made
frequent trips to her parents' house, and always kept
the key in her purse. The only plausible explanation
for Grissom's possession of the key was that he took it
from Christine's purse.

Hinkle and Batt also subpoenaed Grissom's telephone records from the time before Joan Butler's disappearance, to the time after the Rusch-Brown abductions. Specific calls might corroborate other evidence or
testimony. The detectives became particularly interested
in a single phone call made during the early morning
hours of the day Joan Butler disappeared.

The phone call was made from a place known as the Noland Farm, located in Louisburg, Kansas, about twenty miles south of Overland Park. The call was made with the use of a calling card belonging to Grissom and was charged to his home number. The call was made to Marcelais Thibodo who, in due time, remembered it. Thibodo also verified that Grissom had a contract to paint at the Noland Farm and that on the weekend of his call, the owners of the farm were not at home.

Of concern to Batt and Hinkle was that the call was made at 6:38 A.M. on June 18. The reconstruction of the Butler abduction indicated that she was probably taken from her apartment sometime between 4:00 and 5:30 Sunday morning, the eighteenth. The time of the first withdrawal from her Cap-Fed account was 5:59 A.M., and Batt and Hinkle were worried about evidence linking Grissom to two places at nearly the same time. Only thirty-nine minutes separated the bank transaction from the phone call, both of which were believed to have been made by Grissom. Batt was unfamiliar with the distance from the Cap-Fed branch in Overland Park to the Noland Farm in Louisburg. He decided to find out how long it would take to drive the distance.

Batt made two trips from the Cap-Fed branch on College Boulevard to the Noland Farm. The first was to establish the exact distance. The detective measured the route at 25.7 miles door-to-door. The second trip established the time it would have taken Grissom to get from the bank to the farm. Batt was careful to replicate the event as it might have happened, taking the quickest route possible at the same time of day on a Sunday. He left the bank lot at 6:00 A.M. The roads were nearly empty, but Batt stuck to the speed limit as he imagined a watchful Grissom might have. He covered the distance in twenty-nine minutes, leaving plenty of time to step out of the car, enter the farm house and make a phone call. The next Sunday, Hinkle duplicated the effort and got the same results. The detectives were pleased. They had eliminated a defense attorney's attempt to show that Grissom could not have been in two places at the same time.

Days later, another significant call was received by a hot line operator. Kenneth Russell, a steel worker who lived just over the state line on the Missouri side, told the operator that he found something that might be of interest to the metro squad. He had been driving his truck from work when it broke down on I-435 near the Eighty-seventh Street exit in Missouri. Russell said while walking up the on-ramp for Eighty-seventh Street, he found a driver's license in the grass. The license belonged to Christine Rusch.

Detectives combed the area on both sides of the interstate ramp. Nothing additional was found. They wondered if Grissom had been truthful when saying he had tossed out his victim's belongings while driving on the interstate. Or, had Christine Rusch thrown out her license? Had she been trying to send a message, a signal to let someone know where she had been, where she was going? Articles belonging to the other victims were not found along roadways. Why would Grissom have tossed out only Christine's belongings?

Detective Batt next interviewed Christine's close friend, Ellen Dixon, who had been in almost daily contact with Christine until the time of her disappearance. If anyone outside of Christine's family knew about her personal life, her plans and her dreams, it was Ellen Dixon.

She told Batt that Christine was not dating Grissom, that she did not encourage him or lead him on. Christine, in fact, only referred to Grissom once or twice during a time when he was bringing her gifts. Even then, she called him "the maintenance man," Ellen reported. In truth, Ellen had not made the connection to Grissom until seeing his name in the newspaper. "And no," Ellen told the detective, "Christine did not have any plans to run off, or to leave the area at all."

Batt needed Dixon as a witness. He knew that if Christine's body was not recovered, and the case made it to trial, there would be efforts to prove she was not dead, that she simply ran off. The experienced detective knew the tactics of defense attorneys.

Ellen Dixon proved to be a valuable witness for other reasons. She was able to corroborate at least two other elements of the case that were of significance. The first involved the white T-shirt originally discovered among Christine's possessions by Scott Hendricks. Scott had said the shirt had a yellow-brown stain on its front. Ellen Dixon told Batt that the T-shirt was hers, and that she had spilled a Coke on the front of it while she and Christine were getting ready for a party. She had borrowed another shirt from Christine and left the stained T-shirt in Christine's car with the intent of getting it later. Ellen told Batt she had reminded herself time and again to get the shirt but always forgot. To Batt, the information was extremely valuable. Along with the eyewitness testimony from the Metcalf State Bank, it placed Christine's Dodge Colt near the Metcalf storage locker and well away from the Motel 6 where Grissom had said he left it.

Ellen Dixon was also able to positively identify the three rings found in the glove box of Grissom's Toyota as those worn by Christine. Ellen easily picked out and identified the pearl, the opal and diamond solitaire.

Batt set out to determine how Christine had obtained each ring which, in turn, would provide additional witnesses. The first and most obvious person to question was Judy Rusch, Christine's mother. Mrs. Rusch verified that her daughter wore all three rings constantly. She told the detective the history behind each ring. The opal, she said tearfully, had been her and her husband's birthday present to Christine.

Batt also talked to Doug Lucy, a former boyfriend of Christine's. He and Christine had dated more than three years and had, at one time, made plans for marriage. However, they had drifted apart and eventually broke up. In their three-year relationship, Doug had given Christine many gifts, one of them was the pearl ring, encircled by eight small diamonds. The moment Batt showed it to him, Lucy identified the ring. He had given the ring to Christine for her twentieth birthday. He pointed out a flaw in the setting of one of the diamonds. After buying the ring, one of the small diamonds had loosened. It was reset incorrectly and the ring lost its original uniformity.

The history behind Christine's third ring came from Brent Noyes. Brent and Christine had dated just prior to her relationship with Doug Lucy. Brent quickly identified the diamond solitaire he had given to Christine six years earlier, as an announcement of pre-engagement. Their relationship had not survived but was not forgotten. Christine had continued to wear the ring.

21

By mid-July 1989, the metro squad had disbanded. Several detectives remained behind to cover leads and conduct interviews. Detectives Pat Hinkle, Bill Batt and Ken Landwehr stayed on the case to see it through to prosecution. A small task force was set up to review the volumes of paper that had been generated in the case and to assist with leads.

From Dallas, word was received that Grissom intended to fight extradition back to Kansas. This caught investigators by surprise; after Grissom's arrest, he had indicated he would willingly return to Kansas. The consensus around Overland Park headquarters was that Grissom had been assigned an overly aggressive public defender who had decided to demonstrate all of his client's rights to him.

Grissom had decided to stay put and fight. There was no resistance to Grissom's extradition from the Governor of Texas who had to approve the legal maneuver. The extradition process could be lengthy. A variety of motions and appeals were available to the defendant, and most of those could be filed within a thirty-day period. There was no strict timetable for when motions or appeals were considered, but after they were, an additional thirty days would be granted before the next one would be filed.

The detectives and prosecutor's staff in Kansas did not complain about a little extra time. It would help them prepare their case against Grissom. Even so, most of them did not believe Grissom's extradition would take as long as it did.

Prosecutors in Wichita were deferring Grissom's prosecution to Johnson County. They were not giving up on the Terri Maness case, but for now, it appeared that Johnson County had the better case against Grissom. Wichita would wait to see how the case progressed and reserve their own case as a backup. Detective Landwehr began balancing his time and investigative responsibilities between Wichita and Kansas City. Obtaining the needed funds for his juggling act was a problem from the beginning, and the detective often drove his personal car back and forth and spent many nights at Hinkle's house. Landwehr's insights and investigative intuition proved invaluable.

Covering a series of leads that concentrated on the apartment complexes where Grissom did contract work, Landwehr came across a man who had worked with Grissom at several of the complexes. Larry Mickelage was a sheetrock contractor; Landwehr found him covered in white powder and sweat while hanging sheetrock at an area complex.

At first, Landwehr asked Mickelage general questions about Grissom's habits and about any unusual activity around the complexes where they had worked. Mickelage said that he wasn't paying close enough attention to Grissom to notice anything. When asked about seeing Grissom in the Corsica, Mickelage answered, "Yeah, I saw him with that car. He pulled into the Winfield one morning driving this new Chevy Corsica. I walked over to him and said, 'the painting business must be doing a lot better than the sheetrock business if you can afford a new car?"

"What did he say to that?" Landwehr asked.

"He said it wasn't his. A friend let him borrow it," Mickelage replied, dusting sheetrock powder from his clothes. "He said he needed it to get his crews back and forth, and his friend just let him have it."

"The Winfield, that's an apartment complex?" asked Landwehr.

"Yeah, it's in Olathe. That's where he pulled in that morning."

"What morning was that? When did you first see him in the Corsica? Can you remember?"

"It was last month, the Monday after Father's Day," Mickelage replied. "I remember because I just came back from spending the Father's Day weekend in Omaha. I reported to the leasing office at Winfield, and as I was going to my job site, I spotted Grissom and the car." Mickelage said he saw Grissom with the Corsica off and on during the balance of that week. His eyewitness account was significant. It was the earliest sighting of Grissom in possession of Joan Butler's car. Her killer had come back for it less than thirty hours after her abduction.

Landwehr also decided to make a follow-up visit to the South Metcalf Storage Facility. He was covering a lead that Batt and Hinkle had not had time to cover. The detective's only trip there had been to search the locker as a result of Thibodo's revelations. During the follow-up, Landwehr met with the owner of the facility, Richard Mackey, a prudent, unassuming individual. Mackey immediately produced the rental agreement for locker eighteen. The name on the agreement was Randy Rodriguez, a known alias of Grissom's that

Landwehr had seen on other documents. The locker had been rented on June 8 and was paid for until the end of June.

A day after Landwehr recovered the rental agreement, Hinkle asked about the burnt-orange, shag rug he had seen on the locker floor during his first visit. Hinkle knew it would be at least another week before the crime lab could get a forensic team down to the locker. He was concerned about the rug and its preservation. Grissom's rental agreement had expired while everyone was running around the country trying to find him, and no one was sure about what Richard Mackey might have done with the contents of the locker.

Again, Landwehr called Mackey.

"I already picked it up," answered Mackey, when asked about the contents of the locker.

Landwehr's heart skipped a beat. Visions of vital evidence being tossed on the back of a trash truck flashed across his mind.

Mackey added, "I rolled it up and put it in my shed here at the house. It's where I keep things left behind in the lockers in case someone comes back to claim them. I don't keep'em long though, but I still got the rug."

"I need to come down and get that rug as soon as possible," Landwehr told Mackey. "Will that be OK with you?"

"Sure," Mackey replied, not all that concerned about the detective's investigation. "But, I can't wait around here this afternoon. I've got some errands to run. I'll leave it for you on my back porch. You can just go on in and get it"

"I can't thank you enough for your help," the relieved detective replied. "I'm really grateful for your help, and I'll be down right away to get the rug."

Two weeks after Grissom's arrest, and with the knowledge that efforts to fight extradition were under way, the Wichita Police Department sent officer Thomas Mayhill to pay Grissom a visit. The veteran officer was a forensic and document specialist with the Wichita Department, and he showed up in Dallas armed with a warrant for Richard Grissom Jr. His effort would benefit both the Wichita investigation of the Maness murder and the task-force investigation of the three missing women. Mayhill was there for samples of Grissom's chest, pubic and head hair and samples of blood, saliva and handwriting.

Grissom was brought to a holding-cell area in the jail. He wore a white, one-piece jump-suit and appeared relaxed. Grissom was clean-shaven, but his hair remained uncut, because the warrant for head hair samples had been anticipated. Grissom sat through the proceedings quietly and somewhat removed. He said little and offered no objection as blood and saliva samples were taken. At Mayhill's request, Grissom stood and followed instructions to unzip his jumpsuit, reach down inside and pull out his own pubic hairs. He repeated the procedure several times until Mayhill had an adequate sampling. An eventual inspection at the crime lab in Wichita would reveal that, for some unexplained reason, Grissom clipped his pubic hairs.

The procedures for obtaining handwriting samples were varied and tedious. Grissom seemed slightly unnerved at the length of time it took to complete the process. First, he was given forms to fill out. Then, he was asked to write various word and letter combinations. Grissom was instructed to write out sentences and phrases and then print them. He was required to write both strong-handed and with his opposite hand at different speeds. He was told to try disguising his writing. The process dragged on for the better part of an hour with Mayhill standing over Grissom to witness every word put on paper.

The biological samples taken from Grissom were submitted to both the Wichita Crime Lab and the crime lab at the Kansas Bureau of Investigation in Topeka, Kansas. The investigators back in Johnson County eventually would be provided the results of all lab tests. The handwriting samples were filed away at the Wichita Police Department after comparisons were carefully made with known samples on record. Wichita had a case of its own to build against Grissom.

Many detectives continued to make significant contributions in the case against Grissom. One of those detectives was Overland Park's Dan Carney, who was regularly assigned to the Burglary-Theft Division. He had been a member of the metro squad. Carney began reviewing the case files that had accumulated while he was gone, starting with those he had been working when the Grissom case broke. The detective came across a burglary case that caught his eye.

Someone had broken into an apartment at the Comanche Place complex and taken jewelry. With the Joan Butler case still fresh in his mind, Carney checked the report carefully. The victim, Carla Dippel, had told the reporting officer that she believed the break-in occurred sometime during the weekend of June 17 and 18, when she had gone to the Ozarks. It was the same weekend Joan Butler disappeared. Carney checked the victim's address. She lived very close to Joan Butler.

One of the items listed in the burglary report was a gold, Peso-pendant. Carney immediately recalled that Landwehr had recovered a gold coin-pendant of similar description from Cathy Arenal, Grissom's girlfriend, in

Lawrence. She had said the piece was given to her by Grissom.

Detective Carney met Carla Dippel in the administration building of the Johnson County Community College, where she worked. He began his interview by asking about events leading to the discovery that her apartment had been burglarized. He also asked her to describe the items of jewelry she believed had been taken. When Carla Dippel had finished, Carney pulled the pendant and chain from an evidence envelope.

Carla Dippel's face lit up. "Yes sir!" she said with authority. "That's my Peso-pendant and chain!"

"You're sure?" asked Carney. "You're absolutely positive?"

"Yes! Those are absolutely my things. A lot of my jewelry is special order. My mother and I have had some special pieces made. I had the Peso-pendant made. I selected the Peso coin and bail. They were set for me at Reeds and Sons in Missouri. It's a jewelry store on the way to the lake."

"So you can say positively that this is the pendant, the Peso-pendant, frame and all, that you had made special order for yourself?"

"No question," Dippel answered. "I even requested that the eagle on this side face out," she added, showing the detective exactly what she meant. "When I wear it the right way on a chain, the eagle faces out."

"This is great!" exclaimed Carney, knowing how valuable the information was. But, he stopped short of telling Dippel that his burglary suspect was serial killer Richard Grissom. Carney explained that he would have to keep the pendant and chain as evidence, pending the outcome of her burglary case and another investigation. Before he could thank his witness for her cooperation, however, Dippel added another wrinkle to the plot.

"Well, we still have a slight problem with all of this though," she said, waiting for a reaction from Carney.

"What's the problem?" Carney asked, curiously.

"Well," Dippel began and then paused, "the Peso-pendant and the chain are mine, but this chain is not the one I had with the pendant when it was stolen," she added, pointing to the chain.

"This is not the same chain? Are you sure?" asked Carney.

"Absolutely! I bought the pendant and chain back in 1985, and I wear them both a lot. The pendant was always on another chain. Did you find any other chains along with this one?" Dippel asked, hopefully.

"But this one is your chain?" Carney asked.

"Yes, but it's definitely not the one I had with the pendant. I'm still missing another chain."

Back at the Overland Park burglary division, Carney mulled over in his mind what he had learned about the pendant and chain. Something was there, something about the missing chain bothered him, but he couldn't put his finger on it. Grissom had taken Carla Dippel's other chain along with the pendant, but it had not turned up. The suspect could have given the chain to any one of several other girlfriends. But then, thinking of Sherry Cash and a host of other young females who had called the hot line in defense of Grissom, there was no guarantee that a recipient would volunteer information about a chain received from Grissom. Even Cathy Arenal thought nothing of her gift until questioned by Landwehr. But what if Grissom had not given the chain away? Where would he have put it? Carney knew it had not been found in Grissom's Toyota.

Carney's instincts kept telling him there was something right under his nose that he wasn't seeing. He could have let the issue go. He didn't need to recover Dippel's chain to tie Grissom to the burglary of her apartment. The Peso-pendant took care of that. And, the Dippel burglary and Grissom's possession of the Corsica put him at the Comanche Place complex over the Father's Day weekend. The detective's gut instinct, however, would not let him drop it. Carney went back over the Butler case in his mind. What was it that would prove Richard Grissom was inside Joan Butler's apartment. Everything pointed to the fact that he had been in there, but actual proof was still needed.

Carney retraced the crime-scene search of Joan Butler's apartment in his mind. He had accompanied the lab team during their processing. He let his mind drift, retracing his steps from room to room in Butler's apartment. He recalled Joan's black dress which he took down from her closet door and bagged as evidence. He also remembered her pumps from the closet floor. He recalled talking with the forensic team as it went about covering every square foot of the apartment.

Just then, he remembered Bill Chapin photographing the apartment. Suddenly it hit him. Carney came out of his chair. The chain! It was there! They had photographed the chain balled up in Joan Butler's carpet. Carney was euphoric. He had made the link. All he had to do was retrieve the chain from the crime lab, show it to Carla Dippel, and if she identified it as hers, he would have successfully placed Grissom inside Joan Butler's apartment. Carney knew it could be a case-making lead. There was only one remaining obstacle. The lab team had forgotten to pick up the chain at the conclusion of their search. Joan Butler's apartment had been released to the family and cleaned out during the first week of July.

Carney called a task-force detective working on the Grissom follow-up and learned that yes, a photo of the

chain had been taken, and no, the evidence logs did
not show a chain retrieved from the floor of the Butler
apartment. Carney contacted his superior with news of
the dilemma. Detective Sergeant Jeff Dysart, who had
been the lead officer on the metro squad, was troubled
by the unfortunate oversight. Dysart called Ralph Butler
who, after several weeks in Kansas City, had returned
home with his wife to Wichita. The detective learned
that Joan's parents had not taken part in the removal
and storage of Joan's belongings. Ralph Butler did,
however, tell Dysart who had taken care of it.

Detective Dysart contacted Kelly Heintzelman, a
relative of the Butlers, who told him that the packing
and removal of Joan's belongings was handled by her
and several other relatives of the Butlers. Dysart questioned Kelly about whether she or anyone else had
found a gold chain during the move.

"Yes, I did," Kelly replied. "I had been the one
packing up most of the items from the bedroom and
while I was taking a box from the bedroom to the
living room, I noticed a flicker of sunlight bounce off
an object in the carpet. It was a small, gold rope-chain.
I must have walked over it a dozen times, but the sun
hit it just right," she added.

"What happened to the chain?" asked Dysart, hoping Kelly's account would conclude on a positive note.
"Do you still have it?"

"No, I don't have it," Kelly said. "I assumed the
chain was Joan's, so I put it with two other chains that
were already inside a small compartment in Joan's
steamer trunk. The trunk was taken with the rest of
Joan's belongings. Everything is in Wichita."

Dysart thanked Kelly and immediately called Ralph
Butler. He wanted to know if one of the Butlers could
get into the steamer trunk and retrieve the gold chain-
necklace.

Joan's mother, Jada, handled the request. She made the painful trip to the storage locker where her daughter's things had been placed. Once there, she did not dally. Inside the steamer trunk she found three gold chains but had no idea which one the detective wanted. For the sake of accuracy, she took all three chains and bundled them inside one of Joan's small handkerchiefs. She wrapped the bundle in tissue and sealed it inside an envelope. The next day a neighbor of the Butlers, making a trip to Kansas City, delivered the package to Dysart.

Upon receiving the three chains, Dysart paid a visit to Carla Dippel. He asked her if she could positively identify her missing chain. She did so quickly and confidently without the slightest hesitation. She verified that the chain was indeed the one that had been with her Peso-pendant when it was stolen.

The verification completed a large section of the puzzle for investigators. Grissom had robbed Carla Dippel's apartment during the early morning hours of June 18. He then surprised and overpowered Joan Butler who lived just a hundred yards away. During his attack on Joan Butler, he'd lost a piece of the booty. The gold necklace had been partially hidden on the floor for over two weeks and stored inside a trunk in another city for nearly four more. But in the end, it found its way back into the hands of those who would prove that Grissom had been where he wasn't supposed to be.

22

A mong the calls still coming in to the hot line, were those from two psychics with national reputations who called to offer their insights to investigators. Because of their success when working with other police agencies around the country, the detectives considered their suggestions. The psychics had been quick to tell detectives about a few cases that had been solved as a result of their help.

According to the psychics, information came to them in voices directly from one or more of the missing women. To them, it was the missing women's way of saying they wanted their bodies found. Most of the psychics' reports involved information about bodies of water, either rivers or lakes in which the women could be found. The detectives were split between those who felt the psychics could not be ignored and those who believed they could not offer anything substantive.

Hinkle and Batt were two of the more skeptical in the group, which prompted them to call a few of the police references the psychics had given. After three calls, Hinkle and Batt learned that the psychic's claims of "solved" cases could not be substantiated. The detectives decided not to offer psychics any more time and attention, with the exception of one local woman.

Kansas City psychic, Betty Johnson, talked occasionally with detectives after the disappearances. Johnson was a member of the Kansas City Psychic Research Society and had worked with a variety of local police agencies on other cases. The Research Society assembled a group of psychics and accumulated more than one hundred hours of tape recordings of individual psychic impressions and opinions. The data was turned over to the police to use as they saw fit.

Johnson's impressions included a vision of at least one of the women being buried in a rock quarry near Kansas Highway 10, which was the main highway between Overland Park and Lawrence. Johnson also told the media that she had received an impression that Grissom had used a wood chipper to dispose of one of the bodies. She could not provide times or locations, but felt the police should track the lead to determine if Grissom had ever rented such a machine in the metro area. She emphasized that the machine he used still had blood on it and that it remained in storage somewhere.

In Wichita, another woman making claim to substantial psychic abilities contacted the Butler family. The woman, Ruth Silvers, told Jada and Ralph Butler that she knew where Joan had been buried and could lead the police to her. She provided just enough information and background to pique their interest. The Butlers called Hinkle with whom they had developed a good relationship during the early months of the investigation, and asked him to talk to the psychic.

Hinkle listened to the Butlers carefully, but he knew that many who claimed to have psychic abilities simply preyed on emotional weaknesses of others. He also knew that families of missing victims were most vulnerable. He'd seen cases in which "psychics" had milked large sums of money from families by stringing them along with the idea that the "ultimate answer" would be revealed with the "next" discovery. Hinkle cast a suspicious eye on those who offered unsolicited help.

On behalf of the Butlers, Hinkle called Ruth Silvers and asked her to meet him. She met the detective at the task force office. Ruth, in her fifties, was a slight woman and had dark hair and brown eyes. She was extremely talkative, not failing to boast of her ability to communicate with the dead. One of the recent communications she'd had, of course, had been with Joan Butler who told Ruth what had happened to her and where she was buried. "Joan was driven in a small car over a long distance well away from Kansas City," said the psychic.

"Where was she taken?" Hinkle asked. "And who took her there?"

Ruth paused for a moment, clasping her hands together on top of the table. "Joan has told me it was a young, black man. He beat her and raped her and then later he buried her."

"Where did this happen? Where is she supposed to be buried?" Hinkle asked.

"Joan has directed me to an area near Pomona Lake, just south of Topeka. It's an area near the end of Dragoon Creek, where the creek empties into the lake," Ruth said.

"That's quite a distance away," said the doubting detective. "Have you been there to check it for yourself?"

Ruth studied the detective. "I have not been there, no. But Joan has given me very clear impressions of where she can be found. There are certain things there, things that we should look for. If we discover these things, then we are near the body. It's just a matter of Joan telling me where we should dig once we have located the general area."

Hinkle pumped Ruth with more questions. He had his own formula for probing witnesses he had reservations about. If she had information which could be affirmed, he would run with it. If not, he could not afford to play along. He wanted to ensure that the Butlers were satisfied with what he accomplished with the "psychic," but he did not have time to waste with her.

Surprisingly, in contrast to Hinkle's expectations, Ruth provided answers to several questions. Her visions included a road or highway that suddenly ended, going nowhere. According to Ruth, there was a bridge near the road and a gravel road just off the bridge. She told Hinkle that if he took the gravel road he would soon spot another old bridge that would be closed. Near there would be the turnpike and an old stone house on several unkempt acres. Ruth surprised Hinkle with the revelation that the man who had taken Joan had done some painting for the man who lived in the old house.

Hinkle found the information interesting, but it did not completely satisfy his investigative instincts. He let Ruth go, saying that he would check out what she had said and call her if he needed more help from her. Ruth nodded that she understood, but before leaving she insisted that if Hinkle ever wanted to find Joan Butler's body, he had better follow her instructions. Joan was talking to her, Ruth said.

Hinkle placed a call to the sheriff of the county covering Pomona Lake. The sheriff confirmed the closed highway in the area and the bridges Ruth had mentioned, but did not recall an old stone house. He was adamant about the fact that there was no "turn-pike" anywhere in that area. It was almost enough for Hinkle to shelve the lead. However, he gave the lead one last chance, asking the sheriff to check the area and report his findings to Hinkle.

The sheriff called back a few days later and sur-prised Hinkle with his findings. Yes, the sheriff re-ported, everything was there—the bridges, one of them closed, the gravel road and even the old stone house. Further, the road running in front of the old stone house was once called Smith's Turnpike. It had been named after the Smith family who, years before, had lived in the house.

For Hinkle, the gaps had been closed. Ruth had "seen" something that not even the county sheriff knew was there. Hinkle asked the psychic to accompany him and several officers to Pomona Lake. They would search for Joan Butler's body.

When the two carloads of officers and the psychic arrived at the lake, everything seemed to unfold before their eyes exactly as Ruth had said it would. They traveled on the highway which ended suddenly, forc-ing them to take the last exit. They discovered the bridge and then the gravel road. Even Hinkle was feeling a twinge of excitement when the abandoned railroad bridge and the old stone farm house came into view. When they reached the area of Dragoon Creek near the lake, Ruth told them where to concentrate their efforts. Hinkle stopped the car and the officers pulled shovels from their trunks.

As the officers looked over the area for fresh graves, or pieces of clothing, Ruth went into a trance, as if receiving messages directly from Joan Butler. The first message indicated that the officers should dig not far from the creek. They did and turned up nothing. Ruth received another message, and the diggers tried another spot. Again, nothing was found. Another message was revealed, then another and still another, until the officers had dug a lengthy strip along the banks of the creek.

The day's temperature was near ninety-five degrees and by the third dig, most of the officers were drenched in sweat. By the fifth and sixth digs, Hinkle was losing patience with each stroke of the shovel. Then, from the banks of the creek, Ruth directed them to a few open, grassy areas nearby and pointed out locations where she was certain Joan's body was buried. It wasn't.

Over two hours later, Hinkle sat behind the wheel of a police unit and drove his team of tired, wet and frustrated officers from the area near Pomona Lake. Hinkle was angry. About a third of the way into the search, he had realized that Ruth was leading them on. To confirm his belief, Hinkle stopped his unit in front of the old stone house to talk to the owner who was sitting in a chair amidst the tall prairie grass in his front yard.

Hinkle identified himself and asked him if he was familiar with the Richard Grissom case in Kansas City. The old timer responded that he was, that he had been tracking it on the news since it all began. When asked whether Grissom had ever done any contract painting for him, the man replied, "Ain't no nigger ever gonna set foot on my property. If that nigger ever came around here, I'd blow a hole in him before he ever got into the yard!"

Ruth sat in the back seat of Hinkle's car as they drove on. She was as talkative as ever, attempting now to justify herself, her revelations and her abilities. She would not admit that they had failed her. Intent on proving herself to Hinkle, she began a demonstration of her psychic ability by telling the detective a few personal things about himself. She mentioned the color of his house. She was wrong. She talked about his kids. Wrong again.

Hinkle shook his head. As she went on, Hinkle grew angrier and found himself increasing his speed.

Frightened by the speed of the car, Ruth said, "Be careful, there's a sharp turn up here. You'd better slow down!"

Hinkle took a deep breath trying to contain his frustration. "I thought you told me you had never been to this area before? How do you know about the sharp turn in the road?"

"I was down here last week," Ruth responded matter-of-factly. "But I knew if I told you that, you never would have agreed to come down and look."

Detective Batt had a similar experience in which he spent two days baby-sitting a man who claimed to know exactly where the girls were. The man was not an unknown around Kansas City and held a respectable job. Consequently, Batt gave him the benefit of the doubt. The man led the detective to various parts of the city but concentrated heavily on areas that already had been mentioned by the media.

It wasn't until Batt went with the man to the Missouri location near Eighty-seventh Street, where Christine Rusch's drivers license was found, that Batt had seen enough. As they walked near Eighty-seventh Street, the man suddenly began talking aloud to the missing girls. He also began reporting their responses which included their whereabouts and their condition. The detective knew it was time to move on.

Most searches in the Grissom case were the result of solid investigative reasoning from behavioral scientists who concentrated on serial abductions and murders. They told investigators to check areas within a five-to-ten-mile radius of where the victims lived. With topographical maps in hand, Hinkle and Batt plotted and executed several searches, but discovered nothing significant. Detectives believed early on that if Grissom had not mutilated his victims and stuffed them inside trash bags and dumpsters, he had buried them in rural settings or dumped them into a river.

Two extensive searches were conducted around the Noland Farm where Grissom had been working and in the open land areas around 139th Street and Metcalf where Christine's belongings were discovered. In those searches, all available manpower was summoned to help. Even cadets from the police academy were called in. Searchers joined arm-in-arm and walked across fields ensuring that every square yard was checked. Much larger fields outside the metro area were divided into grids and portioned out to searchers who walked the field until every grid had been thoroughly covered. Some search areas were even covered on horseback. In every case, the searchers looked for freshly dug ground or mounds of a suspicious nature. Many suspicious-looking areas were uncovered but none produced results.

One large piece of ground, located off Highway 458 in rural Douglas County near Lawrence, was the sight of a thorough ground search. The search followed a phone call from a woman who owned property adjacent to the parcel. She told investigators she had seen a small, brown Toyota deserted in her neighbor's field. She knew her neighbors were not at home that weekend. It had been just prior to a livestock show that she and her husband had planned to attend. They left for the show on the June 19. The previous Sunday would have been the day Joan Butler disappeared.

The sighting of the Toyota would not, by itself, have sent investigators running to that field. From the inception of the case, there had been hundreds of reported sightings of brown Toyotas believed to be Grissom's. But, what brought the search teams to the Douglas County location was the extraordinary revelation that the Toyota she had seen had a Nebraska license plate. The woman had even remembered the first three letters of the tag. The fact that Grissom's car had a stolen Nebraska license plate had never been made public by the police. The three letters of the tag were identical to those on the Nebraska plate.

The search of the Douglas County plot was intense and thorough. Teams were brought in from various departments and from the training academy. Searchers marched shoulder to shoulder over several acres of land. They dug up suspicious areas and emptied wells to see if anything rested at the bottom.

They also conducted aerial searches using infrared scanners designed to detect slight variations in heat emanating from the surface or just below the ground. A body in the early stages of decomposition would throw off enough heat to distinguish it from surrounding ground temperatures. Several buried animals were dug up, but no bodies were recovered. In the middle of one of the farm fields, however, the searchers found a waded ball of duct tape. A strange place for duct tape to be located, they thought. But still, they were no closer to finding the body of Joan Butler.

From tens of callers reporting strange smells in certain rural areas, hundreds of bones and skeletal fragments were collected. Several items of clothing, mostly blouses, underwear and shoes, were also gathered. The detectives knew the clothing sizes of the missing girls, and most of the recovered items were ruled out as belonging to any of the three victims.

In all, ground search efforts covered more than a dozen locations and spanned four states. The detectives' efforts were tireless. They refused to give up. A few months after the disappearances, when two unidentified bodies were uncovered in Doniphan County, Kansas, Hinkle and Batt responded. They were also on the scene when body parts surfaced in the Kaw River near Shawnee. The duo traveled to Sioux City, Iowa, to determine if a woman found floating in the Missouri River was one of their victims.

They maintained close contact with officers in Benton County, Arkansas, after police there discovered the charred remains of a young woman; the woman's body was found just off Highway 71, the route Grissom was believed to have taken to Texas. The two detectives also attended an autopsy in Minnesota when the early description of a young, unidentified victim closely matched two of the victims in the Grissom case. None of the identifications matched, but the detectives persisted.

23

It was over a month after he told Detective Hinkle about the Metcalf storage locker that Marcelais Thibodo dropped another bombshell. During the sweltering summer week that saw July roll into August, Thibodo called Detective Hinkle and asked him if he would meet him again. Hinkle agreed and waited inside the Lenexa Headquarters building for the sight of Thibodo's truck. When Hinkle saw the truck he went out to meet Thibodo in the lot. Hinkle immediately sensed something was wrong. Thibodo approached with his hands in his pockets and his head lowered. He would not make eye contact with Hinkle.

"What's wrong?" Hinkle asked.

Thibodo stammered and shifted his weight back and forth. "Well, you know, man, there's ah, there's something I didn't tell you about," said the nervous Thibodo.

Hinkle felt his stomach knot. He wondered whether Thibodo was about to reveal his own first-hand knowledge of Grissom's crimes or worse, his own participation. "What is it, Frenchy?" Hinkle asked, attempting to remain as calm as possible. "What did you forget to tell us?" Hinkle demanded.

Thibodo hesitated. "I uh, I found something else, man. I found something else in the locker."

"What!" fired Hinkle, running out of patience. "What was it?"

"It was some tape, man," Thibodo said nervously. "You know, some construction type tape, man. Some of that duct tape."

"Yeah, and?" Hinkle tried to get this witness to fill in the blanks. "What about the tape? Where was it?"

"Well, you know, man. I went to the locker and there it was, in the middle of the floor. It was just there, all balled up and laying there," Thibodo said, then paused again as if waiting for guidance.

"When?" Hinkle asked, thinking several steps ahead to what this new information might do to his case. "When did you see the duct tape in the locker?"

"Ah, you know, it was during that same time I found the sunglasses. The woman's glasses. It was the week before I showed you where his locker was, man," Thibodo responded.

The detective knew there was more to this episode than balled-up duct tape. Duct tape found in Grissom's locker was significant, but something about the tape must have panicked Thibodo. Hinkle knew that no tape had been found in or around the locker by the search teams. Thibodo had done something with the tape, Hinkle reasoned. Was it his own involvement in something? Why was he so concerned about finding the duct tape? "What did you do with the tape, Frenchy?" Hinkle asked, trying to remain as calm as possible.

Thibodo did not want to answer the question. He glanced up at Hinkle and dropped his gaze. He took his hand from his pocket and looked at his watch as if he needed to be somewhere else in a hurry.

Hinkle wasn't at all receptive to Thibodo's stall. The detective grilled Thibodo again about what he did with the tape.

Finally, a shaken Thibodo replied. "I tossed it up on the roof, man. I didn't like it, man. You know, it didn't look good. I had to get rid of it."

"What roof?" Hinkle asked. "The roof of the locker? Is that what you're telling me? You threw the tape up on the roof of the locker?"

"Yeah, man, you know. I had to. It was there and I was the only one around, you know."

Along with another detective from the division, Hinkle rushed back to the Metcalf storage locker within minutes of Thibodo's disclosure. En route, he thought about his witness. Hinkle knew that even if Thibodo was completely innocent, his excuses and untimely surprises did nothing for his credibility. He saw Thibodo's latest act as borderline incriminating.

Thibodo had told the disheartened detective that there was hair on the tape. Long strands of brown hair had stuck to the tape and it scared him. Thibodo had told him that he believed Grissom was capable of anything, and he figured Grissom had purposely left the tape behind to set him up. Thibodo also believed the police would try to "clear the case" with him if they linked him to the tape. Thibodo had made an overt move to destroy evidence at a time when Grissom was pointing an accusing finger and naming him as an accomplice.

Leaning a ladder against the warehouse, Hinkle climbed on top of locker number eighteen. He was not only mad about Thibodo's timing and lack of honesty, he was upset because it was ninety-plus degrees in the shade and worse, Hinkle was forced to climb all over

a tar-and-gravel roof in his new Italian suit. It took the
detective longer than expected to find the tape. It had
melted into the searing tar and gravel. Hinkle imagined
how much better it might have been had Thibodo told
him about the tape when first revealing the location of
the locker. Hinkle knew what the elements could do to
hairs and fibers left exposed. He placed the tape in an
evidence bag, wondering if it could be salvaged and
properly analyzed at the lab.

After the recovery of the duct tape from the storage
locker, the lab team of Chapin and Fahy returned to
process the small locker. They now thought it likely
that Grissom had held one or more of the girls here,
before or after killing them. Chapin snapped photographs and Fahy dusted the locker for latents. From
inside the locker, only four prints of sufficient quality
were lifted. Trace evidence searches were conducted
throughout the locker, including the cracks in the floor
and between the folds of the corrugated metal. No
hairs were found inside the locker, making the discovery of the duct tape all the more significant. A Benzedrine reactive test was performed in the locker and
later on the shag rug taken from it. No traces of blood
were found. When the searches at the locker had been
completed, the detectives did not feel they were much
further ahead.

In early August, Hinkle followed up on leads already covered. He focused on the remaining keys on
Grissom's key ring found in the Toyota. Hinkle wondered how many other doors Grissom had opened
with his keys and how many other crimes he had
committed. The detective first decided to test the locks

at Apple Creek, the complex whose name was on one
of the keys.

Hinkle met with the manager at Apple Creek. She
identified the master key almost immediately. She
pointed out that it was one of the old masters which fit
many of the apartment locks before they were all
changed in mid-June. The reason for the change? A
young woman had been attacked in her apartment in
the middle of the night and there had been no signs of
forced entry. The manager told Hinkle that she and
others at the complex decided that whoever attacked
the woman had a key to her apartment.

Hinkle questioned the manager about the incident
and learned that the victim's name was Michelle Katf.
He also obtained a fair description of the suspect and
was able to draw a relatively easy conclusion. He asked
the manager who had the painting and maintenance
contracts at the complex? The contract had been secured by a company called Metrotech Painting which
Hinkle had learned was owned by Eric Pour.

Hinkle asked if he could get more samples of the
old locks from the complex. He wanted to compare the
key from Grissom's key ring to the type of lock that
would have been on Michelle Katf's door at the time of
her attack. He also wanted the names of anyone at the
complex who might have seen anything that night or
who may have noticed other unusual incidents occurring at the complex during that same period. The manager recalled the names of a couple of people who she
thought may have witnessed something the night of the
attack. She also retrieved two old locks from a storage
room and turned them over to Hinkle. Lastly, she provided Hinkle with a current address for Michelle Katf.

Hinkle met with Michelle Katf during her lunch
hour at a small restaurant. Since her attack, she preferred meeting people in open, public places and did

not want anyone coming to her apartment. Before meeting Michelle, the detective had retrieved a copy of the police report on her case but remained somewhat confused about exactly what had happened to her.

Hinkle initially found Michelle to be less than cooperative. From the very beginning of the meeting he had to continually reassure her that he had her best interests in mind. He believed her uneasiness had to do with her being asked, once again, to relive that horrible night in her life. Hinkle assured Michelle that Grissom was safely behind bars and could not hurt her again. He soon realized, however, that it was not just Grissom that troubled her. It seemed the more he talked, the more apprehensive and uncooperative she became. When Hinkle finally confronted her about her attitude toward him, Michelle admitted that she harbored a deep distrust of police after the way they had treated her the night of her attack.

Stung by the truth, Hinkle tried a different approach. He told Michelle that he was positive that Grissom was the one who attacked her. He also told her that his task force would incorporate her "attempted abduction" case into their own abduction-murder case against Grissom. He added that he had already arranged for the evidence from her case, the knife, the flashlight and the pellets, to be sent to their own evidence lockers for preservation. The detective explained that her case was important, and that they needed her as a witness against Grissom.

After a while, Michelle calmed a bit, demonstrating a greater trust and respect for the detective. She talked openly, and Hinkle learned as much about her attack as possible. When it was time for Michelle to return to work, they arranged to meet again. Hinkle would learn much more from his witness.

At a subsequent meeting, Michelle insisted that she could not positively identify Grissom as the man who assaulted her. Even so, Hinkle had hoped she would be able to identify his car and the pellet gun he'd used during her abduction. Michelle told him that she did not get a good look at the gun, that it had been stuck under her chin and in her rib cage during the assault. She did explain, however, that her attacker had insisted that she feel the gun and she had remembered a few of its features. She told Hinkle that she might be able to identify the weapon by touch.

When they next met to discuss the pellet gun used by her attacker, Hinkle had four guns to show her. In addition to the pellet guns recovered from the Corsica, the brown Toyota and the Grand Am in Texas, Hinkle had taken a fourth gun from Thibodo, who said he kept it for use on aggressive dogs while he was employed at a prior delivery job.

The detective handed a nervous Michelle Katf one pellet gun at a time and asked her to feel them and look them over carefully. She took each one in her hands and felt the undersides of each barrel, searching for those features she felt on that unforgettable night in June. When she had finished, she had confidently narrowed her selection. "If this one is not the one he used on me," Michelle said, "then it's an exact duplicate." Hinkle knew the gun she had selected was the one taken from the glove box of the red Corsica.

Next Hinkle showed Michelle a series of photographs. They were various photos of Grissom's brown Toyota taken from various angles. Immediately she told Hinkle she was almost certain that it was the same car she saw leaving the parking lot at Apple Creek after her escape.

To fill in the remaining gaps in the Kaft case, Hinkle interviewed Thomas Haynes, Michelle's former neighbor at Apple Creek. Haynes not only identified Grissom's Toyota, he identified Grissom himself. He told Hinkle that he was positive that it was Richard Grissom whom he saw crossing the parking lot the night of the attack. Haynes described Grissom—what he was wearing, how he was carrying something wrapped in a towel, and how he got into his car and drove off without turning on his headlights.

Before completing his interview with Haynes, Hinkle asked him one last question. With Michelle Katf having already eliminated Thibodo's gun, the detective would once and for all eliminate Thibodo himself as a suspect in the Katf assault. "Did the man you saw crossing the parking lot that night walk with a limp?" the detective asked.

"No, he did not," Haynes replied, confidently.

In early August, Batt and Hinkle followed-up a previous lead developed from Thibodo. The detectives returned to the town house complex in Overland Park where Thibodo had dropped Grissom off to pick up his Toyota. Thibodo had shown the detectives exactly where the Toyota had been parked and recalled that he had taken Grissom there around June 20. Batt and Hinkle went door to door talking to residents of several townhouses in effort to find someone who may have seen Grissom's car. They found such a witness.

Joann Vermillion lived on Eighty-third Street, just two blocks from Joan Butler's apartment. Joann, an elderly, matter-of-fact woman had not taken kindly to the unauthorized use of her parking space. She definitely remembered the Toyota parked in front of her town house. When Hinkle pointed to a parking space in front of her unit and inquired about it, Joann responded, "Yes, that's my space. In fact, the first two spaces are mine. We have assigned parking here."

When asked if the brown Toyota had ever been parked in one of her spaces, she replied, as if still slightly irritated by the occurrence, "Oh, you bet it was. It was there for several days, and I was getting a little concerned about it. You see, I sometimes let the neighbors or their visitors use my extra space. I live alone and only use one of them. But no one told me they were going to be using it. No one asked me. I just came home from work and there it was in my space."

"When did you first notice it there?" asked Batt.

"It was on a Tuesday. I came home from work and it was there."

"Do you recall the date you first saw the car ma'am, or can you remember a time frame within a certain month?" asked Batt.

"Yes," she answered. "I remember it was in June but I'd have to check my calendar to be positive of the exact dates."

"Did you write the dates the car was there on your calendar?" Batt asked, hopefully.

"No, I didn't write it down. I just remember that the time I saw it coincided with other things I had been doing and those are on my calendar."

"Do you remember much about the car? Was it an older car or newer?" Batt asked, trying not to lead her with too many specifics.

"Oh, it was an older, used model Toyota. I walked out of my house a couple of times to take a closer look at it. It had the darkened windows, and the owner had taken off the license tag while it was here."

"The license plate was not on the car when it was here?" Batt asked.

"Nope," Vermillion replied. "I was getting a little worried about that, too. I wondered if someone had abandoned it. I almost called to have it towed, but told myself that if it was still there over the weekend, I would call someone about it. When I got home from work on Friday, it was gone."

"So, as you recall, the car was first left there on Tuesday and was gone by that Friday, and it was sometime during June of this year?"

"Yes, I'll check my calendar and let you know, but I believe that's right."

The detectives had what they came for, another witness to corroborate the fact that Grissom's Toyota had been left in front of Joann Vermillion's town house while he had Joan Butler's Corsica. However, the new eyewitness testimony did not correspond exactly to the dates reported by Thibodo. He had told Hinkle that he took Grissom there on June 20 to pick up the Toyota. Joann Vermillion indicated that it was probably the twentieth when she first noticed the car. But, at that point, the detectives were happy to have someone in addition to Thibodo telling them about the Toyota parked at the complex. The time frames could be worked out later.

Days later, Ralph and Jada Butler were asked by Paul Morrison, the Johnson County prosecutor, to return to Overland Park to provide blood samples for comparison with blood evidence that might have come from their daughter. The serologists at the crime lab had determined that the tracings of blood found in the trunk area of the Corsica were sufficient enough to test against a known sample of the victim's blood. But since a sample of Joan's blood was not available, the next best step would be to take blood samples from each of

Joan's parents. The samples would then be submitted for DNA typing.

Ralph and Jada Butler wanted to do everything they could to help build a strong case against Grissom, but did they really want to face the certainty that the blood in the Corsica was their daughter's? With emotional ambivalence, the Butlers decided to face the potentially harsh reality. They accompanied a detective to the Shawnee Mission Medical Center and allowed a technologist to draw their blood.

One of the diagnostic labs receiving the blood samples was Cellmark Labs of Germantown, Maryland. Cellmark specialized in a reverse-typing process widely used in cases where paternity was in question. A blood sample from a child could be compared to a suspected father to determine if the man was, in fact, the father. The process itself was time consuming; results would be slow in coming. The wait was just another emotional roller-coaster ride for Ralph and Jada Butler.

24

Mid-August 1989. Johnson County Prosecutor Paul Morrison filed criminal charges against Richard Grissom for three counts of murder in the deaths of Joan Butler, Theresa Brown and Christine Rusch. Additional counts included kidnapping-abduction, robbery, fraud and theft charges from Grissom's multiple check-passing schemes.

Prosecutor Morrison was not breaking new ground in Kansas when filing murder charges in a case where the victims' bodies had not been recovered. Three such cases had been successfully prosecuted in the state prior to the charges against Grissom; however, all three involved only one missing victim. A substantial number of precedent cases also had been prosecuted nationwide. In the Grissom case, however, the lack of any standard prerequisites for the charge of murder made the case extremely difficult.

In most murder cases, prosecutors preferred tightly wrapped cases which contained the three prerequisites: a victim, a weapon and a motive. If the case had even one of the three, the prosecutor's job was made considerably easier. In the Grissom case, all three prerequisites were missing. But Morrison, a career prosecutor, was not going to shy away from the Grissom case. It helped that he had a team of talented police investigators compiling volumes of evidence to support the charges. They could all see the case against Grissom coming together a few pieces at a time. It was far from a ready-made case, but Morrison and the detectives were moving full-speed-ahead with what they hoped would be a strong circumstantial case.

Meanwhile, in Dallas, Grissom's attorney was still pulling out all the legal stops available to his client. By early October, however, several of his motions had been denied, and extradition loomed on the horizon. Grissom's attorney submitted written arguments to the Texas Court of Appeals contending that his client was being illegally detained in Texas. The appeal, of course, was submitted a day before its deadline. With thirty-day intervals between appeals, no one following the case back in Kansas City was surprised to see it drag on.

But then in early November, a window of opportunity opened for the state of Kansas. The Texas Court of Appeals finally denied the motion to free Grissom from custody, ruling that he was not being improperly detained. That ruling, did not surprise the anxious team in Kansas, but what they did find interesting was an order issued by the state of Texas to discontinue all payments for Grissom's legal fees. Suddenly, Grissom's attorney took a much less aggressive approach for his client's rights. The deadline to file a final appeal to prevent Grissom from being extradited was November 5. Grissom's attorney missed it.

Early on November 9, Detectives Batt and Hinkle watched from the terminal as a six-passenger, twin-prop aircraft, furnished by the Governor of Kansas, landed at the Johnson County Airport. The plane had stopped to pick up Batt and Hinkle before continuing to Dallas-Ft. Worth. On board the plane was Scott Morgan, chief counsel to the Governor of Kansas. Morgan had represented the state of Kansas in the months of proceedings to get Grissom back to stand trial.

The plan was to whisk Grissom out of Texas as quickly as possible. With the assistance of the Governor's Office and Prosecutor Morrison, arrangements had been made with Texas authorities to have Richard Grissom ready and waiting near the taxi-way where the plane would be landing. The only wild card in the scenario was that no one knew what Grissom's attorney was up to. The Kansas team assumed the attorney would hold off filing any new motions on behalf of his client, but a motion filed at any time before they got Grissom out of Texas would send them back to Kansas without a prisoner.

The twin-prop landed in Dallas on schedule and taxied to the area where the exchange was to be made. From their seats, Hinkle and Batt watched a trio of detectives escort Grissom toward the plane.

Grissom's appearance had changed. He no longer resembled the photographs and descriptions provided during the manhunt. He had grown a beard and his hair had not been cut, allowing curls to fall below his neck line. He also had gained a little weight.

When the plane came to a stop, the co-pilot left his seat, maneuvered toward the rear of the craft and released the door. Morgan, Hinkle and Batt stepped out of the plane. While Morgan executed the legal paperwork for transferring the prisoner, the detectives replaced the cuffs and leg irons belonging to the Dallas officers with sets of their own. With the process rapidly completed, the teams exchanged thank yous and loaded Grissom onto the plane. They had been on the ground for roughly five minutes. They could not afford to have anything go wrong now.

Even the return flight plan had been pre-filed, with any refueling stops being made outside of Texas. As the plane lifted, Hinkle found himself staring at Grissom, the man who had eluded them for months. To Hinkle's surprise, Grissom appeared calm, seemingly unaffected by what was happening. In typical Grissom fashion, he played along with whatever was happening at the moment.

To say that the detectives were relieved to have Grissom in custody was an understatement. The hunt was over. However, they would keep the trip home low key. They had decided in advance not to question Grissom during the flight back to Kansas. He was advised of his rights even before takeoff but that was simply precautionary. If the suspect decided to blurt out a confession, the detectives wanted to be able to use it.

Batt and Hinkle already knew more about Richard Grissom than he could ever imagine. The two detectives had planned a routine designed to get Grissom to talk to them freely, not about the case, but about anything he wanted to talk about. The idea was to make him feel relaxed around them, feel that he could trust them. The flight back to Kansas would take several hours. It was time they could take advantage of.

Batt and Hinkle spent a lot of time purposefully cutting up and tossing verbal barbs at each other, taking shots at each other's hair or clothes. They asked Grissom non-threatening questions about his athletic ability which he answered freely. They asked his opinion on specific issues and allowed him to voice his concerns about others. By the end of the flight, the three were getting along well.

Finally, around 5:00 P.M., four months and two days after his arrest, Richard Grissom was escorted inside the Kansas State Prison in Lansing, Kansas. Grissom would sit in the holding facility there until being moved to the Johnson County Adult Detention Center to face his accusers and the growing list of charges against him. To the disappointment of those awaiting his prosecution, the final process would be delayed for almost a year.

The morning after Grissom's return, Hinkle was driving along Kansas Highway 10 in Olathe when his car phone rang. It was Grissom, calling from the Lansing Prison. Prior to leaving Grissom the previous day, Hinkle made sure that Grissom had a few phone numbers where he and Batt could be reached. Grissom told Hinkle he needed to talk to him right away. He added that Hinkle would not be disappointed.

Hinkle agreed to meet with him and immediately called Batt, asking him to call the prison authorities at Lansing and to meet him at the prison. Hinkle attempted to contact an attorney at the public defender's office. If Grissom decided to talk and wanted an attorney, then one would have to represent him. Hinkle was unable to reach anyone at the public defender's office.

At the Lansing Prison, the two detectives deposited their guns at the check-in station and were escorted to a holding area to wait for Grissom. Hinkle and Batt were both disappointed with the accommodations made available to them for their interview. The area was not as private as they would have liked. A lot of inmates were passing by within earshot of the holding room. The detectives wondered whether Grissom would feel comfortable talking to them in such an open environment.

When Grissom arrived, he greeted the detectives anxiously. He wore a different jumpsuit but otherwise looked the same. Hinkle immediately laid a "Waiver of Rights" form on the table. He asked Grissom to read it over carefully and, if in agreement with everything, to sign it. The detectives noticed the form shaking in Grissom's hand while he read.

After reading it, Grissom picked up a pen, then hesitated. He would not sign the document. "I want to give you everything! I'm getting too many headaches. I'm upset most of the time." Grissom made eye contact with the detectives. He held out his hands in demonstration. They were trembling. "I want to get right with this thing, man. I know I did wrong, and I want to get right. But, you know, man, I'm going to be in here for a long time, and I just have to know there's going to be some daylight at the end of it."

"What do you mean?" asked Hinkle from across the table. "Are you trying to deal? Do you want a deal for some kind of parole?"

"Yeah, man! Parole, whatever. I want to tell you everything, man. I want to tell how it all went down. But if I do that, and I'm sitting in here for the rest of my life, it's no good. I need to have something to shoot for. I need to know there's going to be a light down the road for me. I know it might be fifteen to twenty, man. But I need the light. I need to know I got a shot some day," Grissom said. Before the detectives could respond, Grissom added, "You know, man, I've been doing a lot of thinking the last few months, and I just don't feel good about anything. I know I did some things, and I want to get right with my God or my Buddha. I'm looking for some kind of forgiveness, man. You know how it is."

The detectives knew that Grissom was laying it on thick. Yes, he was trembling but was also very capable of making that a part of his act. Grissom being remorseful or seeking forgiveness was not possible. The very mention of God or Buddha, or needing to "get right" with what he had done, was all part of the Grissom charade.

The detectives played along. "You know, Richard," said Hinkle. "The best way, maybe the only way, to get right is to get right with your God. Once you've done that, everything kind of takes care of itself. You know, if you come clean and talk to us about everything, you'll be coming clean with your God. If that is what you really think you need to do, then it's the most important thing you can do. If you make amends with your God and he forgives you, then, who knows? Maybe something good will happen for you as a result."

"I don't know," Grissom said, sounding suspicious. "I still would like to know up front if I'm going to see any kind of light down the road."

Hinkle made a conscious effort to steer clear of any continued head-butting on the subject of a deal. He knew a lot of time could be wasted beating the issue into the ground with no results. "Listen Richard, why don't you just think about that for a bit and we can come back to it later. You know, we came all the way out here because you said you needed to talk, so let's talk about some of the things involved in this case. We can use the what-if situation if you're more comfortable with that.

"It's obvious that we can't promise you anything, right. And if there is going to be a deal, it will be because of what we take to the prosecutor, Richard. It will be because of what you want to get right with at this very moment. You know we need to find the girls.

That's extremely important to us and it could be helpful to you. So why don't we just talk, and you can tell us, in a what-if kind of way, the things that will help us all out."

Hinkle did not ask any direct questions. He would not lead the suspect, and he would purposely avoid the Terri Maness case. Hinkle knew that the latest psychological profile revealed Grissom would be very ashamed of the murder-torture and should not be asked about it while he was in a cooperative mood.

"What about the girls, Richard?" Hinkle asked. "Let's talk about the girls. Can you help us with this? I mean this is the best thing you can do for yourself, Richard."

"The girls are dead, man. I mean, you know. I just want to do the Christian thing here," Grissom admitted.

"Where are they, Richard? Can you tell us that?" Hinkle asked, then added, "Help yourself out here, man. Clear the air. Wipe this ugly slate clean, Richard." Hinkle sensed he was close to a response. He needed to keep him on track and focused.

"They're in this country!" replied Grissom, smiling and using a sardonic tone. Grissom quickly changed his tone when he saw the detectives had no tolerance for his humor. "They're in the country, man. They can be found out in the country, out in rural areas," he added.

"You're going to have to do better than that, Richard," said Batt, becoming impatient.

"Hey, man!" Grissom fired back. "I still don't see anything in this for me. I still don't see that light down the road. What guarantees do I have, man? I mean, I'm not the only one in this, but the focus of attention is all on me. I didn't even use the girls' credit cards, man. Somebody ought to be able to sweeten the pie for me if I come clean, tell everything and offer up someone else in the deal."

After an hour of game-playing on Grissom's turf, Batt and Hinkle had had enough. It would forever be a stalemate unless Grissom was handed some sort of deal. The detectives could have lied to Grissom, promised him the deal he wanted just to see if absolution was really what he wanted. Hinkle was aware of a personal letter Grissom sent to an administrative court judge, "…revoking here and forever my right to an attorney.…" They could have played games with Grissom who had essentially waived his right to counsel, but they played by the book. In the end, they were no closer to recovering the missing girls' bodies and were, instead, forced to listen to Grissom's feeble attempts to cast the blame away from himself and to his sudden declarations of need for his God's forgiveness.

Before leaving the room, however, Hinkle took one last shot at getting a truthful answer out of Grissom. He also wanted to get at the real truth about Marcelais Thibodo. "What about Frenchy, Richard? Was he involved in any of this with you?"

"No way, man!" came the quick reply. "Frenchy was just somebody I used when I needed certain things. He helped me out with the business and all. When he was around I had a lot more time to do what I needed. He's OK."

Hinkle came away from the interview with at least something. To him, Thibodo might have been a little difficult to interpret, but he would remain a witness and not a suspect.

The detectives attempted no additional contact with Grissom before his mid-November appearance before District Judge Robert Jones on murder charges.

Grissom, attired in a prison jumpsuit, appeared calm as he stood in front of Judge Jones. When the judge read the lesser charges of theft, forgery and fraud, Grissom appeared unfazed, as if the proceeding was just another tedious event he was forced to endure. When the judge read the first-degree murder charges, each separately, Grissom shook his head. He leaned against the defendant's table for support. As the judge continued reading the charges, Grissom sighed aloud, closed his eyes and kept shaking his head.

25

June 1990. Hinkle, Batt and Landwehr had worked closely with Prosecutor Paul Morrison for several months, scheduling witnesses, arranging necessary reports and documents and preparing more than one hundred other items classified as state's evidence. Hinkle received a call from Frank Denning, a Johnson County Sheriff's Deputy, who had been part of the follow-up task force on the case.

Denning had received word that one of the prisoners at the Johnson County jail wanted to talk to someone about the Grissom case. The prisoner had been incarcerated with Grissom and had received "firsthand" information about his crimes. The prisoner now wondered whether he might be entitled to a little help from the state in exchange for information about Grissom. A meeting was scheduled for Hinkle and Batt to talk to the inmate.

The inmate, Jessie Barnes, was a big man, well over six feet and broad shouldered. Barnes wore his hair long and had a beard. When he first met Grissom in the county lockup, Barnes was very much a seasoned inmate who was part of the prison grapevine and carried a reputation as a "stand-up", one who could be trusted within the system. He had been in prison on and off since the age of fourteen. Time inside was one of the things he and Grissom had in common right away. It didn't take long for Grissom to make the effort to get close to Barnes. Aligning himself with Barnes could mean early acceptance by the more hard-core inmates in the state joint. It was something Grissom knew he needed.

Barnes was brought to a secure interview area at the Johnson County holding facility. He was left to talk to the detectives without counsel. The interview got off to a good start when Barnes opened with, "He told me he killed the girls." Barnes followed that revelation with, "He also killed the one in Wichita. He told me that, too."

The detectives began with questions about the Terri Maness murder. Hinkle and Batt had familiarized themselves with the facts of the case. Barnes's credibility soared when he cited facts of the Maness case, which he could not have known about unless learning of them from the actual murderer.

Hinkle and Batt moved on to what Barnes knew about the three Johnson County victims. What had Grissom told him about the murders? Had he told Barnes how he committed them? Did he talk about his motives, other than wanting money? Did he say what he did with the bodies?

Barnes's answers to most of these questions were emphatic "no's" or responses too vague to offer the detectives much hope. Grissom had admitted to killing the women, but he offered little in the way of details. During his bragging sessions, Grissom also told Barnes that he killed a couple of prostitutes in Florida. He also said he killed a few other women during his travels on the road in various states. Barnes added that, "He did say the three women he did up here in Kansas would never be found."

"That's the way he put it?" Hinkle asked, frustrated by Barnes' lack of details. "He told you they'd never be found, but he didn't say why?"

"No, man," Barnes replied. "He never gave details when he talked about it like that. He'd say they'd never be found and then he'd say some shit like, 'They could siphon the ground and they'd never find 'em.' Hell, I couldn't ask no direct questions, man. I couldn't get in his face and look like I was prying. I had to just let him talk when he wanted to talk," added Barnes, justifying his reasons for offering little in the way of concrete information.

Then Barnes remembered a crucial piece of information. "Wait a minute, man" he told the detectives, excitedly. "The guy did tell me that he drove around with both bodies in the trunk of a car trying to figure out what to do with them. Said he drove like for a few hours trying to figure it all out. He told me he was shitting his pants because he was hanging out in some heavy traffic areas, and he had those bodies in the trunk."

"He must have told you something about what he did with them," said Batt.

"Yeah, he gave me a story about it, man, but I took it as bullshit. I believed him when he said he had the bodies in the trunk, but what he dropped on me later, you know, I just figured he was making things up at that point. It sounded too unreal, you know," said Barnes.

"Well, what did he tell you he did?" asked Batt.

Barnes changed positions. He paused, then said, "He told me he found a deserted spot near the Blue River and then ran the bodies through a tree shredder or a wood chipper or something like that." Barnes caught the detectives glancing at each other. He misinterpreted their response. "See, I told you I thought it was bullshit, man," he declared. " I can see you don't believe it either. I think the man was just talking out his ass, you know, trying to throw some heavy-duty shit my way. It was like he thought he came up with this great idea that nobody else ever thought of, you know. I don't even know if you can do that kind of thing with those machines, so I just played along and told him how cool it was, you know."

Detective Hinkle zeroed in on the comment about the Blue River. "Did Grissom tell you where he got the chipper or where on the Blue River he did this?"

Barnes appeared somewhat surprised that Hinkle had taken an interest in what he had said about the wood chipper. "Yeah, he said he drove around and was cruising the area up near Highway 53 and Blue Parkway. Matter of fact, he told me it was around the intersection at 6600 Blue Parkway, that he knew a man there named Bob who had the wood chipper. He said some other shit about a coal mine, but I can't remember exactly what that was all about. He did say he went to Bob's place, which was near the intersection, and then took an old road down to the Blue River. He said he went back and got the chipper and then shredded the bodies and let the pieces flow right down the river, man. That's the story. I mean, that's how he gave it to me, believe it or not," said Barnes, completing the picture for the detectives.

Changing course for the moment, Hinkle asked Barnes about any other activity involving Grissom that might be of help to them. Barnes's reply was not at all what they had expected.

"Well, he asked me to help him set up a hit on an FBI man," Barnes said casually. Barnes told of Grissom's expressed hatred for FBI Agent Mike Napier. "He told me it was the agent who busted him in Dallas and then grilled him for the rest of the day. Grissom said he was proud about the way he led the FBI guy on, saying he gave him just enough to keep him interested but never really gave him shit, you know. But it's true, he wanted him hit. He can't stand the guy."

"Did he say why?" Hinkle asked. "Was it just because he was the one who busted him?"

"Well, I think that was part of it, man. But it wasn't just that he busted him; it was the way that the FBI guy was shaking when he busted him. Grissom said the guy was a wimp, a discredit to his badge, you know. That's how he tells it anyway. He's into all this macho shit, man. He figured the guy shouldn't have been shaking."

"How did he set it up?" asked Batt, sensing an opportunity to nail Grissom with another serious felony. "What did he want you to do?"

"He wanted me to arrange it through some of my connections on the outside, you know. I didn't take it seriously. It wasn't like he kept coming after me to set it up. He just mentioned it once or twice when he was blowing off steam, you know, and the FBI guy suddenly popped into his head. I was never going to do anything about it, trust me."

Barnes went on to disclose an elaborate escape attempt being planned by Grissom. Grissom was slowly tearing away thin strips of bed sheets and weaving them together into a rope. According to Barnes, Grissom would not use the rope to lower himself from a prison window. He was using it to get specific carbide-tipped tools with the help of other inmates. The inmates worked in the machine shop where they took the tools and bits periodically and tied them on to Grissom's rope which he left dangling at specific times from his holding area. Grissom was then using the tools to file away at various parts of his holding cell. Grissom at one time told Barnes that when he escaped, one of his first moves would be to kill Napier.

Barnes also told the detectives about Grissom's sexual preferences, emphasizing that Grissom was fanatical about anal sex. "He was always a pitcher, man, not a catcher," Barnes said of Grissom. "I think he got his first taste of it when he was in the juvenile facility. I'll tell you, man, he can't talk about sex without talking about what sticking someone in the butt does to him. That's why he's always hanging with hookers, man. He talks them into giving up what he wants. If they don't, then they have to hope he can just walk away and forget about it. He gets a little in the joint, but to hear him tell it, he was getting a lot during his last bit, and getting some on the outside too. He's a freak for it, man."

The psycho-sexual profile on Grissom corroborated what Barnes had revealed. It also explained why Grissom was not sexually aggressive when dating women. Grissom was not interested in sex unless it was the kinky kind, generally where the recipient of his aggression was getting hurt in some fashion.

Barnes went on to reveal that Grissom asked him to use his connections on the outside to make contact with one of Grissom's girlfriends. The contact was to instruct the girl to write a letter to Grissom's attorney. The letter was designed to implicate Eric Pour in the murders of the missing women. The letter was to have no postmark and no return address, but was to be signed "Tiffany." Grissom told Barnes that the letter should be purposely written in poor English since "Tiffany" was a foreigner and would not be able to write well. Grissom knew that "Tiffany" was a friend of Eric Pour's, information he hoped would become available to investigators through his attorneys once the letter was received.

Grissom had also asked Barnes to use his outside influence to make contact with Sherry Cash. The instructions were to have Sherry purchase a Mexican Peso-pendant. Grissom was insistent that it be a 1985 Peso-coin that would match the coin turned over to detectives by Cathy Arenal. He gave Barnes a detailed description of the piece. After the purchase, one of Barnes's street players was to "plant" the pendant at the house of another girl named by Grissom. This girl was also known to be a friend of Eric Pour. The long-range plan was to have Grissom's private investigator recover the Peso-pendant from the girl's house, raising questions about the testimony of Cathy Arenal and the evidence she turned over to Detective Landwehr.

The Barnes account provided the detectives with additional insights about their suspect's capabilities and the lengths he would go to subvert the investigation. Grissom would not stop with the initial requests to Barnes. More attempts would be made in the weeks preceding his trial. One of them would have the effect of breaking the case wide open.

Hinkle and Batt considered everything Barnes told them. What Barnes may have thought were lies from a jailhouse braggart were, to Hinkle and Batt, additional leads to be checked out. The likelihood that Grissom was setting up Barnes with the wood chipper story was high. Nevertheless, the lead had to be covered.

Before going to the area described by Barnes, the detectives did their homework. They learned that at the time Grissom was thought to have used the wood chipper, there were only ten available for lease through companies around the metro area. A check with all of the metro area police agencies for reported crimes during that same time period revealed that no wood chippers had been stolen. The detectives also knew a little something about the wood-chipping machines. Grissom would have had to ·freeze his victims' bodies before running them through if he wanted to keep the chipper from jamming. Wood chippers were geared to accept rigid, dry objects. It was more likely that if Grissom was anywhere near a deserted section of the Blue River, he was indeed looking for an opportunity to dump the bodies into the river. The Blue River had a fairly strong current and eventually emptied into the Missouri River. A body dumped into the Blue at the location described by Barnes, would likely be carried all the way to the Missouri.

When the detectives reached the area on Blue Parkway described by Barnes, they could not find anything remotely resembling a dirt or gravel road leading to the Blue River. They drove back and forth through the intersection dozens of times with the same results. They stopped and questioned merchants, gas-station attendants, even other police officers, but found nothing. They drove several miles in both directions along the Parkway, as well as up and down Highway 350 looking for the road described by Barnes.

On the second day of their search, having decided to take a last pass through the area on foot, they found the road. Its entrance had been completely covered by bushes, overhanging trees and weed growth. Back in their car, the detectives passed through the intersection and turned into the jumble of weeds and branches which, within yards of the highway, gave way to a dirt road. The road dropped off, making a gradual descent toward the river. The detectives began discussing the probability of Grissom's account being more accurate than not as they drove down the narrow, one-lane road. After rounding the first big turn, their doubts about what Grissom told Barnes were reduced considerably.

They spotted an older, two-story house directly in front of them. Thick, tall vegetation covered the side yards of the house, but the front had been cleared and maintained. A pickup truck sat in the gravel driveway. It was apparent to them that someone was at home. As they approached the house, they noticed a small sign, faded and worn by age and weather, tacked to a tree near the driveway. It read, Joe-Bob's Woodchip Service. They paused, glanced silently at each other and then pulled into the driveway, a bit nervous that Grissom's version of events might just have a shred of truth.

Bob, the owner of the house, was at home. Although no longer in the business, Bob admitted to detectives that the summer before he did have a wood-chipping business. No, he had not loaned or leased the equipment to anyone else during that period. He admitted, however, that he had gone out of town during the last ten days of June in 1989. He added that no one had used his equipment during that time, at least no one he was aware of. In response to whether his machine could have been stolen, Bob replied, "well, it was here when I left and in the same place when I got back home, but I did leave the keys in the pickup and the chipper was hitched up behind it. I figured who's going to steal the truck with a big wood chipper hooked on the back?"

Bob showed the detectives how to get down to the bottom of the road and next to the river. They drove down to have a good look around for themselves. Grissom's version of events was looking more and more probable, except that he still would have had difficulty running the bodies through the shredder. At the bottom of the road, another road veered off in the direction of a concrete plant a short distance away. The road heading to the plant was Coal Mine Road, a reference that Jessie Barnes had tried to recall. Just off the road was an old, unkempt parking lot and a concrete platform that spread out over the Blue River. Neither detective spoke while surveying the area. Both knew that if ever an opportune setting existed for one to dispose of a body, either through a shredder or by dumping, the concrete platform over the river was it. The detectives once again called out the search and dive teams.

The scuba search teams battled currents and poor visibility but stayed with it for several hours. They brought in a sifter and dug up the bottom in various grid patterns until they had sifted a large portion of the river. Bones were recovered, even a near-complete ribcage, which the lab later reported were the bones of a large animal. One set of recovered bones was determined to be from a pig, which had been tossed in the river more than thirty years before.

Hinkle dug up some soil samples of the surrounding area, making certain to gather some from Coal Mine Road. He wanted to have it analyzed and compared to the clumps of dirt found on the floor of Christine Rusch's Dodge Colt. If Grissom had been driving around with bodies in the trunk of a car, he likely would have been using Christine's Colt.

Hinkle sent the soil samples from the Colt to Mid-Western University lab, which specialized in soil analysis. Hinkle would have to wait a few weeks to find out about the samples but the wait would be worth it.

Before leaving the area, Batt and Hinkle returned to the old house on the entry road for another chat with Bob. They questioned Bob about exactly where he had leased his wood chipper the year before. He willingly told them.

The detectives eventually found the exact machine Bob had leased. It had stains which looked a lot like blood splattered around the inside area near the blades. They scraped off samples of the stains and secured them in evidence bags for testing at the lab.

Eventually, the detectives learned that the stains on the wood chipper were blood, but it was the blood of some kind of animal. The university test results revealed that the soil samples from Coal Mine Road and that from the floor of the Colt were a reasonable match. In fact, they matched in more characteristics than any of the other samples submitted for comparison. Both had large quantities of Bithumus powder, derived from coal. The old road must have, at one time, led to a coal mine, as its name implied.

26

Within ten days of his trial, Grissom was working fast and furiously to set up an alibi defense, which he no doubt hoped his defense attorneys would spring on the prosecution. Grissom had maintained steady contact with at least four individuals outside of prison whom he wanted to bring into court to testify on his behalf. Two of the individuals were women. Two were ex-cons whom he knew from prison or from the street. In addition, a private investigator named Joe Collins came into the picture under contract by the defense.

One of the two women was a young prostitute, whose preferred location for drumming up business was the area around the Country Club Plaza. Both of the women had hung out with Grissom during the months he lived with Eric Pour and frequented the Plaza and Westport areas. According to pre-trial reports, the two were prepared to take the stand and testify that Richard Grissom was with them during one or more of the critical time periods linking him to the missing women. Grissom's intent was, of course, to offset or completely refute the testimony of critical prosecution witnesses. He was not telling his attorneys that one of his alibi witnesses was a prostitute who had been busted more than once, or that the men were ex-cons working on his behalf to plant evidence and lie on the witness stand.

In orchestrating a scheme to create alibis, Grissom was willing to pay the two men $10,000 for their testimony and for planting evidence. In one scheme, Grissom smuggled a letter out of prison to one of his co-conspirators. The letter clearly spelled out where items of clothing and jewelry were to be planted. Once planted, an anonymous call would be made to the private investigator telling him where to find the evidence.

The ex-con, however, more down on his luck than Grissom realized, was way behind on his rent and had left his apartment abruptly without notice. In his rapid departure, the man left behind a few personal items, including Grissom's personal letter to him. It was discovered by his landlord and turned over to detectives on the Grissom case.

Grissom's attorneys were not aware that he was fabricating stories about alibis and secretly scheming to "buy" testimony and have evidence planted. Nor were they aware that he had arranged for bogus information to make its way into the hands of the private investigator, Joe Collins.

Collins drove to the Mini Warehouse in Raytown, Missouri, and introduced himself to Ruth Porter, the manager on duty. Collins was nicely dressed, wore a jacket and tie, spoke softly and smiled a lot. He was a broad-shouldered man in his mid-thirties and looked the part of a TV private eye. He initially told Ruth he was a private investigator looking into some personal dealings of a client and showed Ruth a list of names. He wanted to know if anyone on the list had leased a storage locker during the period from June to July of 1989. Collins' smooth approach and generally pleasant appearance helped convince Ruth Porter that the request was on the up and up.

Ruth Porter didn't consider the request unreasonable. She could not give out information about current warehouse clients, but the dates in question were more than a year before, and it was unlikely that anyone on Collins' list would still be clients now. It was not an unusual occurrence having police or private investigators at the facility asking questions about previous clients.

Porter checked her Rolodex file. She was surprised when one of the names on the investigator's list appeared. She told Collins that yes, a Christine Rusch had leased locker number 7-21 on June 26, 1989. She added that the lease was not renewed, and a refund check for her deposit had been sent out months before. When asked whether she could recall any of the details of the rental, Porter explained that the contract agreement was made before she began working at the Mini Warehouse. He would need to talk to someone at the Shryock Office who managed the facility. Or, he could talk to the previous manager, Jackie Faught, who was now working for another storage facility called AA Northland Store All, in Northmore, Missouri.

Joe Collins did not ask many more questions. He thanked Ruth Porter, took a brief look around the facility and left. Within two days of Collins' visit, events would take place at the Mini Warehouse that would work against Grissom rather than for him.

Collins' intent was to avoid management and deal directly with anyone who may have been a witness to a transaction involving Christine Rusch or Theresa Brown. That same afternoon he located Jackie Faught at the AA Northland facility. She and her husband John were live-in managers, and both were behind the counter when Collins approached. Unlike the previous encounter with Ruth Porter, Collins was less than straight forward with the Faughts. He did not identify himself as a private investigator.

Collins laid a folder on the counter and informed a curious Jackie Faught that he was investigating the theft of a large quantity of TVs and VCRs. He pointed out that his investigation encompassed the Mini Warehouse in Raytown, and he wanted to talk to Jackie because she had worked there. Collins felt he had successfully convinced Jackie that he was a cop without having to break the law and introduce himself as such. He did not, however, want to deal with John Faught, who Jackie had mentioned also worked at the Mini Warehouse. He knew Jackie had been the counter manager at Raytown, and he needed to determine what she remembered about the Christine Rusch rental in June of 1989.

Continuing his ruse, Collins opened the folder. Intentionally displayed on top were two large photographs of Christine Rusch and Theresa Brown. The investigator set the pictures aside but left them clearly visible to Faught and pretended to shuffle through his papers. He took his time, allowing the photos to register with Jackie Faught.

Conveniently, Jackie Faught took his bait. "Aren't those two of the girls that were missing last year from Overland Park?" Jackie asked, curious about why the photos would be displayed in the folder.

"Excuse me," Collins replied, feigning ignorance. "What are you talking about?"

"The girls!" said Jackie. "The girls in those pictures. Those are the girls who've been missing since last year."

"Oh, I think you're mistaken," replied Collins. "These women are involved in another matter. They couldn't be who you say they are."

"Oh come on," replied Jackie, certain that she was correct. It had been awhile since she had seen any news accounts of the girls, but she remembered them.

It was what Collins was counting on. All he needed then was for Jackie Faught to detail what she remembered about them at the warehouse.

"John, come over here and look at these girls' pictures. Tell me these weren't plastered all over the TV and newspapers for several months last year," Jackie said emphatically.

"They can't be," insisted Collins. "To my knowledge, these pictures have never been shown in public before."

"Those are the girls who were reported missing," said John Faught, sure of himself.

"There's no doubt in my mind either," added his wife.

"All I know is that I'm investigating some robberies, and these women here are figured into it somehow, but we haven't established just how yet," answered Collins.

"No way!" said Jackie, unable to believe that after this much time and hearing nothing new about the missing women, they were somehow still alive and involved in an investigation. "That's impossible! They've been missing over a year! Everyone who knows anything about the case believes they're dead. The guy who's supposed to be involved has been locked up for over a year. I can't believe you don't know that!" Faught insisted, still believing Collins was a cop.

"Well, I'm just doing my job, but you've really got me interested," replied Collins. "How could something like that have been in the papers and I missed it?"

Collins had what he came for. He had coaxed Faught into talking about the missing girls and what she knew about them. She eventually admitted that the man responsible for the girls' disappearance had rented a locker from them at the Raytown facility, but it had been several months before the disappearances. When Faught could not place Grissom at the storage facility with either of the two women whose photos were displayed on the counter top, Collins tried yet another tactic. He asked Faught a series of questions about Eric Pour. The inference was slight, but its intent was to link Eric Pour and the missing girls together in a robbery scenario.

Faught told Collins that Eric Pour had rented several lockers from her at Raytown. He had a used-car lot nearby, and occasionally leased one or more of the larger lockers to store cars. Collins subtly asked if locker 7-21 might have been one of the lockers leased by Pour. Faught could not remember which lockers Eric Pour may have rented. John Faught volunteered that, to his recollection, 7-21 was one of the larger, two-door, drive-in lockers.

Collins had learned from Ruth Porter that Christine Rusch's name appeared on the rental agreement for locker 7-21 in June of 1989. He had also learned from Grissom that Eric Pour leased lockers at the Mini Warehouse in Raytown and that locker 7-21 was somehow involved. Collins left convinced that Jackie Faught could not place Grissom at the warehouse beyond the February 1989 date she remembered. He left also failing to tell Jackie or John Faught that he had tape-recorded their conversation.

During the afternoon of October 5, 1990, an anonymous phone call was made to Prosecutor Paul Morrison's office. The caller said that Grissom's defense team had discovered the origin of the blue paint previously found on the side of Christine's Dodge Colt. The caller said that Private Investigator Collins had stumbled on to the source of the paint while checking leads in the Raytown area. The call was apparently designed to get investigators on the Grissom case to the warehouse. From there, they would learn what the defense team already knew.

The call sent detectives scrambling to cover this newest lead just ten days before the beginning of Grissom's trial. By noon the next day, Batt and Hinkle had interviewed Ruth Porter at the Mini Warehouse and had collected paint samples from the posts at the entry and exit areas to the lockers. From there they called Jackie Faught at AA Northland to tell her they were on their way to talk to her.

They arrived, fully prepared to get to the bottom of whatever was exciting the defense team about the Mini Warehouse. The first order of business was to determine who had been there talking to Jackie Faught and what they had learned. When the detectives learned about Joe Collins' approach and the tactics used to glean information from Jackie Faught, they were upset. They were actually disappointed that he had not openly said he was a cop, which would have given them the opportunity to nail him to the cross. As it was, all they had was a case of low-grade subterfuge, and however unethical, it was not criminal.

Upon learning that Joe Collins was not a cop but a private investigator working for Grissom's defense team, Jackie Faught got mad. The short, 200-pound woman paced back and forth behind the counter trying to find some sort of release for her fire. She grew angrier by the minute at the thought of Collins' pretense that the murdered women were still alive. "How could anyone be so tactless and cold as to even suggest such a possibility for the sake of helping a merciless savage like Grissom?" she asked.

Jackie Faught gained her composure as the detectives resumed their questioning. She related the things she had told Collins the previous day. When she said that she had told the PI that Grissom had rented a locker at the Mini Warehouse in February of 1989, the detectives were taken slightly by surprise. When they questioned Jackie about how she had remembered that it was Grissom, she startled them even more.

"You guys should know this! I called the Tips Hot Line back in July of 1989, and told them I recognized one of the aliases Grissom was using," she explained. "He used one to rent a locker from us at the Mini Warehouse, and I remembered the name."

"Did anyone respond to the tip?" Hinkle asked, caught completely off guard by Faught's revelation.

"No, not at first," answered Faught. "But eventually they did." Then Faught dropped another bombshell. "You see, I got a call from one of the missing girl's mother. I don't remember which one. She told me she had been going through the telephone book and calling all the storage facilities in the metropolitan area. She said she knew Grissom had used a storage locker during the time her daughter was taken, and she was checking around to see if he had leased any others. Well, I told her he had rented one from us the previous February, and then I told her I had called the Tips Hot

Line but nobody responded. She got real mad and said, 'They will, you just sit tight. Somebody will be out there real soon!' Sure enough, the next day two detectives came out, asked me a few questions about Grissom and the locker I rented him. They were going to go and have a look around the locker, and then they left."

The two detectives searched their own minds for answers to this new wrinkle. They knew they'd be going back through volumes of paperwork to see if a report had been filed on the lead she had just described. "When did you call the hot line?" Batt asked.

"It was around July fourth of that year," said Jackie. "My husband and I had taken my mother to Colorado to celebrate her retirement. When we came back, I heard on the news that the police were hunting for Grissom. When the news mentioned Grissom's aliases, I recognized one of them as the name he used to rent the locker. It was then that I called the hot line."

Batt and Hinkle each knew what the other was thinking. That July 4 was when the metro squad would have been at only half-force, covering the entire metro area. It was a critical phase in the investigation when half the squad had scattered to other parts of the country to cover leads. If there was ever a time for a lead to be missed or hurriedly covered, it would have been during that period.

Faught explained that she remembered the incident vividly because the man calling himself Rikki Yoon Cho got angry with her when he came into her office to collect his refund check on the locker. When Jackie wrote out the check she misspelled Yoon, replacing the "Y" with an "H". Grissom had made a big issue of the error.

Next, the detectives showed Faught a series of photographs of both Christine Rusch and Theresa Brown.

She studied the photos, commenting that many of them looked like the ones she had seen on TV and in the newspapers. It wasn't until Jackie had gone through most of the photographs that she focused on one of Theresa Brown. The shot showed Theresa standing among a group of friends in a bar-restaurant. In the photo, Theresa's hair was straight and somewhat unkempt, her makeup was not as neatly applied as it was in the other photos.

"Wait a minute," said Faught. "The girl in this picture looks like a girl who came in and rented a storage locker at the Mini Warehouse. And from what I'm remembering, Richard Grissom was with her. It may be that the last time he rented from us wasn't in February last year, but maybe right around the time the girls disappeared," said Faught, shaken by the realization that the killer and one of his victims had stood across the counter from her.

"How do you know, Jackie?" asked Hinkle. "How can you be sure?"

"Well, that one photograph helped me recall the transaction for the locker. The whole procedure for completing the agreement was just different. It was real strange. It was one of those episodes that stays with you for a while," Faught answered.

"Which photo was it? Was it this one here?" Hinkle asked, picking up the photo of Theresa Brown.

"Yeah, that one in particular. In that picture, she doesn't look like she does in all the others. She looks like the girl who came in to the office to rent the unit. When she came in, she looked the worse for wear. Looked like she had fallen on hard times. I remember she was with this guy, but she was the one filling out the rental agreement. But it was strange because she kept looking over at him for help with some of the questions on the form, like place of employment or address. She seemed nervous about the whole thing, like she didn't want to screw things up or make him mad, you know. I helped her a little bit, but he still kept giving her the answers to a lot of the questions." Faught studied the photo again. "What sticks out in this picture is the stringy hair and the unkempt look with no makeup. It's exactly how the girl looked when she came in that day."

"Was there anything else about her that you recall, other than the hair and the makeup?" asked Batt, trying to sort through the troubling details.

"She was a tallish girl and thin like she looks in this picture. Of course, everyone is taller than me," Jackie added, laughing. "She had kind of a rough-looking complexion and looked like she hadn't slept very well. What really made me think that she was down on her luck was when I told her that the rental was for a minimum of a month, and a deposit was required. She looked over at the guy and then told me she only needed the locker for a few days."

"So they left a deposit and took one of the units?" Batt asked.

"Oh yeah! I can't let a unit go without a deposit. They took it, she filled out the form and paid the fee."

"What kind of locker did they get?" asked Hinkle. "They're not all the same size, right?"

"Well, if I remember right, the deposit was for twenty dollars, which would have covered one of the bigger lockers. In fact, I think she insisted that they needed one of the big units. Those have double doors and they're big enough for a car to be kept inside."

"You're sure it was this girl and not the other one?" asked Hinkle, pointing to the picture of Theresa Brown. "There's not a chance you could be confusing them? "

"No way!" said Jackie, certain that she was not confused. "Don't get me wrong. This whole thing is not exactly crystal clear in my mind, but from what I'm recalling about the woman who came in to rent the unit, it looks just like the one in this picture."

"The guy with her that day, was it Richard Grissom?" Hinkle asked, point blank.

"I want to say that it was, but you'd better give me some time to think that one over," said Faught, nervously. "In my mind it's him, but it doesn't look like the same guy in all the pictures. I had recognized him when I called the Tips Hot Line. When he rented from us in February as Yoon Cho or Rikki Yoon Cho, whatever, he was smooth and well-dressed and his hair was neat—oiled and curly. But the guy who was with this girl, looked in about the same shape as she did. He was dirty and his hair was matted down, and he looked exhausted. I want to tell you it was him, but I need to think about it."

Batt looked at Hinkle while placing the photos back in his folder. They understood that even though Christine's name appeared on the rental contract, it had been Theresa with Grissom during the rental of the locker. They realized that Grissom probably had her sign Christine's name to confuse investigators covering the trail. They also realized that they had much more than they ever thought they'd have from this lead.

Turning from the women's photos, Batt pulled out a series of color photos of Christine's Dodge Colt and laid them on the counter. He asked Faught if she recognized the car.

"Not really," replied Faught. "The car doesn't ring any bells, but I can probably tell you where that scratch running along the side of the car came from." Faught told them about the posts which lined the entry and exit gates of the Mini Warehouse lockers and about the numerous drivers who scraped their cars while coming through the gate and inserting their cards in the key pads. According to Faught, all the scratches were about the same length and were blue.

The detectives exchanged glances. Faught's corroborating information was music to their ears. For more than a year the two detectives had stopped at almost every post, pole, gate or wall they'd passed that had been painted blue. They had scraped untold samples of blue paint and had sent them off to the lab for comparison against the paint scrapings from the Dodge Colt. Even the wives of Batt and Hinkle had been known to comment to others in their social circles that it had become quite routine for their husbands to stop and retrieve samples of blue paint during trips around town. Whether going out to a restaurant or to a store, if either man saw a blue post or pole or any blue object near a roadway, he stopped to investigate.

Before Batt and Hinkle departed, Faught gave them another bit of valuable information. She explained the key-pad entry system used at the Raytown facility. The gate had a computerized box with a slot for a coded access card to be inserted to gain entry. Everyone leasing a locker was given a card that had seven numbers—three assigned by the facility, the last four being the renter's own private code. The date and times of anyone entering or exiting was automatically recorded. In other words, if Richard Grissom had leased the locker in June of 1989, a record of every entry and exit he made would be on file. An irrefutable timetable for his activities at the warehouse could be established.

The detectives next paid a visit to Shryock Realty & Management in Overland Park, where they retrieved the rental contract of June 26, 1989, for Mini Warehouse locker 7-21. They also received printouts of all the entry and exit activity for the locker during the contract period. Now, however, the detectives were beginning to unravel the scenario which Grissom's defense team had not been able to piece together. Grissom's scheme to show that one of the missing women had rented a storage locker used by Eric Pour was falling apart at the seams.

Early on October 8, Batt and Hinkle returned once again to talk to Jackie Faught. Having had time to rethink the events of June, 1989, she was much more confident that the man there had been Richard Grissom. Faught told the detectives that Grissom could look like two completely different people, depending on whether his hair was long or short. "The length of his hair even seemed to alter the color of his skin," Faught had said adding, "when he wore it longer, his skin looked darker, and he's not that dark."

In less than forty-eight hours, Batt and Hinkle had successfully shut the door on any final attempts by Richard Grissom to create an alibi defense or cast the blame for his crimes on someone else. They had learned that Joe Collins had planted the seed linking Eric Pour to the missing women and to the lockers, based on the bogus information Grissom had provided. They knew Grissom had dealt a serious blow to his own defense.

The investigative teams and members of the prosecution team were ready for trial and were overjoyed by the news of the early October findings. The latest discovery enhanced their case immeasurably and gave everyone a much-needed lift as they made final preparations during the week before the trial. Before finding the Raytown locker, many questions remained about Grissom's location and his activities immediately after the Rusch-Brown abductions. The warehouse not only brought to light the timetable, it explained why he had spent so much time on the Missouri side of the city.

Pandora's box had been opened, and the prosecution was prepared to take full advantage of it. Last-minute reports and evidence pertaining to the Raytown locker were placed among the volumes already amassed in a conference room utilized by the prosecution. Morrison and his assistant, Deb Vermillion, gathered in the conference room for a final meeting with the lead detectives the weekend before the trial. Detectives Batt, Hinkle, Landwehr and Carney, covering leads until the end, had reserved weekends for strategy sessions with prosecutors. The seven-day work week had become routine since the task force had disbanded months before.

The detectives took seats around the conference table and on the floor. They were literally surrounded by volumes of police reports, witness statements, photographs and evidence envelopes. The materials were stacked so high around the room that maneuvering about was not accomplished easily. As usual, an abundance of hot coffee and doughnuts were available.

The detectives and prosecutors had assembled a solid case against Grissom, and each of them knew it. Nevertheless, it was important to discuss the final witness list and the order of appearance. The number under consideration was staggering. Between 250 and 300 people were on the "endorsed" witness list. Reducing that to a manageable number had been no small task.

Each witness had been interviewed and evaluated for testimony and impact. Morrison pointed out, for example, that Jessie Barnes could provide damaging testimony against Grissom, but his jury appeal was suspect. He would be viewed as a career criminal out to cut a better deal for himself. Likewise, Thibodo could be valuable, but the defense would surely review his statements to police which contained inconsistencies and often, outright withholding of information.

The group also discussed the chronology of the upcoming trial. Hinkle and Carney went over details of the "time-line" chart they had painstakingly prepared over the previous weeks. The final product was a four-by-sixteen-foot bulletin board with sheets of foam core serving as a backdrop for photographs. Stencils and bold lettering outlined key events as they occurred throughout the case. The photos included those of the three missing women, vehicles involved in the case, storage lockers, apartment buildings and key geographical areas. The bold lettering revealed the names of people, places and dates. The "time-line" provided a visual chronology for the jury to follow as the prosecution unfolded its case. Everyone in the room understood its value.

As the final meeting wound down, team members found themselves reminiscing. It began when a comment was made about Landwehr's incredible ability to recall exactly where, amidst the mountain of paper, a particular file or witness statement could be found. On several occasions during previous meetings, when someone had needed to review a report, Landwehr could locate the right stack of material and recite the volume and page on which the material could be found. The ocean of paper that intimidated most members of the group was to Landwehr, a private library he accessed at will. Whenever he performed, others in the room shook their heads in amazement.

Team members also told stories about the people they had met and the varied and unique places they had visited during the case. Hinkle and Batt remembered stories about the many untimely searches conducted in the strangest places to find a match for the blue paint on the Colt. The detectives joked about the different kinds of food they had eaten and the unique, out-of-the-way places where they dined. They also remembered the lengthy stretches of time occurring between meals when they did not stop for lunch or dinner.

The attempts to keep the conversation lighthearted was purposeful. Each was in touch with a nagging trepidation. Did they have enough to convict Richard Grissom? Could they present the case as they had hoped? Why hadn't Grissom confessed? He had been so close on more than one occasion. Was it possible that he could go free? Was it enough to have the Terri Maness case as a backup? After so much time, so much work and so many sleepless nights, why did so many questions remain? Perhaps it was because the case was circumstantial. Their case would move forward with no victims' bodies and no murder weapons. Only the next two weeks of the Grissom trial would tell whether or not their case was strong enough for a conviction.

27

Finally, on October 19, 1990, after fifteen months of legal arguments and maneuverings, the trial of Richard Grissom was set to begin. Judge William Gray, a distinguished, fair-minded arbiter with several years of experience on the bench in Johnson County, was to preside.

On opening day, the courtroom was jammed to capacity. A number of seats had been reserved, limiting seating for the general public. Seats were reserved for the victims' family members who were not scheduled to testify, including the Maness family who had traveled from Wichita.

Security throughout the courthouse was tight, with exceptional precautions taken to ensure the defendant's safety. Numerous threats on Grissom's life had been called in. In addition to a tight escort on Grissom, metal detectors had been installed, and hand searches were conducted when warranted.

Grissom was led into the courtroom through a side entrance and seated at the defense table. He wore a dark blazer, a white dress shirt and colorful necktie.

His hair had been neatly trimmed, and his beard had been shaved. He appeared calm, sitting motionless and silent, staring straight ahead. When Judge Gray opened by reading the charges against him, Grissom did not move. He kept his eyes lowered and focused on a notepad on the table in front of him.

Grissom appeared to start taking notes as Paul Morrison began his opening statement to the jury. However, he was doodling.

Prosecutor Morrison understood the courtroom. He was a career prosecutor who worked his way up through the assistant ranks to become chief. Confident and energetic, Morrison faced the jury. The experienced prosecutor stood seemingly taller than his lean, six-feet-two-inch frame as he outlined the state's case against Grissom. Wearing a conservative, dark suit with button-down white shirt and subdued tie, he paced in front of the jury box, never losing eye contact with the jurors.

It took Morrison less than twenty minutes to give the jury the road map they would need to follow his case. He informed them that in the course of the trial they would hear in excess of one hundred witnesses and would be asked to review many pieces of evidence. He carefully outlined his case in the chronological order in which he would present it, informing the jury that they would have the opportunity to follow a "time-line" carefully positioned in the front of the court room. The large board was completely covered. Morrison's intent was to reveal a piece at a time. Each section represented a portion of the case as it unfolded.

Morrison also had purposely ordered that an extra chair be placed next to the prosecution's table. The chair would remain empty throughout the trial. It was entirely symbolic. It represented the three missing women whose lives had been cut short by Richard Grissom.

Richard Grissom was represented by two highly qualified attorneys who had been assigned his case by the Johnson County Court. Tom Erker and Kevin Moriarty were not strangers to either side of the courtroom. Following law school, both worked for the Johnson County Prosecutor's Office. Tom Erker's tenure with the state lasted just over two years before he made the move to private practice. He was a New England native who moved to Kansas to pursue a career in law. At the time of the Grissom trial, Erker was around forty years old. He was five-feet-ten-inches tall with a large, muscular frame, and a receding hair line. Erker was known as a solid, hard-nosed attorney who knew his way around the courtroom.

Kevin Moriarty shared a law practice with Erker in Overland Park. He stood six feet tall, weighed 170 pounds and kept himself in shape. He wore his thick, brown hair conservatively and sported a mustache. Prior to leaving the prosecutor's office, Moriarty's specialty was the prosecution of sex crimes, making him a worthy choice to structure a defense for Richard Grissom.

With the selection of Erker and Moriarty, Judge Gray knew the issue of adequate defense for the defendant would not be raised before or after the trial.

Following opening arguments by Morrison, the defense team exercised its option not to present its arguments until after the prosecution rested its case. The move allowed Morrison to begin calling witnesses on behalf of the state. Morrison knew the defense team would argue that the women were, after all, "only missing." No bodies had been recovered, and the state could not say positively that they had been killed. Who really knew that they had not taken off on their own? Morrison needed to counter that argument repeatedly throughout the trial.

He began his prosecution with the case of the first missing victim, Joan Butler. From Celeste Becker, one of the last of Joan's friends to see her alive, to Joan's employers and family members, witnesses were called to lay a foundation in the state's case—that Joan Butler loved her family and friends and would not have disappeared on her own.

Ralph and Jada Butler did their part convincingly. Their descriptions of Joan as a responsible, dependable daughter were not at all exaggerated. A crushed, but determined Ralph Butler described his daughter's last phone call to him. His voice breaking, he told the jury of Joan's disturbing call to him just after her car accident. He paused and gathered himself before telling jurors that Joan had said, "I guess my luck is running out, Dad." Ralph Butler also described the last time he saw his daughter. He had traveled from Wichita and met Joan in a restaurant for a glass of wine. Joan sat across the table, talking about her job and her life. She smiled all evening, Ralph Butler said. It was just two weeks before she disappeared. She was very happy.

Prosecutor Morrison continued to piece together the Joan Butler case, calling witnesses to verify her bank accounts and the simultaneous transactions that had depleted them. He also called Officer Brian Edwards, a strong witness, who appeared in uniform and described his confrontation with Grissom at the Trailridge complex in Lawrence. He was the first witness to point a finger toward the defense table and positively identify Richard Grissom as the man who had held the keys to the Corsica and who ran from him in Lawrence.

Morrison continued with a string of witnesses linking Grissom to the Joan Butler murder. From Carla Dippel and Dan Carney to Cathy Arenal and Ken Landwehr, the prosecution tied Grissom to the jewelry found inside Butler's apartment, placing him at the crime scene. Cathy Arenal provided additional damaging testimony by explaining how Grissom had left Lawrence for Kansas City in the early morning hours of June 18, and had returned to Lawrence on Monday driving Joan's Corsica. "He was really exhausted, he even said he was," Arenal told the jury, adding, "He told me he hadn't had any sleep since I had seen him that last Saturday at Pizazz."

Morrison was unable to present a clear-cut re-creation of the actual crimes. Just how Richard Grissom committed his crimes remained speculation, but what Morrison had was the next best thing. Through the testimony of three witnesses to attempted abductions by Grissom, the prosecution demonstrated the cold brutality and boldness of the defendant.

The first and strongest of the three witnesses was Michelle Katf, who had narrowly escaped from Grissom. Under careful questioning by Morrison, she zeroed in on the man who assaulted her at gunpoint and dragged her from her apartment. As she related her account, she glared at Grissom who kept his eyes lowered, unable to meet her incisive stare. It was Michelle who first spoke about the use of a master key by Grissom to gain entry into her apartment. She told an attentive jury that it was the only possible way he could have gotten in without breaking and entering. Her testimony set the stage for other witnesses, who testified a master key to Apple Creek was found on Grissom's key ring.

Those witnesses, Bill Mayo and Stephanie Foster, testified about their experiences at the Stonybrook complex the night of June 27. Mayo's revealing account of a crouching Grissom hiding under the darkened stairwell outside Foster's apartment gave the jury another look at the defendant's tactics. Mayo's testimony about finding Grissom's Toyota opened the door for additional witnesses who would expose the damaging evidence found inside by forensic search teams.

Stephanie Foster also pointed a finger at Richard Grissom. She verified that Grissom had performed contract work at Stonybrook and had possession of a master key, which would have allowed him access to her office and apartment. The jurors stirred as Foster spoke of her fear upon learning that Grissom had been just outside her apartment waiting for her. "I knew right away that he had keys to my apartment. I knew why he was there. I couldn't spend another night in my apartment until he was captured."

Day four of the trial produced incriminating testimony on the blood found in the trunk of the Corsica. Officer Gary Dirks, a forensic serologist with the Johnson County Crime Lab, outlined the initial presumptive tests he performed to prove the material from the trunk was indeed blood. He also explained the follow-up immunological, or Precipitin test, which proved the blood was of human origin. He told how genetic marker tests were conducted to determine blood type for an individual. In the Joan Butler case, he obtained type B blood.

Dirks told the jury when and why he sent the blood samples to Cellmark Labs in Germantown, Maryland, for DNA analysis. "The reason Cellmark was selected," said Dirks, "was because of their background and expertise in the type of analysis needed, a special paternity or reverse-type paternity testing." Dirks knew that

Cellmark could analyze the blood samples for various Restriction Fragment Link Polymorphisms (RFLP). Dirks testified that he also submitted the duct tape recovered from the roof of the Metcalf storage facility to determine if Cellmark could obtain RFLP analysis from the hairs attached to the inside of the sample.

Before disclosing the results of the DNA testing in the Butler case, Morrison wanted the jury to know DNA typing was performed. He called Robin Cotton, Director of Research and Development at Cellmark. According to Cotton, the primary agenda of Cellmark Labs was to use DNA typing to answer either of two questions—those of paternity identification or those identifying individuals. Cotton explained that, "It is through the DNA that the genetic information from two parents is passed onto their children. The chromosomes which include DNA, reside in the nucleus of all cells." She added that even the cells that make up a hair follicle have DNA. She was sure to point out that DNA is unique to each individual with the exception of identical twins who share the same genetic markers. Cotton also confirmed it could determine if individuals were related.

Finally, David Walsh, the technician at Cellmark who completed the DNA typing of the blood samples, testified. "The samples revealed a complete match to the bands of both Butler parents. There is simply no other explanation than that being the blood of the biological child of those two parents."

Robin Cotton returned to the stand to support those conclusions, stating, "There is no question that a match was found between the blood sample provided and the blood issued from the parents. The sample provided had to have been the offspring of the Butler parents."

The afternoon of day four brought the beginning of testimony relating to the abduction-murders of Christine Rusch and Theresa Brown. The first two witnesses on the stand were the last two friends to have seen Christine and Theresa alive.

Deputy Mike Raunig, Theresa Brown's boyfriend, testified that Theresa had been with him during the night before she disappeared, that she left his apartment around 6:00 A.M. to go home and get ready for work. Raunig identified the KU T-shirt and baggy surgical scrubs Theresa had worn. They were found on the floor of her bedroom, indicating she had made it home.

James Grooms, a friend of Christine's, told the jury about Christine's activities the night before she disappeared. Grooms had met with Christine and a group of their friends at the Backstage Bar in Overland Park. He testified that he last saw Christine when she left the bar around 12:30 A.M. No one knew whether Christine made it all the way home.

Morrison next called a succession of Rusch and Brown family members. He structured his questions with the intent of painting a reasonable picture of the missing women's habits, personalities and their loyalty to family and friends. Each family member's testimony emphasized how unlikely it would have been for either Christine or Theresa to have taken off on her own.

In addition to telling the jury about her close and loving relationship with her daughter, Judy Rusch positively identified the three rings found in Grissom's Toyota as belonging to Christine. She spoke about each ring, where each came from and how long Christine had been wearing them. She also identified the sheepskin seat covers from Christine's Colt as those given to her daughter the previous Christmas. She verified that her daughter's credit card had been found on the floor of Grissom's car.

On day six of the trial, Deputies Chapin and Fahy returned to the witness stand. Each had previously testified about his role during the processing and searching of the apartments, cars, personal items and storage lockers. According to Chapin, the blue paint samples taken from the posts at the Mini Warehouse and the samples from Christine's Colt matched. Chapin said, "That in all of the tests that I performed, the two samples were entirely consistent."

Now they talked specifically about the items found in Grissom's Toyota. With the use of photographs taken during processing, the deputies showed the jury the hundreds of items recovered, including the victims' credit cards, numerous keys including several masters to apartment complexes and two that fit locks to Joan Butler's apartment and the Rusch family home. Also shown were: a pellet pistol and cartridges, black leather gloves, a nylon rope with a smear of blood on the tip and a silver knife with an eight-inch blade. When the jury later saw similar items that were part of Grissom's "kill kit," seized from the stolen Grand Am in Dallas, they were able to piece together a pretty clear picture of Richard Grissom's mode of operation.

Morrison next brought several witnesses forward who could testify that it was indeed Christine Rusch who, battered and under duress, withdrew money from her roommate's account at the Boatman's Bank in Raytown. Morrison displayed a photo of the victim wearing sunglasses over bruised eyes and a bandage over part of her forehead. The photo was taken around 10:00 P.M. on June 26 by a bank security camera.

Postal Inspector Richard Meuten took the stand to verify that Richard Grissom, using the name Rikki Cho, rented a post office box on February 6, 1989. Linking

Grissom to that box was significant since he forced Theresa Brown to use the box number when filling out the application for the storage locker at the Mini Warehouse in Raytown.

Meuten's testimony was supported by Jackie Faught, who testified that she handled the rental of the locker on June 26, 1989. She identified a photograph of Theresa Brown and pointed out Grissom in the courtroom. Faught told the jury the circumstances behind the rental of the Raytown locker. "The address was given to the woman by the man with her." she said. "He told her to write down P.O. Box 300761, in Kansas City, Missouri, for her address." Faught had the jury's undivided attention as she related how Theresa Brown looked and acted that morning in Raytown. "She seemed a little distressed, like she needed help. She looked like she had kind of fallen on hard times."

Responding to Morrison's questions about the request for a particular locker Faught indicated, "She said she really didn't want to rent the unit for a whole month, and I felt like maybe she was hurting for money. She got instructions from the guy and said she wanted a ten by thirty unit, the drive-in kind. I suggested that maybe she could use a smaller locker and she said no, she needed the biggest one I had." Faught added that when the woman whom she identified as Theresa Brown leased the locker, she signed for it using the name Christine Rusch.

It was through the testimony and records of individuals associated with the management firm handling the Mini Warehouse that Grissom's activity was revealed for locker 7-21 during the four-day period beginning June 26. All activity for the locker while in the Rusch name ceased on June 29. A printout of the computer records provided a record of Grissom's entering and leaving the facility. His entry began a few hours after the abduction of Christine Rusch and Theresa Brown and ended in the pre-dawn hours a little more than a day after he had stolen the Grand Am. The picture drawn for the jury suggested that one or both of the victims were probably kept in the car inside the locker for most of the day and part of the night on the June 26 and 27.

Deputy Rick Fahy once again took the stand to reveal the conclusions reached from examination of checks written by Christine Rusch. The courtroom was set up with enlargements of checks and other documents mounted on tripods. Enlargements of the signatures allowed Fahy, pointer in hand, to demonstrate his findings to the jury. Fahy began by telling the court that when comparing and analyzing handwriting, he needed both "known" and "comparison" samples. "There are a certain number of points of comparison that must be made before one can say he has a match," Fahy indicated.

Demonstrating with enlargements of the four checks written in succession during the morning of June 26, Fahy showed the jury that the same person had written all four checks. Using the "known" samples for comparison, he was able to say that the person was Christine Rusch. "I was not able to find any distinct dissimilarity in the writing," Fahy said.

Fahy testified that there also was a detectable variation in the writing that grew more extreme with each check. "It's definitely the same writer, but the writing seems to break up more, seems to be more choppy and lose its naturalness. There is a slight change between each check, but if you go straight from the first to the fourth, you can see a radical change," the deputy indicated. With the jurors keying on every word, Fahy talked about some of the factors that might have influenced such disparity. "Writing taking place in a moving vehicle might cause it, so might one's writing position or the surface they're writing on or the writing instrument," he noted. Fahy also mentioned contributing factors such as fatigue, lack of eyeglasses, duress, injury and breakdown as factors that might have influenced the changes in Christine's writing.

Before he was finished, Deputy Fahy verified that the signatures on various rental contracts, key identification tags and the post office box agreement were definitely those of Richard Grissom. He also verified that the signature of Christine Rusch on the rental contract at the Mini Warehouse was definitely not written by Christine Rusch.

Specialist Bill Chapin followed his partner to the stand for a final time to testify about how he and his lab associates processed the items of bedding from the Rusch-Brown apartment. He demonstrated a technique called "particle picking." It involved taking an article and going over it a section at a time and "picking" items of possible evidentiary value using tweezers. They also looked for biological fluid stains from semen, blood or urine. Chapin was setting the stage for follow-up testimony on evidence found in the bedding.

Morrison's next witness, Officer Gary Dirks, told the jury about findings needed to declare hair samples a "match." He explained that testing could reveal not only whether a sample was of human origin, but what part of the body it came from and its racial origin. He emphasized that there were over twenty specific characteristics the lab looked for when attempting to "match" a piece of evidence to "known" hair samples. "Not one of the characteristics can fall outside the range of the known sample. If they fall outside, it's an elimination," Dirks said.

Dirks pointed out that Grissom's samples "displayed primarily Negroid characteristics, although some characteristics were suggestive of Mongoloid, Asian and Indian, origin as well." There was enough difference, however, to distinguish Grissom's hair from that of purely Negroid origin, Dirks said.

Dirks testified that hairs of the Negroid-Mongoloid "mix" were recovered from Christine's sheepskin seat covers, the bedding of both Theresa Brown and Christine Rusch and from Grissom's apartment. Two of the hairs, determined to be pubic hairs, found in the women's bedding were positively matched to Grissom.

The case against Grissom continued to build as Dirks revealed the results of tests performed on hairs recovered from the shag carpet at the Metcalf Storage locker and the duct tape recovered from the locker roof. Eight hairs from the carpet were compared with "known" samples taken from hairbrushes of the three victims. Four of the hairs were found to be indistinguishable from those of Christine Rusch. No hair from the carpet could be matched to Theresa Brown or Joan Butler.

As for the hair samples attached to the duct tape, Dirks explained that the hairs stuck to the tape had apparently been pulled from the victim's head when the tape was forcibly removed. More than one hundred hairs had been found on the tape. Many of the hairs were damaged, but others remained suitable for comparison. The hairs, Dirks announced, were consistent with the "known environment" for Christine Rusch, but not for Theresa Brown or Joan Butler.

The day's last witness limped to the front of the courtroom to take the stand. Marcelais Thibodo was, if anything, a precarious witness for the state. His testimony could be damaging to the defendant, but his credibility was suspect. The risk, however, was felt by the prosecution to be worth it.

After identifying Richard Grissom, Thibodo revealed that he knew of at least three aliases used by the defendant. He mentioned the names, Yoon Cho, Rikki Cho and Randy Rodriguez. He pointed out that Grissom owned and drove the brown Toyota and explained how he had helped Grissom get the car. He talked about the Apex painting contracts and how Grissom conducted business. Thibodo answered questions about Grissom's possession of the Corsica and how, during the week after Father's Day, Grissom worked odd hours and frequently alone. When asked by Morrison about the time he drove the Corsica, Thibodo told the jury, "He eventually told me I could drive it, but to be careful with it and don't go looking through the trunk or in the glove box, and to just take my time and come right back."

Thibodo told the attentive jury about the time Grissom led him into the missing women's Trafalgar Square apartment using a master key and pretending to look for water damage. He revealed how Grissom eventually started going through the women's personal items and then held up a pair of panties to Thibodo saying, "Yo, man, check these out!"

At the defense table, Grissom lowered his head and shook it from side to side as Thibodo testified.

Thibodo also told the court about Grissom's flight from Lawrence the night of June 25, and how he bragged about escaping from the police. He retraced their steps, spelling out the hurried packing of Grissom's belongings, the meeting at the Motel 6 lot and Grissom's last words to him.

Eventually, Thibodo talked about finding the duct tape in the storage locker and throwing it up on the roof. "I thought it was a plant." Thibodo said, adding,

"I was concerned about Richard, and I wasn't sure about what was going on with him." Thibodo admitted that initially, under questioning by police, he had not told them everything. When asked why, he replied, "You know, I just wasn't sure about what was going on. I thought they might try and clear the case with me." When asked by Morrison if he lied to the police or purposely withheld information, Thibodo responded, "I cannot remember."

One of the last witnesses to take the stand against Grissom was the FBI agent who arrested him in Dallas. Agent Mike Napier recalled the circumstances of the arrest and the process leading up to Grissom's interrogation. Napier led the jury through the interrogation, emphasizing most of the incriminating statements made by the defendant. The agent explained how, at first, Grissom objected to any insinuation that he could have been involved in the women's deaths, but later made statements about their not being dead and then saying, "Well, they're probably dead by now."

The agent recounted other damaging statements made by Grissom, such as, "You'll dig them up," and "You won't find any bodies in Missouri, only Kansas," emphasizing Grissom's awareness that Kansas did not have the death penalty. Napier held the jury's attention when he told how Grissom frequently rubbed his eyes and looked away when shown photographs of the missing women, as if trying to block the images from his mind. Napier revealed how Grissom wanted to use him to "make a deal" with the prosecutor. The agent explained that Grissom's attitude fluctuated from one of "What's in it for me?" to one of "I can give them the whole thing, man."

Grissom's defense team of Tom Erker and Kevin Moriarty actively challenged every witness called by the prosecution. They questioned even the victims' parents.

As expected in a trial where the victims had not been found, Erker and Moriarty took advantage of every opportunity to point out that the state could not say positively that the women had been killed. Under questioning by the defense, Celeste Becker, a long-time friend of Joan Butler's, had to admit that she did not know Joan was changing apartments. And, James Grooms, Christine's friend, could not say positively that Christine made it home from the Backstage Bar the night before she disappeared. The defense team questioned how it was that everyone could say for certain that the women had not taken off.

The defense attorneys also put forth an argument of crime-scene contamination in response to such evidence as the gold neck chain found in Joan Butler's carpet and Grissom's pubic hairs discovered in the Rusch-Brown apartment. In the Butler case, they emphasized that seven to eight people had roamed through the apartment prior to the police. They grilled Bill Chapin for failing to inform his partner about the gold chain and for not collecting it as evidence.

In challenging his client's pubic hairs being discovered in bedding at the Rusch-Brown apartment, Erker peppered the investigators with questions about their processing of the evidence. Had any of the bedding been on the floor prior to their arrival? Had any parts of the blankets touched the floor while being bagged? Did the officers know how many people had touched the bedding before or after the girls disappeared?

Further, the defense questioned the fact that no other trace evidence—blood, saliva or semen—had been found. It was improbable, they argued, that only pubic hairs would be found.

Finally, Erker insinuated that both Christine and Theresa had known Grissom much better than had been suggested. His partner Moriarty had also reminded jurors that early in the investigation, David Rusch gave police information about a "maintenance man" from Trafalgar Square, who had befriended his daughter and brought her gifts. Christine had known Grissom long before her disappearance, they argued.

Even Michelle Katf who had courageously stared down Richard Grissom and had won a degree of sympathy from the jury, was not immune from cross examination. Tom Erker was quick to focus on Katf's inability to positively identify Grissom as her attacker. Erker had Katf admit that she could not be certain whether her attacker was a light-skinned black man or a dark-skinned white man. She also could not say whether the gloves worn by her attacker were black or brown. Erker questioned Katf's selection of the pellet pistol as the one used during her attack since the one she identified had never been broken. Erker also challenged Katf's identification of Grissom's Toyota from the photo spread shown to her. The fact that the spread contained photos of only the Toyota and not a variety of cars was seen by the defense as significantly biased.

Grissom's attorneys disputed little of Officer Brian Edwards's account of Grissom's possession of the Corsica and his flight from Trailridge Apartments. They emphasized that Grissom simply knew the car was stolen and did not want to be apprehended for auto theft.

Moriarty spent several hours challenging the DNA testing performed by Cellmark Labs. Initially, he concentrated on the size of the blood samples taken from the trunk. He argued that it was nearly impossible to draw the firm conclusions outlined by witnesses since much of the blood sampling was consumed by Dirks and the Johnson County Lab team before being sent to Cellmark. Unable to sufficiently dispel the results from Cellmark, however, Moriarty attempted to muddy the waters by forcing witnesses from both Cellmark and the crime lab to outline every aspect of their procedures, which were extremely technical.

Tom Erker had a relatively easy time challenging Jackie Faught's testimony. He emphasized the size of the Mini Warehouse facility and the number of customers she must have dealt with over the course of a year. Erker questioned Faught's sudden, independent recollection of the single transaction occurring June 26, 1989.

He also pointed out the discrepancies between Faught's courtroom testimony and statements given to police the year before. According to the defense, when Faught was shown photographs of Grissom by metro squad detectives within a month of the disappearances, she picked out the man she knew only as Yoon Cho who had rented a locker from her the previous February. Yet, she did not place him back at the facility during the June incident. Then, over a year later, she was nearly certain that Grissom was the man who was in her office with the "distressed" woman on June 26.

Erker questioned how Faught could have come face to face with Grissom, "He stood there as big as life in front of you, asking for his refund check in March of 1989," and not have placed him back at the facility until after substantial prodding from others jarred her memory. The attorney mentioned more than once that Faught had told the metro squad detectives that her only contact with Grissom had been in February to March of 1989.

Erker's intent when cross examining Marcelais Thibodo was simple. He needed to impeach him. Erker opened by forcing Thibodo to admit that he had, at one time, been told by police that he was a suspect in this case. The opening paved the way for the jury to doubt whether anything the witness said could be considered truthful. It also gave Erker the chance to reveal the numerous discrepancies in Thibodo's early statements to police. More than ten police reports had been completed by investigators who had questioned Thibodo. The defense team had studied them thoroughly, following the progression of Thibodo's statements as they ranged from highly questionable to believable.

It wasn't long before Thibodo was stumbling and hesitating in search of answers to Erker's rapid-fire questioning. The witness simply never appeared ready to stand firm behind his responses. Growing increasingly frustrated, Thibodo's responses became, "I don't know" or "I can't remember." When asked if it had, in fact, been him, and not Grissom, who transported the shag carpet to the Metcalf locker he replied, "I cannot remember."

"Didn't you also have keys to the apartments at the complexes where you worked?" Erker asked.

"Not at first," Thibodo responded.

"Well, when did you get them?"

"It was later. I don't know the exact date."

"What apartments did you have keys to?"

"I don't remember. Richard gave me the keys."

When asked how it was that, after being in the Rusch-Brown apartment only once, he could draw such an accurate drawing of the entire layout for police, Thibodo replied, "I don't know."

Asked why he threw the duct tape onto the roof of the locker, Thibodo answered, "I don't know. It was just something I thought shouldn't be there."

One of the final arguments presented by the defense during cross examination was offered in response to testimony given by Agent Napier and Detective

Langer. The defense noted that no notes or tape recordings could be provided. The agents could not, they argued, demonstrate that what they said were the actual statements made by Grissom.

It was after Prosecutor Morrison had called his last witness that everyone in the courtroom sat in anticipation of the defense team's opening arguments and the witnesses who would testify on behalf of Richard Grissom. The defense segment of the trial, however, was not to be. Their case would be limited to the previous cross examination of the prosecution's witnesses. Tom Erker and Kevin Moriarty formally rested their case.

In spite of last-minute juggling and attempts to create alibi witnesses, not a single witness would take the stand for Richard Grissom.

28

It was mid-afternoon on Friday, November 2, 1990, when the jury in the Richard Grissom case received its final, pre-deliberation instructions from Judge William Gray. By the following Saturday evening, less than thirty-six hours later, it had returned with a unanimous verdict. The jury found Grissom guilty of all but one of the twelve felony charges against him.

Grissom stood beside his attorneys as each charge and corresponding verdict was read aloud. Typically, he showed no emotion and stared straight ahead throughout the declamation.

Upon hearing the verdicts, Paul Morrison turned toward his assistant, Deb Vermillion, and broke into a broad smile. He looked on as Ralph Butler embraced Detectives Hinkle and Batt. The men's eyes were glassy with tears of joy and, most likely, relief. Members of the victims' families embraced each other and hugged the detectives.

Twenty days after the verdicts, Richard Grissom returned to the Johnson County Court for sentencing. The defendant appeared once again with his attorneys. He wore a bright blue shirt, yellow tie and dark slacks. He appeared, as always, calm and collected. His demeanor reflected the attitude of a man who had done nothing wrong, a man who believed that, at any moment, the judge and prosecutors would finally see the error of their ways and set him free.

Judge Gray offered Grissom the right to address the court in mitigation of punishment, explaining that Grissom could speak for himself or through counsel if desired. The judge reiterated the charges, their corresponding verdicts, and then recited the maximum punishment allowed under law for each one. He then acknowledged the state's motion for sentencing Grissom under the Habitual Criminal Act, which carried a greater penalty for each count.

Speaking for Grissom, Moriarty addressed the court. He acknowledged that Grissom "was not unmindful of the grief that the families are suffering and friends are suffering as a result of the loss of their loved ones." Moriarty went on to talk about Grissom's continued denial that he had any involvement in the missing women's deaths. "The backdrop that must be remembered by all is Mr. Grissom denies his involvement in this particular case and as a result, his comments will be viewed and reviewed by many in a different light." Moriarty added, "The court has a brief understanding of his family background and the difficulties he had as a child being raised and transferred about. The home environment, needless to say, was deplorable. And that, of course, has an impact on anyone and everyone." Moriarty stressed how Grissom's entire life, beginning with abandonment by his natural mother, had been a series of bad breaks.

Moriarty, however, could not demonstrate his client's remorse; his client could not admit to being sorry for something he said he didn't do. Yet, he found it necessary to utilize Grissom's past and his upbringing to defend his client against those very actions which his client supposedly had not committed. "He has always been one step behind, always seemed to have received the most unfavorable light at the most critical times," Moriarty said of Grissom. "It is very difficult for us at this time to tell the court very much about what has occurred here or for us to tell you how sorry we are, because Mr. Grissom maintains his innocence."

Moriarty summed up by describing his relationship with the defendant. "Throughout the trial people would ask Mr. Erker and myself, what is Mr. Grissom writing all the time? What is he taking down there? They would ask, how come he didn't show any emotion? Mr. Grissom has shown emotion. He did it at the appropriate time and in the appropriate manner. He remained a gentleman throughout the proceedings in this courtroom and that is the same way he has interacted with Mr. Erker and myself."

Paul Morrison countered with his own pre-sentence address, stating that throughout his entire career as a prosecutor, he had never confronted a defendant like Richard Grissom. "The side of Richard Grissom that I have seen is completely different, apparently, from the side that Mr. Erker and Mr. Moriarty have seen." Morrison described Grissom as a sociopath who had been incarcerated numerous times, once previously for murder. He outlined aspects of the Hazel Meeker murder, mentioning the many wounds inflicted on her with a railroad spike after Grissom had bound the elderly grandmother. "I have seen the pictures, Judge. They're horrible!"

Morrison spoke of various contacts with probation officers who had handled Grissom and how each had warned Morrison to be careful, that "Mr. Grissom was an extreme manipulator who, throughout his life, had used the excuse that he was abused as a child." Morrison countered the defense's claims to Grissom's "deplorable" background by explaining that the man and woman who raised Grissom were still together and had afforded Grissom a good and supportive home environment. Morrison spoke of his pity for Grissom's adoptive parents, stressing the guilt they were now forced to live with as a result of their son's actions.

The prosecutor also cited Grissom's two escapes from the juvenile center and how, after each escape, he broke into the homes of two other women but bragged at his parole hearing that he had not killed the women, implying that he was rehabilitated and fit for release. "That is the reason he gives," Morrison said. "I think that gives us a lot of insight into his mentality."

Morrison did not fail to mention the Terri Maness murder. He pointed out that the crime involved "a binding and brutal murder," and that Richard Grissom was a prime suspect. Grissom was, Morrison stated, one of the few people who he was certain would kill again if ever released from prison.

Ralph Butler addressed the court on behalf of the victims' families. He told of his and David Rusch's efforts to lobby the Kansas legislature to institute the death penalty for certain criminal offenses. As a result of their efforts, the state had enacted two new mandatory sentencing laws creating more stringent penalties for murder. (The State of Kansas eventually passed the death penalty but not until the Spring of 1994.)

Butler told the court about the "terrible feelings of deprivation and longing that we feel with the loss of Joan and Theresa and Christine. We have been deprived of their laughter, their smiles, their joys and their sorrows. We have been deprived of walking down the aisle and watching them get married and loving the grandchildren they would have produced." He emphasized that the girls could not even feel safe inside their own apartments. He mentioned "the loathsome way Grissom disposed of the bodies, secretly, so they would never be found." Ralph Butler told the court, in no uncertain terms, that the time for courteous treatment of Richard Grissom had reached an end. "The time has come to dispense the punishment prescribed by the state for these horrible crimes."

Following arguments by Morrison and the defense team both for and against the court's adopting the provisions of the Habitual Criminal Act, Judge Gray announced that a sufficient amount of evidence had been presented to warrant adoption. The judge then read every count against Grissom and imposed a sentence for each guilty verdict. When finished, the judge had sentenced Richard Grissom to four life terms plus 361 years, to be served consecutively in the Kansas State penal system.

Epilogue

Richard Grissom is serving his multiple, life sentences in the Kansas State Prison at Lansing. The prison has three cell-blocks: A, B and C, with the latter considered the most desirable, general population section. Having served brief periods of adjustment time in both A and B blocks, Grissom is now assigned to C, where he enjoys somewhat of a celebrity status inside the prison.

Because Grissom is a lifer, he's accorded a special standing by many inmates. Add to that Grissom's reputation and the notoriety of his case, and his position is elevated. To many on the inside, he carries considerable clout. Grissom has been known to decide who sits at his table during meals and who hangs out with him in the prison yard.

Grissom also has followers outside prison walls. Over the years, his visitor list—mostly women—has grown by leaps and bounds. The number of his visitors prompted prison officials to adopt new regulations, limiting the length of time a visitor could spend with Grissom. He has made no effort to shorten the list. The number of women visitors has helped increase his popularity among peers.

Grissom continues to play sports at Lansing. On more than one occasion, when a visiting baseball team has played the prisoners, several of the outside players have approached Grissom and asked for his autograph. Others have wanted to talk to him, so they could say they'd met him.

Legally, Grissom has exhausted his appeals at the state level. Federal appeals remain available to him; however, he has not had the money to retain legal representation. He could be afforded assistance through the Indigent Defense Program, but funds are not guaranteed to everyone. Money for the program is approved by the state legislature, and a review board decides who receives assistance.

With or without funding for appeals, it's not likely that Grissom will ever be set free. Still, for virtually everyone involved with the investigation, the case continually lingers in their minds. Pat Hinkle worries about whether Grissom will remain behind bars for life. He also admits that never a day passes without him thinking about the missing women and where they might be. What does he think Grissom might have done with the bodies?

Hinkle believes that at least one of the women, probably Joan Butler, was buried in rural Douglas County, somewhere off Route 458 near the Clinton Lake Dam. Grissom's Toyota, bearing the Nebraska license plate, was spotted there. It's possible that he was in the area, scouting for a place the hide his victim. This is the same area where a wad of duct tape was found during the land searches.

Hinkle believes that Grissom may have disposed of the other two women in the Blue River. He does not believe the story about the wood chipper.

Like Hinkle, Detective Bill Batt places little credence in the wood chipper scenario. He, too, thinks Grissom may have buried the bodies in Douglas County. Batt surmises that after Grissom buried Joan Butler, and her body went undetected, he would have considered it a "safe" place to hide or bury his other victims. The detective admits, however, that "there are a lot of possibilities."

Many people have asked the detectives why neither Christine nor Theresa cried out for help or attempted to escape when at the bank ATMs, the Raytown storage facility or the pay phone in the mall parking lot on Metcalf.

Hinkle and Batt figure Grissom threatened each girl, telling her he would kill her roommate if she failed to cooperate with him. When forcing Theresa to lease the Raytown locker, Grissom likely had left Christine, tightly bound and her mouth taped, in the Metcalf locker. Theresa's cooperation was the only thing that could keep her roommate from harm.

Entry and exit logs at the Raytown facility allow for a reconstruction of probable scenarios during the day and night of June 26. Shortly after leasing the Raytown locker, it's possible that Grissom returned for Christine, and then kept the two women together in the Raytown locker for the remainder of the day.

When the ATM video camera photographed Christine at 10:00 P.M. that night, it's likely she had been given strict instructions. Theresa may have been in the Dodge Colt with Christine and Grissom during the transaction, and Christine may have feared for Theresa's safety if she tried to escape.

Even though Batt and Hinkle base their theories on first-hand knowledge of the investigation, both admit that a lot of questions still exist. They hope to someday have the answers.

Meantime, Hinkle still serves on the Lenexa Police force, where he has been promoted to sergeant of the Directed Patrol Unit. He has sixteen years of service with Lenexa and remains active in major criminal investigations.

Detective Bill Batt has marked his twenty-third year with the Overland Park Police department. The tenacious detective remains hooked by this case and its seemingly endless reservoir of leads. Six years later, an average of a lead a week is still funneled to him. Batt diligently responds to almost every one. "Even after I retire, this case will stay with me," Batt insists. "I want to find those girls just as much as their families do."

Paul Morrison continues to head the Johnson County prosecutor's office and recently celebrated his sixteenth year there. He remains active in both legal and community projects.

In Wichita, Lt. Ken Landwehr is close to retiring from the Wichita Police department, but continues to work multiple-murder investigations. He is active in the "BTK" serial-killer investigation in Wichita and offers his expertise to other jurisdictions covering the case. Landwehr is glad to have participated in the Johnson County case; however, he, too, had hoped to get Richard Grissom in a Wichita courtroom.

Meanwhile, the Terri Maness case does remain open and pending in Wichita. However, unless Grissom's convictions are reversed or an appeal is granted, it's not likely he will be prosecuted. Investigators believe, however, that enough evidence exists to to put Grissom on trial for the Maness murder.

In June of 1991, a memorial mass was held in Wichita for Joan Marie Butler. The card announcing the mass contained two quotes. The first was written by

Joan's brother Tim. The Butler family requested it be included at the end of this book.

The quote speaks for the Butler family and those who knew Joan, and for those who survive Terri, Theresa and Christine.

"May her untimely death teach us
    the value of the time we have remaining
on this earth as God's servants."

The second quote was from Joan, who had offered these words in a letter to her younger sister Julie during a time when Julie was suffering a personal crisis.

"I ask God for all things that I might enjoy life,
He gave me life that I might enjoy all things."

The Brown and Butler families have established scholarship funds in the names of their daughters. Anyone wishing to contribute to the Brown scholarship fund, established for those pursuing health-care careers, may send donations to:

The Theresa Brown Scholarship Fund
c/o The First National Bank of Camdenton,
Camdenton, Missouri 65020

Donations to the Butler scholarship fund, created to assist students of advertising at the University of Kansas, may be sent to:

The Joan Butler Fund
c/o The Kansas University Endowment Association

P.O. Box 928
Lawrence, Kansas 66044-0928

Today, the victims' families take life one day at a time. They have coped with a pain that has stretched their levels of endurance and rationality and will likely remain with them, in some measure, until they have taken their last breaths.

A sense of closure has been denied the families as well. The Manesses recovered their daughter's body and were able to provide Terri an appropriate burial. They were, however, denied an opportunity to see the man believed responsible for Terri's death prosecuted and convicted.

On the other hand, the Brown, Rusch and Butler families were given their day in court, but the bodies of Theresa, Christine and Joan have never been found. Even though finding the women would never fill the void created by their absence, it would alleviate the grief caused by not knowing. The uncertainty is like an emotional roller-coaster, rising and falling through levels of hope and despair each time a body is found somewhere.

At times, the surviving family members bombard themselves with unanswerable questions—how could he intentionally take their child's or sister's life? Why did he choose her? Is he laughing at their pain? Is it possible that he could be without remorse?

The harsh, day-to-day reality is that Terri, Christine, Theresa and Joan are no longer participating in their lives. The young women are with them in spirit, but they no longer share life's journey, its mysteries and its joys.

One day...one hour...one minute...the young women were with them. Then, they were suddenly gone.

About the Author

Dan Mitrione is a native of Indiana, but was raised in Brazil, where his father worked for the State Department. Mitrione graduated from the University of Maryland with a degree in international affairs, and later served with the United States Marines in Vietnam.

A former federal investigator, Mitrione lives in the Midwest with his wife Janet. He is currently at work on a new project.